Learning the Law

Learning the Law

Success in Law School and Beyond

Steven J. Frank, Esq.

Revised and Updated

A Citadel Press Book
Published by Carol Publishing Group

A Citadel Press Book
Published by Carol Publishing Group
Citadel Press is a registered trademark of Carol Communications, Inc.

Editorial, sales and distribution, rights and permissions inquiries should be addressed to Carol Publishing Group, 120 Enterprise Avenue, Secaucus, N.J. 07094

In Canada: Canadian Manda Group, One Atlantic Avenue, Suite 105, Toronto, Ontario M6K 3E7

Carol Publishing Group books may be purchased in bulk at special discounts for sales promotion, fund-raising, or educational purposes. Special editions can be created to specifications. For details, contact Special Sales Department, 120 Enterprise Avenue, Secaucus, N.J. 07094.

Manufactured in the United States of America

10 9 8 7 6 5 4 3 2 1

Library of Congress Cataloging-in-Publication Data

Frank, Steven J.
  Learning the law : success in law school and beyond / Steven J. Frank.—Rev. and updated.
     p. cm.
  "A Citadel Press book."
  Includes index.
  ISBN 0-8065-1871-5 (softcover)
  1. Law—Study and teaching—United States. 2. Law schools—United States. 3. Law students—United States. 4. Law examinations—United States. 5. Lawyers—Vocational guidance—United States.
I. Title.
KF283.F73   1997
340'.071'173—dc21   96-50115
                                                                      CIP

To Andrea
Wife, best friend, editor in chief

Contents

PART ONE
LEARNING THE LAW

PART TWO
LEARNING THE ROPES

PART THREE
LIFE AFTER LAW SCHOOL

Contents

Introduction

SOMETHING VERY STRANGE is going on in the legal profession, and no one can quite put a finger on it. The economy has emerged from recession. The practice of law is booming again. Lawyers are the highest-paid professionals in the nation, right up there with computer service providers. In 1995, law firms collected $108 billion in revenue. Starting pay at top Wall Street firms now exceeds $85,000. And law students are smarter than ever. The class of 1994 entered law school with the highest Law School Admission Test scores in history and among the highest college grade point averages. Bar exams have been getting harder lest everyone pass.

So what's the general mood out there? Gloom, pessimism, and despair. Hiring is down relative to the 1980s. Starting salaries have dropped at the less-glamorous firms. Raises are smaller, partnership tracks longer. Many firms have hauled up the ladder entirely, simply refusing to make new partners. Clients are more demanding and frugal than ever. Job satisfaction is down. *L.A. Law* is kaput.

Basically, the legal profession is suffering from an acute case of short-term memory. It's true: the 1980s are over, and the ranks of lawyers may never again expand as vigorously. That's hard to accept for a lot of people whose expectations were shaped by a seller's market. But for those just starting out or sitting on the fence, deciding whether or not to pursue a career in law, the current outlook provides a healthy measure of the future. All in all, employment prospects are brightening. In fact, what you see today bears a much closer resemblance to the historical picture—that is, before the previous decade warped everyone's outlooks. Not everyone gets a job. Not everyone keeps the one he or she gets. Only a very few become partners at big-time firms. The binge is over, but so is the purge. Welcome to the way things have (nearly) always been.

Since those of you contemplating law school today are an unusually smart bunch, you instinctively recognize what you're in for. The most encouraging statistic of all is the decline in law-school applications over the past couple of years. Fewer aimless graduates are stumbling into the law for want of a more solid career alternative. More people than ever recognize the limited value of a *juris doctorate* outside the corridors and corner offices of the legal profession. In short, informed choices are being made. Self-selection will ultimately nudge those job-satisfaction stats back up.

This book is about making that momentous career decision with open eyes. It's about starting off on the right foot. The law is an extremely competitive profession, beginning with law school. Career horizons can be fixed by the end of your first semester. That leaves precious little time to get comfortable with the material, to find your moorings. New students enter law school with widely varying backgrounds and experiences. And many begin with a leg up. They've majored in jurisprudence, Shepardized cases as paralegals, researched statutes for attorney Dad or judge Mom.

Learning the Law will give *you* that leg up. We'll cover the basics of how laws are enacted, shaped, and enforced; law professors assume you're already a whiz at civics. We'll explore practical logic, the techniques lawyers use every day—whether they realize it or not—to express and dissect principles. We'll have you perusing some of the same cases you'll encounter in first-year classes. And you'll find yourself thinking twice, maybe three times about what you've just read. When you're done, you will have acquired the general background and familiarity you'll need to succeed. You'll also know whether this stuff is sort of fun or makes you want to scream.

The second part of this book is about negotiating the day-to-day of law school. We'll help you organize your time and develop worthwhile study habits *before* you find yourself buried under a barrage of cases, lectures, critical materials and unanswerable questions. We'll lead you through the world of study groups, outlines, commercial study aids—we name names—and law-school folk wisdom, separating truth from myth, helping you decide what's right for you. We'll discuss commercial outlines, case briefs, and the latest computer study tools. Once again, students with close relatives or friends who have gotten a legal education frequently possess maddeningly thorough familiarity with the ins and outs. Soon you will too.

Finally, we'll outfit you with some provisions for the long and sometimes lonely journey into the real world. Finding a job, passing the bar, succeeding in a new environment that bears about as much resemblance to law school as that experience did to your LSAT prep course—these are the subjects of the final chapters in this book. You'll get the inside story of law-firm structure and management: partnership tiers, leverage, and billable hours. You'll find out about different career choices and how they feel when you try them on. You'll scout the early hazards before you stumble. And we'll give you some tips on navigating perhaps the most revolutionary resource since the *American Lawyer* started its salary survey: the mammoth pastiche of computer links called the Internet. Overwhelming in scale and constantly growing, the Net can help you find answers to almost any question. On the Net you can search the collections of university and law libraries, locate career opportunities, hook up with like-minded law students, check bar-exam deadlines and requirements, or quickly bone up on that breaking insider-trading scandal you just fibbed awareness of . . . if you know how to use it. Most lawyers don't.

So take heart, aspiring paper-chaser. There's still plenty of opportunity out there, many ways for you to distinguish yourself. It's what real lawyers do every day—lest their clients reattach themselves to someone trying just a little harder. Law is a challenge, whether you're swallowing great gulps of legal doctrine or deploying it in the service of someone who needs your help. It's a profession of advice, advocacy, and constant learning; that is, after all, why it's called *practice*. But if you develop good habits early and dedicate your talents to the demands of that practice, you'll find law one of the most rewarding and meritocratic professions. Last names, gender, skin color—they don't count for much in the heat of a proxy fight or cross-examination. Neither do excuses afterward. Get used to standing on your own two feet and thinking on them, too.

Now let's get to work.

Acknowledgments

Special thanks to my parents, both for bringing me up right and for their insights on the world of solo practice; to Jennifer Sobel, for her enthusiasm and helpful perspectives on law school; to Gary Fitzgerald, my editor and chief motivator; and to George Jakobsche and Andy Epstein for some great Internet sites.

A Note on Footnotes

You will find a fair number of footnotes in this book. Better get used to them. Legal journals, treatises, and cases are replete with them. To avoid being second-guessed by judges or by the opposition, lawyers get pretty compulsive about backing propositions with cited authority.

Maintaining brevity and consistency among the welter of legal sources requires a specialized form of citation. To the rescue have come the editors of the Columbia, Harvard, University of Pennsylvania, and Yale law reviews with *A Uniform System of Citation* (better known, affectionately or otherwise, as the Blue Book). This encyclopedia of citation covers virtually every type of source and has earned the allegiance of lawyers and judges throughout the country. The Blue Book system differs from most generally accepted bibliographic styles, however, and a word of explanation is in order.

The general form of a case citation is:

<volume> (Reporter) <first page of case>, <page of quotation>

Citations also tell you the year the court rendered its decision, usually in parenthesis at the end of the cite.

Case reporters, which contain the full texts of legal rulings and not much else, are abbreviated according to conventions adopted (you guessed it) in the Blue Book. You will encounter the following common citations in this book:

U.S. = United States Reports (U.S. Supreme Court cases)
F.2d = Federal Reporter, 2nd Series (federal Court of Appeal cases)

F.Supp. = Federal Supplement (federal District Court cases)

An abbreviated state name (e.g., "Conn." or "Minn.") denotes the official state reporter containing decisions of the state's high court

Hence, "334 F.Supp. 497, 502" means that the case may be found in volume 334 of the Federal Supplement reporter starting on page 497, and the cited quotation appears on page 502.

A jurisdiction's 'official code,' or complete body of statutes, is usually divided into separate titles or chapters, each of which deals with a particular topic and is itself divided into sections (denoted by the symbol §). The general form of a statutory citation is:

<title or chapter> (Official Code) §<section>

So 35 U.S.C. §112 refers to Title 35 of the United States Code (the official code of the federal government, which contains all federal statutes), section 112.

PART ONE

Learning the Law

┌─────────┐
│   1   │
└─────────┘

The Institutions

THE FIRST FIVE CHAPTERS of this book will acquaint you with the basics of legal reasoning—what goes on in the minds of lawyers. We'll also fill in some likely blanks in your data banks. Oh, sure, law school isn't supposed to require any particular educational background; there's no such thing as a pre-law course of study. But law professors assume some background in political science and philosophy, even if they don't admit it. The first blanks we'll fill in have to do with basic civics. Understanding law is difficult, but should not be mysterious. Laws and cases have little meaning without an appreciation for the processes that create them and make them work.

Before they enter law school, most people think they have a pretty good idea of how government operates. Law school shows us how much we *don't* know about government in general and its effects on law in particular. Unfortunately, law-school professors expect you to have acquired this knowledge somewhere else or to pick it up on the fly. That's not easy, and hence this first chapter. A word of warning at the outset: this stuff ain't sexy. But you can't find your way around the law without first touring its institutions, and this first chapter will serve as an introductory (and relatively painless) guide.

We all know that the coordinate branches of national government enact, enforce, and decide the law. We've all learned the basic functions of each branch and recognize the separation-of-powers principle that frees them to operate autonomously. That's where simplicity ends. Sometimes the branches coexist peacefully and reinforce each other. At other times the unitary entity we call "government" behaves like a newborn foal unable to synchronize its independently-minded legs. The drafters of the U.S. Constitution hoped that the system of checks and balances they introduced would act like a set of hopples to ensure an orderly gait. But hopples work no better on noisy democratic governments than on confused young pacers, and when government breaks stride, the effect on law and lawmaking can get rather knotty.

Compounding the complexity is the fact that the federal government represents, at most, only half of the story. Sharing power with the federal legislature, executive, and judiciary are the independent regimes that govern the individual states. The interrelationship among all of these somewhat unruly government entities gets every bit as intricate and testy as the associations among their individual components. At times it appears that states and the federal bureaucracy act as individual sovereign bodies, each within its own separate sphere. In other contexts a two-step hierarchy seems more accurate, with the federal component exercising a dominant, supervisory function.

In this chapter we'll explore some of these interactions and their effects on the creation, application, and interpretation of law. We focus primarily on the federal legislature and executive, since state versions are ordinarily quite similar and don't mingle much with their federal counterparts. However, significant federal-state overlap occurs in the judicial context. State and federal courts are highly interdependent, and we discuss their relationship in section 1.3.

1.1. The Legislature

The Congressional Neighborhood

The business of Congress is to make law and oversee various aspect of government operation. Here we'll focus primarily on the lawmaking function, although oversight will become important as we explore the various roles played by administrative agencies. Congress, as we will soon see, is free to enact laws only within certain defined spheres. But that's jumping ahead. For the moment let's consider generally the confluence of political factors that must occur in order to propel someone's suggestion into statutory law.

Legislators exist in a world of lobbyists, special-interest groups, internal political hierarchy, and the often indifferent but occasionally strident voices of public opinion. It requires a special set of conditions to arouse busy legislators and the cumbersome body they inhabit into motion. Perhaps an influential lobbying group will mount a vigorous campaign to attract congressional attention; or a strong public opinion might coalesce on a certain matter, mobilizing broad support or the enthusiasm of key legislators. But institutional inertia and internecine politics can be difficult obstacles to overcome. The chances that a proposed measure will succeed increase when opposing forces are weak or absent and legislators demonstrate willingness, at all stages of passage, to negotiate with one another.

In fact, compromise is perhaps *the* critical feature of the legislative process. Yet as accommodation and conciliation increase, so do the vagueness and obscurity of the final statutory product. Compromise often expresses itself in ambiguity. When courts later attempt to interpret a law in a manner consistent with the intent of the enacting body, they are unlikely to encounter a unified set of purposes and goals, and the law's very indeterminacy may invite the judiciary to inject their own clarifications. More on this in chapter 2. What follows is a brief description of legislative protocol that explores some of the institutional sources of compromise.

The Congressional Lawmaking Process

Proposed legislation is introduced in the form of a bill. With the exception of measures to raise revenue, which must originate in the House of Representatives, bills may be presented by an elected member of either the House or Senate chamber. This sponsor generally follows the bill as it proceeds, explaining its terms to colleagues and soliciting their support. A newly introduced measure is first referred to a *standing committee*. These are specialized, permanent units established in each congressional chamber, formed to research and evaluate the terms of new legislation (see Figure 1–1). The chairman of each committee oversees its operation and exercises great power over both the committee's membership and the ultimate fate of bills passing before it. A bill that is in committee faces its most critical test and, not surprisingly, generates the greatest amount of lobbying at this point. After study and probably alteration, the committee may (1) recommend passage, sending the bill to the floor of the chamber and placing it on the agenda for debate; (2) recommend killing the bill; or (3) simply let the bill languish, which will end consideration for that session of Congress and probably for good.

In the House, survival through a standing committee places the bill at the mercy of the House Rules Committee, which sets its chamber's agenda. Ordinarily a bill cannot reach the floor unless it has first received a "rule."[1] The Rules Committee thus acts as an omnibus screening panel. It may end a bill's life despite its recommendation by the standing committee, or condition granting of a rule on addition or deletion of particular provisions.

The Senate has no counterpart to the Rules Committee. Any senator may move to consider a measure at any time. As a practical matter, however, Senate leaders exert considerable control over their chamber's legislative agenda. Bills typically reach the floor only after receiving the endorsement of a standing committee and a time slot from the Senate leadership.

---

1. Certain measures, such as revenue bills originating in the Ways and Means Committee, hold privileged status and do not require a rule.

House	Senate
Agriculture	Agriculture, Nutrition and Forestry
Appropriations	Appropriations
Armed Services	Armed Services
Banking, Finance and Urban Affairs	Banking, Finance and Urban Affairs
Budget	Budget
District of Columbia	Commerce, Science and Transportation
Education and Labor	Energy and Natural Resources
Energy and Commerce	Environment and Public Works
Foreign Affairs	Finance
Government Operations	Foreign Relations
House Administration	Governmental Affairs
Interior and Insular Affairs	Judiciary
Judiciary	Labor and Human Resources
Merchant Marines and Fisheries	Rules and Administration
Post Office and Civil Service	Small Business
Public Works and Transportation	Veterans' Affairs
Rules	
Science, Space and Technology	
Small Business	
Standards of Official Conduct	
Veterans' Affairs	
Ways and Means	

FIGURE 1–1. STANDING COMMITTEES OF THE CONGRESS

Introduction on the floor begins the process of debate. Due to its smaller membership, Senate procedures are much less restrictive than those of the House, where the rule issued by the Rules Committee governs the duration and scope of debate. Members of both chambers offer and approve amendments during debate, and may also add *riders*—unrelated amendments attached to a bill well on its way to passage.

At the conclusion of debate, legislators vote on the measure. The requirements for passage depend on the nature of the matter. In most cases, a majority of those present will suffice; however, the number present and voting must first constitute a *quorum*, or majority of the total chamber's membership, to produce a valid vote. Certain subjects require the assent of an extraordinary majority, such as the two-thirds vote in the Senate needed to ratify a treaty.

Passage by one chamber sends the bill to the other chamber for its approval. A number of factors make the second chamber's affirmance easier to secure than that of the first. One is legislative momentum; popular support may have surfaced after the initial favorable action, or the counterpressures necessary for defeat subdued. Another is the previous opportunity for the bill's opponents to offer their input, perhaps resulting in a compromise package. And yet another is interchamber relations.

But harmony does not always reign. The other house may pass the bill with specific amendments, sending the onus back once again to the first chamber. And sometimes the houses simply cannot agree, period. In that case a special conference committee, composed of members of both chambers, is assembled to try to devise a compromise.

Opportunity for persuasive influence by the President occurs at virtually every stage of passage. The President's most important power, however, is negative: a *veto* will overturn congressional passage of a bill (although the veto may itself be overridden, and the bill reinstated, by a two-thirds majority of each chamber). The President's veto power has traditionally been nonselective; a bill must be accepted or rejected as a whole (hence the importance of riders). State governors, on the other hand,[2] often enjoy the prerogative of a *line-item veto,* which permits them to turn down portions of a bill.[2a] Disfavored bills may be spared the indignity of outright rejection if Congress is close to adjournment, in which case the President can simply withhold signature; this is known as a *pocket veto* and is every bit as effective as an ordinary veto.

1.2 The Executive

Executive Responsibilities

The primary and traditional tasks of the executive branch relate to administrative supervision and implementation of public policy. Federal executive power derives from Article II of the Constitution and from special congressional delegation. Article II makes the President commander in chief of the armed forces; it also authorizes the President to make treaties and appoint public officials (subject to Senate approval), and to "take Care that the Laws be faithfully executed."

As chief executive officer, head of state, head of government, and head of a titular political party, the President holds perhaps the greatest locus of power in the world. Yet in many ways, presidential power also remains subject to potentially sharp limitation. While the President may appoint public officers, he may not create the offices themselves. His administration retains control over the methods and degree of law enforcement, but the laws

---

2. Throughout this book and throughout the law, you will find there is always another hand.

2a. Admist a chorus of constitutional misgivings, the President at last acquired a relatively limited line-item veto on January 1, 1997.

themselves originate in Congress. And, of course, executive action may not violate the Constitution.

As a practical matter, presidential power has increased substantially in the last century. The many voices of Congress cannot ordinarily articulate a coherent policy agenda, and the need for secrecy in sensitive areas can silence those voices entirely. It is not surprising, therefore, that the executive administration has become responsible for initiating and garnering political support for national policies. It is the President to whom those seeking introduction of new programs inevitably turn. Congress may ratify, reject, or modify the President's proposals, but it initiates few of its own. And the President, for his part, may reject any congressional formulation by veto.

The executive exerts control over policy in other ways as well. The executive Office of Management and Budget (OMB), for example, prepares the initial draft of the federal budget, since the fiscal schedule represents the financial embodiment of national policy. And although Congress alone has the ultimate say over how the money—and how much of it—is spent, OMB's first cut sets the stage; deviation from its recommendation is common but complete overhaul rare.

Executive Organization

The executive branch, through a multilayered arrangement of bureaucratic offices, discharges the enormous task of compiling and processing the information necessary to run the federal government. Closest to the President are members of the White House staff. These special assistants and aides perform a wide range of functions that include speech-writing, congressional liaison, and press relations, to name but a few. The staff forms one unit of the Executive Office of the President (EOP), a group of counselors and committees that provides advice to the President and helps coordinate policy. Other EOP units include the OMB, the Council of Economic Advisers, the Domestic Council, and the National Security Council (see Figure 1–2).

The President maintains a more formal relationship with the Cabinet, whose member-ship consists primarily of the secretaries who head the fourteen executive departments. The Cabinet originated as a forum for discussion of policy proposals and the budget, but personnel of the EOP have largely captured this role (although the advice of individual Cabinet members may be valued greatly). Today the Cabinet is more a creature of Congress. Cabinet posts and their accompanying bureaucratic regimes generally find their origins in congressional legislation. While the President appoints members of the Cabinet, he has little say over their responsibilities, which tend to focus almost exclusively on departmental management. The Senate also retains the right to approve the President's Cabinet appointees.

The executive office you will encounter most often in law school is the Justice Department, which serves as law firm to the entire federal government (see Figure 1–3). Headed by the Attorney General, the department investigates violations of federal law and

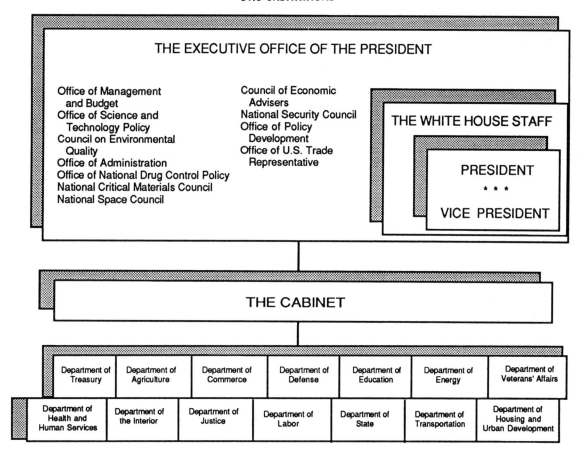

FIGURE 1–2. EXECUTIVE ORGANIZATION

represents the United States in court. The Federal Bureau of Investigation, an agency reporting directly to the Attorney General, probes criminal conduct; other divisions of the department oversee operations directed against illegal immigration, drug traffic, monopolistic and other unfair business practices, tax evasion, and violations of civil rights. The Solicitor General takes responsibility for all litigation in the Supreme Court to which the federal government is a party; most of these cases have first been argued in the lower federal courts by the staffs of the nationwide system of U.S. Attorneys' offices. Ninety-one such offices serve the judicial districts of the U.S. district courts.

The Justice Department is a massive bureaucratic entity. If that surprises you, remember that rule by law is an empty concept without some comprehensive and reliable mechanism for its enforcement. As we'll see later, the policies and temperaments of the personnel who run enforcement agencies can have almost as great a practical impact on the lives of the governed as the text of the laws they enforce. Lethargic execution leads to disrespect for the law just as surely as its arbitrary and harsh application; only when people feel confidence in the way justice is administered can the rule of law function effectively.

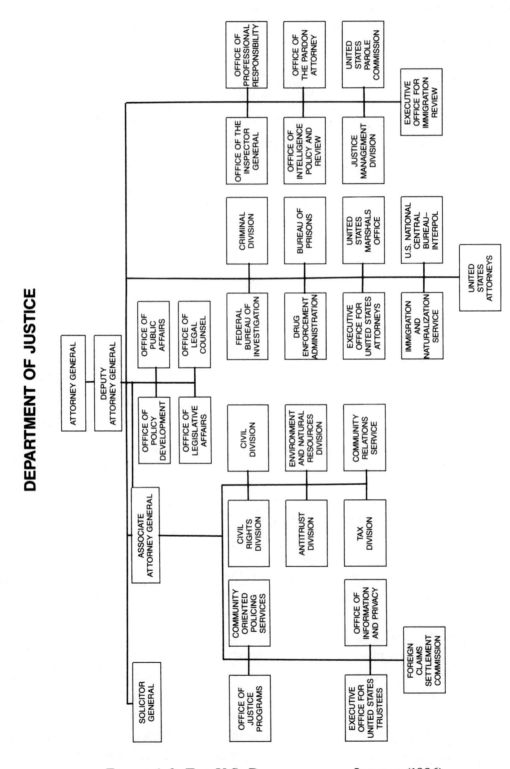

FIGURE 1–3. THE U.S. DEPARTMENT OF JUSTICE (1996)

1.3 The Judiciary

Dual Systems of Law

One of the more confusing facets of the United States legal system is the simultaneous existence of two entirely distinct types of law that coexist in each of two separate spheres of authority. *Statutory law,* the codes enacted by legislatures, and *common law,* that made by judges, are features of both the federal and state systems of laws. How do these kinds and regimes of law interact with one another?

State Law The power of state legislatures to enact laws must yield to the coequal rights of other states and the supremacy of the federal government. With respect to other states, each legislature is expected to keep its law to itself. New York has no authority to tell dairy farmers in Vermont how to produce milk. Nevertheless, one state's legislation can seriously intrude on the affairs of another without overtly appearing to do so; for example, if New York taxes all Vermont milk entering New York so as to make it unprofitable, the effect on Vermont dairy farmers will be both significant and direct. In such a case, provisions of the federal Constitution come into play to prevent states from legislating warfare with one another: the Commerce Clause[3] has been interpreted to demand economic fair play among states; the Privileges and Immunities Clause[4] protects various rights of out-of-state residents; and the Full Faith and Credit Clause[5] ensures that a judgment rendered by one state's courts may be enforced in any other state, regardless of whether the other state has different legal policies. Federalist issues such as these are often delicate but rarely easy: it can be tough to tell whether one state has enacted regulations in order to meddle deliberately in another state's interests or simply to protect the health and well-being of its own citizens.

State laws are *always* subject to the terms of both the state and federal constitutions. These two overarching documents act as "superstatutes." If a state law is found to conflict with either, it gets bumped. Federal laws need only satisfy the federal version. Now, who decides what's constitutionally acceptable and what's not? *Marbury v. Madison*[6] gave this responsibility to the courts in 1803. That decision was not based on any requirement of the Constitution itself, which says nothing about the issue. Responsibility for assessing the constitutionality of a law could just as easily have fallen to state legislatures, or perhaps to the governors. But Chief Justice John Marshall considered judges best qualified to determine whether a statute nudges the constitutional boundaries too strongly, and the rule remains to this day.

---

3. Article I, Section 8. For your reading pleasure, the U.S. Constitution is included as Appendix A.
4. Article IV, Section 2.
5. Article IV, Section 1.
6. 1 Cranch 137 (1803).

So far we've only discussed statutes. Yet any legal code can only cover precise topics, and no state has attempted to codify all possible legal questions into statutory form. Judges themselves have for centuries filled in the gaps by developing and refining areas of law basic to society's fundamental organization. States generally adhere to this *common-law* foundation in such fields as contract, property, and tort law. Common-law doctrine is based entirely on precedent. Because they need not answer to a legislature, judges remain free to reinterpret past decisions in light of changing circumstance. And should the legislature feel dissatisfied at any point with the judicial common-law formulation, it can simply reverse or modify existing case law by statute.

Federal Law It must be borne in mind constantly that the principles underlying federal law and the federal system's organization differ radically from those operating within the states. While states have general power to legislate in all areas except those specifically *withheld* by the Constitution, the federal government's very existence is limited to explicit constitutional *grants* of power. Hence, federal law is better thought of as interstitial rather than general. Congress cannot pass a law on any subject unless it can trace its authority to a specific provision of the Constitution. Most such provisions can be found in Article I and, to the delight of eager lawmakers, are quite broad. They include the power to lay and collect taxes, borrow and coin money, regulate commerce, establish post offices, regulate standards of weights and measures, create courts, declare war, create an army and navy, provide for a militia, set up a government for the capital district, and adopt laws concerning bankruptcy, naturalization, patents, and copyrights—a diverse smorgasbord, though hardly sufficient to fully regulate a society. The Tenth Amendment puts the brakes on federal lawmaking power, reserving to the states all powers not expressly delegated to Congress.

But when federal power to make law *does* exist, it supersedes state *laws* and *constitutions* by virtue of the Supremacy Clause of the U.S. Constitution.[7] Federal law thus rides roughshod over its competitors, but only within the narrow corridors where it is permitted at all, and only to the extent that it avoids conflict with the U.S. Constitution.

Most federal law is statutory. There isn't much federal common law around these days. In fact, federal courts aren't supposed to fashion their own law unless it's absolutely necessary.[8] When they do, though, federal common law has the same force over state law as a federal statute, but it can be overruled by Congress.

Systems of Courts

Given the simultaneous existence of two independent sets of laws, it should not astound you to find two equally independent systems of courts to apply them. What is by no means obvious, however, is which courts have jurisdiction over whose laws. The simplest

---

7. Article IV, Section 2.
8. If you're interested in why, have a look at Erie Railroad v. Tompkins, 304 U.S. 64 (1938).

arrangement would be one in which federal courts hear issues of federal law only, leaving state questions to state courts. Ah, would that life were so simple, but history and the Constitution have wrought otherwise. State and federal courts overlap considerably in their respective jurisdictions.

Federal Courts Federal courts hear federal cases—that is, cases arising under the Constitution itself, a federal law, or a United States treaty. But state law can also find its way into federal courts under certain circumstances. The first such circumstance is narrow: federal district courts assigned to the territories of the Virgin Islands, the Northern Mariana Islands, the Canal Zone, and Guam retain jurisdiction over local matters. If a plaintiff and defendant reside in different states, *diversity jurisdiction* permits federal courts to hear the case even if it involves issues only of state law. This jurisdictional grant was written into the Constitution to provide out-of-state litigants with an alternative to local courts, which were viewed as susceptible to regional interests and bias. If a state claim is interwoven with a federal one, a district court *may* decide to entertain both issues by exercising *pendent jurisdiction*. The idea here is to promote economy in litigation by getting the whole affair wrapped up in one proceeding. The fourth circumstance occurs in cases where federal law explicitly incorporates relevant state law. In all of these instances, federal judges must venture into unfamiliar territory and endeavor to interpret state law in a manner consistent with state policies.

Even when a case admittedly involves a federal question (or an allowed state-law question), federal courts do not automatically have power to decide it. That's because federal courts are limited not only as to the kinds of law they may consider, but also the types of cases they are empowered to hear. Article III, Section 2 of the Constitution restricts the federal judicial power to "Cases" and "Controversies."[9] At first blush, these words seem to state the obvious—after all, every lawsuit is a case, and why would anyone go to court in the absence of a controversy? There's more to it, of course. Numerous decisions have given substance to these seemingly hollow terms, imposing a series of prerequisites for federal jurisdiction.

For example, federal courts cannot issue *advisory opinions*[10]—that is, naked requests for legal interpretation unrelated to any actual dispute—since no controversy exists to adjudicate. But because the line separating requests for advice from actual dispute resolution can be quite indistinct, courts have developed the requirements of *adverseness* and *standing*. These concepts reflect the conviction that full and fair resolution of a legal issue requires the clash of parties whose stakes in the outcome are real and immediate. There must also be some sort of genuine disagreement on the merits; if two parties without actual quarrel file a "friendly" suit

---

9. This discussion focuses only on courts created pursuant to Article III. Congress also has limited authority to create *legislative courts* pursuant to its Article I powers, and such courts are not subject to the restrictions of Article III. More on the distinction between Article I and Article III courts in chapter 4.

10. These are discussed more fully in chapter 5.

just to see how a judge will rule, they may lack the necessary incentive to make their best arguments.

A fundamental tenet of United States constitutional policy is the concept of an independent federal judiciary. Federal courts exercise their day-to-day power without interference from the political branches. To ensure this, federal judges are appointed for life and assured that their salaries will not be reduced. At the same time, however, federal courts do not exist entirely outside the political process. All federal judges are appointed by the President (subject to Senate confirmation), and Congress completely controls the shape of the federal judicial structure. Article III, Section 1 of the Constitution mandates the existence only of the Supreme Court and "such inferior Courts as the Congress may from time to time ordain and establish." And only the Supreme Court has its jurisdiction set in constitutional concrete. Congress can specify not only the number and types of other federal courts, but also the areas to which they may address themselves.

Two centuries of congressional tinkering have produced a set of general federal courts, which may consider everything the Constitution allows, and a sprinkling of specialized tribunals. The general courts are organized into three tiers: (1) ninety-one *district courts* hear cases on the broadest jurisdictional level; these "lower" federal courts conduct full trials, hear motions—you name it. (2) Appeals from the district courts as well as from many federal administrative agencies are taken by thirteen *courts of appeal.* (3) Final review of all federal cases is reserved for the *Supreme Court.* That review is not automatic. Access to the Supreme Court comes only by way of a *writ of certiorari,* with which the Supreme Court grants discretionary review, or as a result of few statutory provisions that require the Supreme Court to review certain cases. In a very few special situations,[11] the Supreme Court will listen to an entire controversy instead of exercising its usual appellate role.

Congress has responded to the changing needs of an increasingly technical (and litigious) society by creating specialized federal courts. These tribunals, which decide nothing but precise, narrow aspects of federal law, have over the years included the Tax Court, the Customs Court (now known as the Court of International Trade), the Court of Customs and Patent Appeals, and the Court of Claims (which handled cases filed against the United States).[12]

State Courts Because the constraints governing the federal courts do not bind the states, the range of issues considered in state courts can be quite broad. The Massachusetts high court, for example, will issue advisory opinions on important matters of state law to

---

11. These include cases "affecting Ambassadors, other public Ministers and Consuls," and cases between states.

12. In 1982, the new Court of Appeals for the Federal Circuit was given the appellate jurisdiction of the Court of Claims and the Court of Customs and Patent Appeals. Another new court, the U.S. Claims Court, assumed the trial jurisdiction of the Court of Claims.

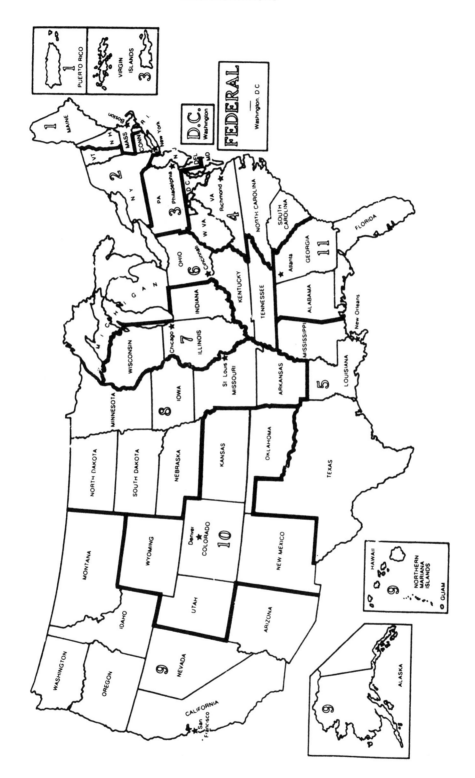

FIGURE 1-4. THE FEDERAL JUDICIAL CIRCUITS

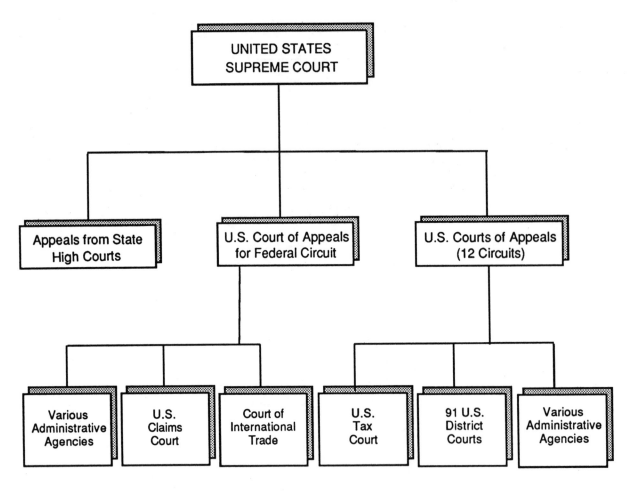

FIGURE 1–5. THE FEDERAL JUDICIAL SYSTEM

other governmental departments. Unlike federal courts, whose jurisdiction is limited by the U.S. Constitution and the judgment of Congress, state courts entertain *all* types of cases. Federal claims often wind up in federal court because such tribunals may be perceived as more sympathetic toward federal rights or capable of greater expertise in their application, but state courts possess concurrent jurisdiction over federal matters unless and until Congress says otherwise.

The organization of state courts varies considerably (see Figure 1–6), but there are always two or three tiers of general review. The lowest level may share its jurisdiction with subsidiary tribunals that hear only specific types of cases (such as traffic, family, juvenile, or probate matters). States are also free to set the terms under which state-court judges serve. Many state judgeships are elected offices; although the judiciary ordinarily tries to hold itself above the political fray, judicial elections occasionally engender some vigorous campaigning and public debate.

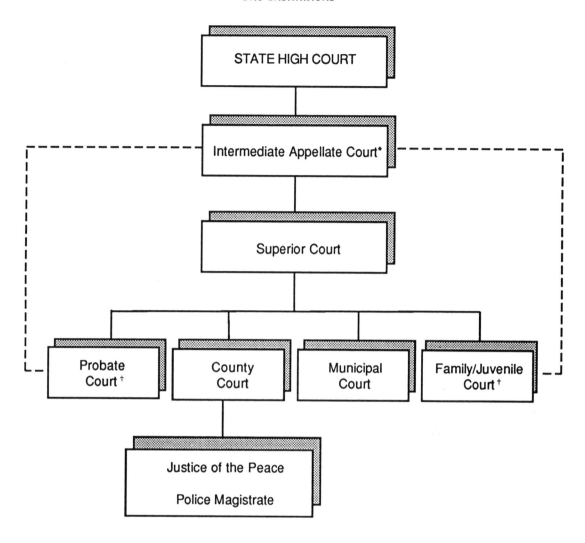

*Twenty-three of the fifty states have intermediate appellate courts.

†These courts may be considered subsidiaries of the trial court, or are treated as separate entities with review by the higher tier.

FIGURE 1–6. TYPICAL STATE JUDICIAL SYSTEM

The Supreme Court How does the U.S. Supreme Court, a federal tribunal, fit into this scheme? Is its jurisdiction confined to federal issues, or does it have the last word over state law as well? The answer is neither, sort of. *No* federal court, including the Supreme Court, may tell a state what its law says—the state high court's interpretation is final. But the nine justices of the Supreme Court retain full jurisdiction over all *federal* issues, and whether a state law offends the Constitution or a federal statute is itself a federal question. Hence the Supreme Court can review the *validity,* though not the substance, of state law—as well as any federal issues that state high courts consider.

1.4 The "Fourth Branch"

The complex nature of many private activities and areas of government service precludes regulation by the traditional mechanism of congressional lawmaking and executive implementation. It would be impossible for Congress to formulate the detailed rules needed to supervise, say, the production and distribution of energy. Likewise, it would overburden the Justice Department to investigate and litigate energy-related violations nationwide. Federal and state legislatures often delegate authority over narrow fields of regulation to an *administrative agency.* Such an agency may be inserted into the executive structure or set up as an independent commission, the difference lying in the degree of control accorded the incumbent executive administration over agency operations. Often, the distinction is more apparent than real; for example, Congress may create a new executive agency but impose restrictions on the President's discretion to dismiss agency personnel. Figures 1–7 and 1–8 depict the political location of some major agencies.

Agencies offer a number of special advantages. First, they may be staffed with individuals possessing special expertise in the agency's area of oversight; particularly when that area involves technical issues, such acumen can be critical to effective decision-making. Second, in creating an agency, the legislature can concentrate a great deal of governmental authority over a very limited domain. An independent administrative agency may be accorded *legislative* power to issue its own rules which have the force of law and carry heavy penalties for violation; *executive* authority to investigate violations of law (or the agency's own rules) and prosecute offenders; and *judicial* power actually to adjudicate the cases initiated by its enforcement arm. Finally, this array of authority permits the agency to select its own mode of policy-making. It may choose to promulgate rules, issue advisory opinions, or examine situations case by case (possibilities which we'll consider further in chapter 5).

A companion issue to the scope of agency authority is the degree of oversight reserved by the body that created the agency in the first place. Congress, for example, must constantly evaluate whether it has created any Frankenstein monsters. The House and Senate Government Operations Committees perform investigative assessments of agency activity, and other congressional support bureaus (such as the Congressional Research Service, Office of Technology Assessment, and General Accounting Office) also provide data.

What, then, does Congress do when it discovers a monster? One option is to restrain a few limbs. As original creator of all federal agencies, Congress may amend a particular one's *enabling act*—the law that originally establishes an agency—to prevent or mandate a particular action. The amendment may be as specific as desired; if Congress disapproves of

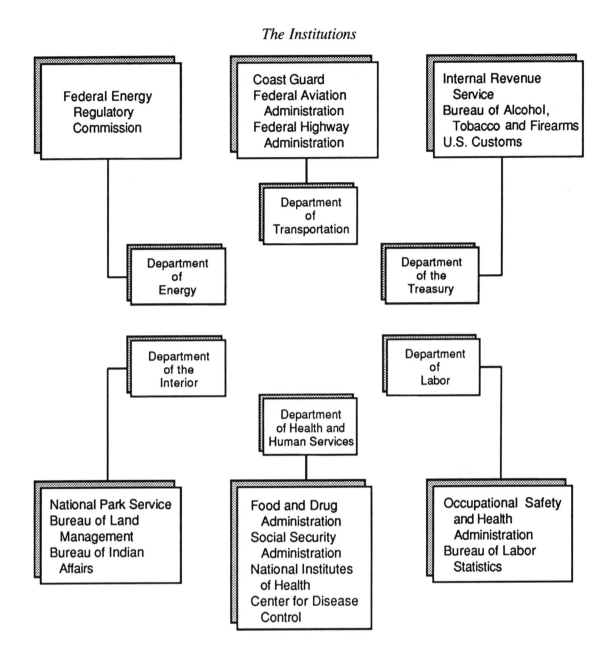

FIGURE 1–7. SOME EXECUTIVE AGENCIES

an agency's Rule 42, it can simply withdraw the agency's ability to make Rule 42 but leave general agency authority otherwise intact. Congress can also starve the monster until it behaves; a cruder oversight mechanism, congressional power over the purse can be used to effect wholesale curtailment of agency authority by reduction of funding. The least specific form of oversight is lifespan control—the inclusion of a "sunset" provision in the agency's enabling act, which terminates its existence at a specified date unless the act is renewed.

The executive branches of the state and federal governments also monitor the shape of

Central Intelligence Agency
Commission on Civil Rights
Commodity Futures Trading Commission
Consumer Product Safety Commission
Environmental Protection Agency
Equal Employment Opportunity Commission
Farm Credit Administration
Federal Communications Commission
Board of Governors of the Federal Reserve System
Federal Trade Commission
General Services Administration
Interstate Commerce Commission
National Aeronautics and Space Administration
National Foundation on the Arts and Humanities
National Labor Relations board
National Science Foundation
Nuclear Regulatory Commission
Securities and Exchange Commission
Small Business Administration
International Trade Commission
U.S. Postal Service

FIGURE 1–8. SOME INDEPENDENT FEDERAL AGENCIES

agency policies. The President, for example, receives evaluations of agency rules and overall performance through a regulatory-analysis group of advisers, and also possesses a number of means to restrain wayward agency action. The most important is the President's power of appointment. Article II, Section 2 of the Constitution gives the President sole discretion to appoint the central leadership of the federal bureaucracy (subject to Senate approval), including the heads of federal agencies. The appointment power probably confers the correlative ability to remove those previously appointed, but the President typically wields this power only to change agency leadership as terms expire. The executive may also reorganize the structure of its bureaucracy, again subject to congressional approval. And executive influence over the budget through OMB provides a degree of financial influence.

So where do the courts stand in the process of agency oversight? As might be expected, the judiciary's role is the most detached. Judicial review of agency action primarily involves verifying its accord with the will of the political branches. A court's inquiry typically begins with an examination of the enabling legislation, which defines both the agency's mission and the subjects that courts are allowed to look into. Those subjects may be virtually nonexistent—a complete snub by the legislature—or can include just about everything. (Of course, since judges interpret an agency's enabling act, they ultimately wind up with the last word.)

Regardless of the extent of their role, courts review some issues more closely than others. For example, judges are likely to defer to an agency's factual determinations but not to its legal conclusions. They will not question an agency's findings of fact so long as they are "reasonable," if some "rational basis" exists to support them, or if they are not "arbitrary or capricious." However, they will feel freer to reevaluate the agency's view of the law and the way it has applied the law to concrete facts.[13]

Full utilization of the many benefits of agency regulation obviously requires broad delegations of power and responsibility to these administrative units. Many feel that such delegations unduly threaten the fundamental distribution of governmental authority set forth in the U.S. Constitution. Our system of checks and balances depends on a true separation of powers, which ensures both governmental accountability and restraint. With all responsibilities fused into one governmental body—even one confined to a limited area of law—the traditional paradigm of separateness disappears.

In addition, broad authority usually implies large bureaucracies and their attendant costs. Excessive agency jurisdiction may encourage overregulation, a burden both to those directly regulated and to taxpayers generally.

When do the benefits of the agency concept outweigh its civic risks? Agencies work best when created in response to urgent pragmatic needs and with a view toward meeting those needs efficiently. It is perhaps wiser to ask, in each case, whether it is possible to imagine an effective alternative. The administrative process is dynamic and evolving; new governmental exigencies are constantly being recognized and met with an ever-expanding array of administrative solutions. Each new innovation calls for review of these same basic issues.

Lest this discussion of agency function and oversight appear academic and remote, it is well to emphasize the degree to which administrative agencies can influence our everyday lives. The Environmental Protection Agency, for example, sets the ecological agenda for the entire nation; state environmental agencies augment EPA surveillance at the local level. The Federal Reserve System controls the nation's money supply, a responsibility that touches the lives of countless employees, consumers, business people, and investors the world over. Even an area as seemingly rarefied as freedom of expression finds its way into the prerogatives of several federal agencies: the U.S. Postal Service issues regulations aimed at restricting the flow of certain materials deemed obscene, the Federal Communications Commission limits the hours during which radio stations can broadcast "adult-oriented" (you know what that

---

13. These distinctions will become clearer in chapter 4.

means) programming, and the National Foundation on the Arts and Humanities (which administers both the National Endowment for the Arts and the National Endowment for the Humanities) directly influences the output of the nation's artists through discretionary funding outlays.

It may not be sexy, but this stuff can definitely get provocative.

2

Reading Cases and Statutes

2.1 Stop and Smell the Roses

This chapter takes you from legal institutions to their handiwork: judicial opinions and statutes. Lawyers and law students learn primarily by reading cases, each containing the decision of a court as expressed in a ruling and supporting discussion. As you read on you may begin to think we are unduly obsessed with them. If so, that's because law students seem obsessed with them.

Enter any law-school dorm or cafeteria and you'll hear law students laughing, arguing, and whispering case names. Those little titles become a medium of exchange—almost a culture. The reason is data compression. To keep pace with the vast amounts of material they must master, law students tend to think about entire bodies of law in terms of the important cases. Then (they hope), when it comes time to reconstruct the rich, detailed picture, all those cases will coalesce like the stipple dots of a printed illustration.

In this and the next four chapters, we'll assume you've decided to take the plunge into law school. We'll look at the way cases are studied, organized and thought about. But first a bit of advice. The practice of law is about people, not words on paper. As you become immersed in a deepening sea of cases, try to remember that each represents more than a formal opinion, more than an abbreviation for a legal principle. Each is a slice of life. In the real world, parties to a case are not algebraic (P)laintiffs and (D)efendants, but individuals (or entities) with some sort of problem. Unable to resolve their dispute between themselves, they have sought the aid of professional advocates, fact finders, and our system of adjudication. So take a moment to view each case in terms of parties and process. What made these people so upset that they resorted to the courts? What would you, as a lawyer, have done if the file had landed on your desk? And don't forget to think about the actual characters and their personalities; let yourself be entertained. Some cases, like *Guilford v. Yale University*,[1] surprise with their unintended humor. The deadpan opinion speaks for itself:

> The plaintiff [Dudley Guilford, a graduate of the class of 1899] had returned to New Haven for the fortieth reunion of his class. On the night in question, at about 12 o'clock, he, accompanied by one of his classmates, proceeded to [the reunion headquarters] and there met a number of younger men of the class of 1936. After arriving he spent a pleasant period with those gathered there, remaining until about 2 o'clock, at which time it was suggested that the place be closed. Those of the party then remaining left the building and proceeded to the sidewalk in the street where they talked for five or ten minutes. While they were conversing, the plaintiff expressed a desire to urinate [and was informed that there was a toilet in the basement. At this time, the lights in the building had been turned out. The plaintiff did not reenter the building but] stepped back upon the premises, crossed the curb between the Trumbull Street walk and the grass plot [near the entrance] and proceeded across the grass plot, walking about midway between the side of the building and the [one-foot] stone [retaining] wall enclosing the property on the Trumbull Street side. There was a tree growing from the lower level [of the building] beyond the retaining wall at the east of the grass plot. The shape of the tree was such that its top projected above the level of the top of the retaining wall. The plaintiff thought that the top of this tree was a bush growing on the grass plot, and walked towards it. He tripped over the parapet at the top of the retaining wall and fell [about ten and a half feet] to its bottom at the lower level. The region generally was well lighted at the time, but the plaintiff claimed that, while he was able to see the street and the sidewalk very well, the ground under his feet was in dark shadow and that he was walking into the shadow to find a secluded place near the bush to urinate.

> [The appeals court, in affirming the lower court's ruling, concluded:] It does not subject the defendant to an undue burden to require that it exercise reasonable care to see that not only the buildings assigned for headquarters but also the surroundings are free from traps dangerous to life and limb.

---

1. 128 Conn. 449, 23 A.2d 917 (1942).

2.2 Elements of a Case

Before you can approach any case intelligently, you must be able to separate its component parts. Mechanical as this may seem, it is the only way to get a firm grasp on exactly what the opinion stands for. Sorting out the different pieces helps to cut through confusion.

This skill is not acquired overnight. After reading enough cases, though, you can't help but become an expert. By investing some extra effort in the beginning, consciously identifying the elements listed below as you read a case, you can reduce the time it takes to become an efficient and knowledgeable case reader (a talent everyone respects!). When you actually write down this information, you produce the hallowed case brief. Whether and to what extent case briefs will be useful to you are considered in chapter 6.

Procedural Facts

Being able to plot just how the particular case you're reading wound up before the tribunal that wrote the opinion is essential to understanding the legal system's structure and how various courts interact with one another. With that said, it may now be admitted that these procedures become rather routine in a short time, and soon you won't pay much attention to where a suit originated or how it made the judicial rounds. But don't get cocky. Special procedural devices often lurk inconspicuously amidst the mundane phrases that you're tempted to skip. Not only might these be important to the eventual outcome, but they're part of the legal vocabulary you must assimilate as you progress.

The *Guilford* case that you just read has a pretty mundane procedural pedigree. It represents the opinion of the Connecticut Supreme Court of Errors, to which Yale had appealed after the New Haven County Superior Court found in favor of Dudley Guilford.

Substantive Facts

Part of thinking like a lawyer is being able to separate pertinent information from irrelevant rubbish. The factual descriptions found in judicial opinions invariably contain, shall we say, more background than we might wish to know, so the objective becomes to discern the important features of a case. This takes practice. For basic courses, where fact patterns tend to remain fairly confined and similar to each other, one strategy is to start by reading the case through quickly, noting facts that appear significant. After isolating the court's holding, read through the case again and add any facts that now seem more salient; eliminate the ones that turned out to be unimportant after all. But don't be too stingy! The world is not so clearly divided into significant and insignificant facts.

Keep in mind, also, the *reason* that knowing the facts is so important: a case's usefulness as precedent in a future controversy will depend on its similarity to that controversy (more on that in chapter 3). Law-school exams test your ability not only to recognize cases that appear relevant to a particular factual situation, but how *strongly* they apply to the given facts. When you emerge into the real world of lawyering, your power to advocate a legal position effectively will depend strongly on your facility with cases.

The version of the facts that a court accepts for purposes of its opinion can depend on how the case got to that court. For example, say a defendant moves to dismiss for failure to state a claim—in other words, he contends that the plaintiff doesn't have a case. The court will consider, *for the sake of argument,* the facts as asserted by the plaintiff, in order to assess whether she has any chance at all of presenting a winning case at trial. The *Guilford* court stated its intention to view the facts "in the light most favorable to the plaintiff" so that, when it slammed Yale, it did so without appearing to have jumped to any unfair conclusions.

After trial, however, an appeals court will accept the lower court's version of the facts rather than one of the parties' accounts. This is because both sides have already been given the opportunity to be heard; fairness, therefore, does not demand deference to the loser's story. The court can then avoid dabbling with the facts and concentrate on pure questions of law.

Although uncovering the important facts of a case is a skill that develops with experience, several avenues of general inquiry often provide worthwhile starting points.

1. **Parties:** Who are they? If there are more than one on either side, what characteristics and interests do they share? What are the relationships among co-parties and between opponents? Are any special duties or obligations attached to these relationships? In the *Guilford* case, Dudley had been invited to the reunion by the Yale administration, who hoped both to elevate his spirits and loosen his wallet. As such, the court considered him a "business invitee" to whom Yale owed a higher degree of care than it would to an uninvited visitor.

2. **Places:** Is there a geographical location relevant to the lawsuit? For example, does it matter that the parties are from the same or different city, state, or country?

3. **Events:** What is the transaction or occurrence that resulted in the lawsuit? What details, if changed, would alter the tenor of the claim?

Advanced courses often involve cases with complex factual backgrounds. Understanding the reasoning behind one of these beasts is usually impossible without thorough comprehension of the facts. Unfortunately, the simple technique described above will not help you unravel a multiparty transaction involving several financial, corporate, or commercial exchanges. It becomes necessary to roll out some heavy artillery: a pencil, an eraser, and some creativity. The only efficient way to represent an elaborate scheme such that it will be mentally accessible in the future (say, at exam time) is to draw yourself a diagram that tells the whole story. It should be as simple and visually understandable as possible, so it is good practice to devise figure elements that always designate the same concept. Because each case is unique, of course, it will be necessary to come up with some new ideas here and there. But remember that these diagrams function merely as mnemonic devices; they don't have to be works of graphic artistry.

To see how this might work, consider the following excerpt from *Estate of Franklin v. Commissioner.*[2] This is one of those mercilessly intricate tax-shelter cases, in which two parties (Twenty-Fourth Property Associates, referred to simply as Associates, and the Romneys) attempted to steer merrily through the tax law by means of a clever real-estate scheme. As to the outcome, suffice it to say that the court took a rather humorless view of their antics. The immediate task for us is merely to figure out what the transaction was all about.

But first, a few preliminaries. A *nonrecourse* purchase means that the seller, who has parted with his property on the promise of installment payments to be received from the buyer, agrees to look only to the property itself for satisfaction of the debt should the buyer fail to make the required payments. In other words, he has no recourse against the buyer personally; the best he can do is foreclose and retake the property, hoping its value is sufficient to cover the remainder of the debt. A *leaseback* refers to an agreement where the buyer, upon receiving title to property, immediately leases it back to the seller.

The court reported the facts as follows:

> Under a document entitled "Sales Agreement," the Romneys agreed to "sell" the Thunderbird Inn to Associates for $1,224,000. The property would be paid for over a period of ten years, with interest on any unpaid balance of seven and one-half percent per annum. "Prepaid interest" in the amount of $75,000 was payable immediately; monthly principal and interest installments of $9,045.36 would be paid for approximately the first ten years, with Associates required to make a balloon payment at the end of the ten years of the difference between the remaining purchase price, forecast as $975,000, and any mortgages then outstanding against the property.
>
> The purchase obligation of Associates to the Romneys was nonrecourse[.] The sale was combined with a leaseback of the property by Associates to the Romneys[.] The Romneys were responsible for all of the typical expenses of owning the motel property including all utility costs, taxes, assessments, rents, charges, [etc.] Finally, the Romneys were allowed to propose new capital improvements which Associates would be required to either build for themselves or allow the Romneys to construct with compensating modifications in rent or purchase price.

---

2. 544 F.2d 1045 (9th Cir. 1976).

Figures 2-1 and 2-2 might be suitable alternative depictions of this fact pattern:

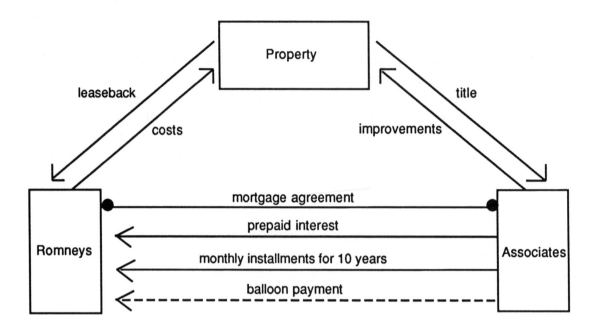

FIGURE 2–1.

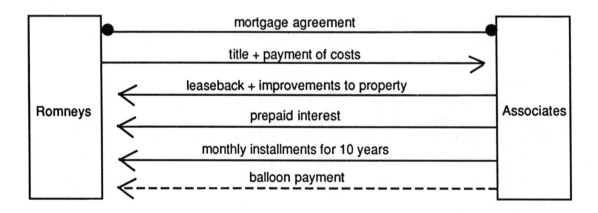

FIGURE 2–2.

A dashed line is used for the balloon payment to emphasize its prospective character (more accurately, its fictitious character: the parties never intended for it to be paid!).

So, as the diagrams show, the Romneys sell the property and immediately rent it under the leaseback. But the drawings also suggest something further. If the costs and improvements are of equal value, and if the Romneys' rental payments are equivalent to Associates' loan payments, then nothing seems to have occurred except some paper shuffling. This recognition was critical to the court's holding, which denied the desired tax benefits, and can be readily appreciated from Figure 2–2.

If this tax case did not prove sufficiently entertaining, here's a secured transactions example. Once again, some background first. Secured transactions bear great similarity to the transaction encountered in the *Franklin* case above, in that collateral is used to support a debt. However, the subject matter involves personal property (like cars and refrigerators) instead of land.

In a typical transaction, the buyer walks away with goods on the promise of paying for them in installments. The seller, called the *secured party,* retains a *security interest* in the sold goods, meaning that she can retrieve the goods should the buyer default. The agreement covering the transaction is called a *conditional sales contract.* It is almost never nonrecourse, because the seller knows that the value of already-used property will probably not suffice to offset the buyer's remaining obligation after default; therefore, the buyer remains personally on the hook. Like any debt, the conditional sales contract can be sold or assigned to a third party for collection.

Security interests often arise in contexts other than sales of goods. A bank, for example, might agree to extend credit to a borrower only if it can obtain a security interest in the borrower's personal property. Since no sale is involved, the agreement in this case is called a *security agreement,* rather than a conditional sales contract (but the bank is still called the secured party). In either case, the seller or lender is required to give public notice of her security interest by filing a *financing statement* with the appropriate governmental office or offices. This document tells the world of the existence of the security interest.

Sometimes, a security agreement can cover the same goods as a conditional sales contract. When the borrower/buyer goes bankrupt, the bank and the seller both want the goods. Who wins depends on which agreement was executed first, who filed the necessary financing statements first, and a few other factors. These were the circumstances of the following case, *Cain v. Country Club Delicatessen of Saybrook, Inc.*[3]:

> Defendant [Country Club Delicatessen] opened its restaurant in Old Saybrook on July 26, 1962. At that time it was fully equipped. [By the time it declared bankruptcy, Defendant had purchased additional equipment] from Hewitt Engi-

---

3. 25 Conn. Supp. 327, 203 A.2d 441 (Super. Ct. 1964).

neering, Inc., referred to herein as Hewitt. On August 16, 1962, defendant corporation borrowed $35,000 from First Hartford, giving a promissory note secured by a chattel-mortgage type of security agreement covering a security interest in "All goods, personal property, equipment [etc.]."

The day previously, viz., August 15, 1962, First Hartford had filed a financing statement with the secretary of state, Uniform Commercial Code division, showing the defendant as debtor and First Hartford as the secured party.... Also on August 15, 1962, First Hartford executed another financing statement, being a duplicate of the one filed in the office of the secretary of state, and filed it with the town clerk of the town of Old Saybrook....

On August 30, 1962, defendant corporation and Hewitt Engineering, Inc., executed a conditional sale contract covering property sold by Hewitt to defendant.... Some of this property is expressly mentioned in the financing statement and security agreement of the defendant with First Hartford, above mentioned. On August 30, 1962, a financing statement was filed with the town clerk of the town of Old Saybrook showing Hewitt Engineering, Inc. as the secured party, and General Electric as assignee of Hewitt, and defendant corporation as debtor. The description of the types or items of property covered by it read: "Complete restaurant and delicatessen including kitchen equipment and display equipment."

There are two ways to approach this parade of documents and filings. If you consider the timing of the various components to be most important, you can construct a simple time-line diagram like this:

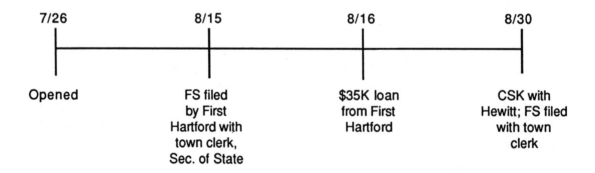

FS = financing statement
CSK = conditional sales contract

FIGURE 2–3.

30

By contrast, if you want to become familiar with the substance of each individual transaction, the following form would be more useful:

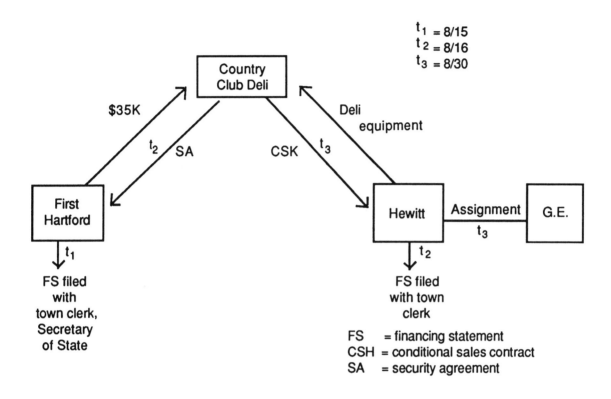

$t_1 = 8/15$
$t_2 = 8/16$
$t_3 = 8/30$

FS = financing statement
CSH = conditional sales contract
SA = security agreement

FIGURE 2–4.

What can each diagram tell us? If the court's decision turns on the order and official bureaus in which the parties filed their financing statements, the first diagram illustrates all we need to know. If, however, the case involves broader questions (such as validity of the contracts, or which parties should actually be in court at this time), the more comprehensive second diagram will be more helpful. As it turns out, the case involved the first set of considerations. Who won? First Hartford, and for a rather mundane reason: Hewitt filed its financing statement in the wrong office!

Now is this stuff fun or what?

Issue

You can't feel comfortable with a case until you have a reasonably precise idea of the *legal issue* being addressed by the court. Often it can be boiled down to a single question of

31

law whose application is contested by each side, such as "Whether the invention represents a sufficient advance over prior work to deserve a patent." Sometimes, however, the parties will not have conceded that the case reduces to one element. Each will have a distinct theory. In such situations, both or all theories should be noted; the fact that someone lost doesn't mean his argument is interred forever.

Returning to *Guilford v. Yale*, the plaintiff framed the issue as one of negligence: the university should have been more careful about keeping its grounds safe. Yale contended, more or less, that it could not possibly have foreseen the muddleheaded peregrinations of every inebriated, weak-bladdered alum.

Holding

Trying to extract the actual decision from a legal opinion can be the most difficult aspect of case reading. The judge's thoughts may digress into seemingly distant issues or soar effortlessly to lofty heights of jurisprudential philosophy. We'll have more to say about separating the actual decision from *dicta*—that is, extraneous commentary or marginalia—in chapter 3. For now, remember that the holding does not exist independently of the issue(s) and facts of a particular case. Courts, after all, decide specific controversies between real litigants; be careful not to overgeneralize what you think a case stands for.

Reasoning

How did the court arrive at its holding? Was it applying or overruling precedent? Often, trying to follow a judge's application of law to facts can seem like a treasure hunt. She may not announce her reasoning boldly. She may disperse it through the opinion. The facts may be ambiguous.

The lines separating a judge's holding, reasoning, and dicta are rarely distinct. For example, the court found for Dudley Guilford because of the "free and easy hospitality which exists in New Haven at reunion time," and which apparently places a special burden on Yale to foresee the muddleheaded peregrinations of every inebriated, weak-bladdered alum. But just how the university failed to meet this burden is never really spelled out in the opinion.

Understanding a court's reasoning involves two analyses: (1) the judge's own logic and conclusions, and (2) his use of earlier judges' ideas in the form of case citations. A court that wants to get around a previous decision can read it narrowly, focusing strongly on the specific facts rather than the opinion's underlying logic. Courts occasionally "reinterpret" the reasoning of their predecessors, supposedly (but not really) without disturbing previous holdings or reasoning. At the other end of the spectrum, courts seeking to apply a previous ruling expansively may generously ignore significant factual differences, or treat language that is quite plainly dictum as if it were part of the earlier holding. And the variations go on. Most often, courts choosing to apply precedent will remain true to the earlier case's reasoning and distinguish it only when the facts are different in a legally relevant sense. But don't be too sure.

Dissents and Concurrences

More than one judge listens to each case brought before an appellate court. Judicial minds do not always agree. Accordingly, do not be surprised when you find that many of the opinions you read are not unanimous. The *majority* opinion speaks for the court and expresses its holding. If a judge agrees with the majority's ultimate outcome but not its reasoning, she may write a *concurring* opinion explaining her differences. Disagreement with the majority's outcome (and possibly, though not necessarily, its legal reasoning) is expressed in a *dissenting* opinion. While neither concurrences nor dissents carry formal precedential weight, they are frequently influential. Legal doctrine[4] is always changing. Today, the majority prevailed; no one can be sure about tomorrow.

2.3 Recurring Themes

Some legal motifs are so fundamental that they consistently permeate entire bodies of law. These themes represent universal background issues that continue to shape the thoughts of judges and scholars even as the law itself changes. You must reckon with them each time you analyze a case. Three such recurring themes are described below. Remember them as you progress; you will undoubtedly discover others for yourself.

The Slippery Slope

A concept you will encounter repeatedly as a rudiment of legal analysis is the quandary of the slippery slope. It is often introduced in the course of Socratic dialogue, a technique employed by professors to needle nervous novices and expose sloppy reasoning. As discussion of a case proceeds, the professor selects a student at random—yourself, for example. Your views on the case are solicited. The professor probes your analysis with questions to expose its weaknesses. You are then invited to reconsider. Just when you think your newly modified conclusions have afforded you a means of escape, your professor slices the salami ever more

---

4. Lawyers use the word *doctrine* to connote legal rules and principles. *Black-letter* doctrine refers to those fundamental, "meat and potatoes" aspects of the law that have gained widespread acceptance.

thinly, proceeding to a deeper level of analysis and exposing the frayed edges of your reasoning that you still have not tucked away.

The purpose of this exercise is not (usually) meanness, but mind-sharpening. As your reasoning is dissected, you and your classmates (who, you are sure, must be snickering by now) learn that there are far more questions in law than answers and that you must think twice about your conclusions before embracing them too firmly or categorically.

The slippery slope problem stems from an intellectual inability to avoid the next logical step, much as we would like to stay put. Any conclusion or rule has implications reaching beyond its own narrow little world. We are often forced to admit that acceptance of one proposition carries with it *implied* approval of other, undesirable propositions that are "logically compelled," and perhaps the truly bizarre awaits us at the end of the slide if the proposition is "taken to its extreme."

We encounter the slipperiest and steepest inclines when we attempt distinctions based upon degree alone. Let's say you live next door to Arnold, a successful corporate executive. One day Arnold decides that the rat race is taking too much out of him. He yearns for the simpler life: The obvious solution, Arnold decides, is to convert his house into a pig farm. As he is nailing a sign above his door that reads ARNOLD'S PIG FARM, you attempt to reason with him. You stress the character of the neighborhood, the prospect of declining property values, the personal imposition, and your mother who keeps kosher. "Bourgeois bellyaching," he replies, adding: "Besides, no judge will support you. Why, think of the parade of horribles that would follow. Any modification or use of property would require full neighborhood approval. Should I be able to veto the color you choose for your house? Should you have the right to prevent Little Johnny from running his lemonade stand?" And, with a snort, Arnold gets back to work.

The simplest way to conquer the slippery slope is with a *bright-line rule*. Zoning regulations establish specific guidelines for permissible property usages. Their language is generally clear. Undoubtedly, the operation of a pig farm would run afoul of some prohibition, perhaps against unhealthful or unaesthetic activities, or even a complete ban on all commercial undertakings. The slope is flattened, not because of any argument of logic, but because people—through their elected representatives—have made a choice and enacted a clear restriction.

If you can find no bright-line rule on which to rely, you must try to convince a judge that closing the pig farm will not open Pandora's box to wild and unruly restrictions in the future. You might suggest a *limiting principle* that would include Arnold but not Little Johnny. One suitable precept is a famous and enduring property maxim: a person should use his or her property only in such a manner that will not injure another.[5]

But the judge may be skeptical of limiting principles, which can themselves lead to more slippery slopes. Instead, she may prefer to be as explicit and forthright as possible,

---

5. *Sic utere tuo ut alienum non laedas,* for you Latin lovers.

insisting on a *balancing test* to expose all competing values. Often the common-law doctrine of nuisance, poignantly applicable here, is used by landowners to prevent interference with the use and enjoyment of their land. The *Second Restatement of Property*[6] defines one type of actionable private nuisance as an "intentional and unreasonable" invasion. If we stopped here, we would have a simple limiting principle. The *Restatement* goes on, however, to define reasonableness with a balancing test that weighs the "gravity of the harm" alongside the "utility of the actor's conduct." These expressions are then further defined:

Gravity of Harm—Factors Involved

      (a) the extent of the harm involved;

      (b) the character of the harm involved;

      (c) the social value which the law attaches to the type of use or enjoyment invaded;

      (d) the suitability of the particular use or enjoyment invaded to the character of the locality;

      (e) the burden on the person harmed or avoiding the harm.

Utility of Conduct—Factors Involved

      (a) the social value which the law attaches to the primary purpose of the conduct;

      (b) the suitability of the conduct to the character of the locality;

      (c) whether it is impracticable to prevent or avoid the invasion, if the activity is maintained;

      (d) whether it is impracticable to maintain the activity if it is required to bear the cost of compensating the invasion.

While the limiting principle focuses its main inquiry on the extent of injury and only implicitly considers the value of pig farming, the balancing test reaches further. It demands detailed analysis of all factors relevant both to the conduct and to the harm it produces. You would have to demonstrate not only that Arnold's enterprise is causing harm, but also that its social contribution falls short of rendering that harm acceptable to the larger community.

The Normative/Empirical Distinction

Though it sounds rather pedantic, this often subtle judgment provides the key to understanding a great deal of legal discussion. An empirical or positive proposition is one which seeks simply to describe, without drawing any conclusions, the state of a piece of the

---

6. Section 822. A Restatement represents the efforts of the American Law Institute to summarize the contents of an entire area of law and to suggest its future direction. Typical Restatements occupy many volumes and are updated periodically.

world. Empirical methods are detached and scientific. They do no more than measure and present data. A survey of the average salaries of first-year associates is an empirical study. A *normative* proposition, on the other hand, does more than merely report; it concludes and suggests. Normative ideas incorporate analysis, inference, and personal views, although they may be based on empirical suppositions. A suggestion that average salaries of first-year associates are, based on our empirical survey, too low represents a normative statement.[7]

In short, the normative/empirical distinction maintains the boundary separating *ought* from *is*. At first, perhaps, the difference appears too patently obvious to warrant a technical term describing the distinction. However, a purportedly empirical conclusion that really camouflages a normative stowaway can prove quite insidious. By exploiting the respect accorded scientific observations because of their precision and impartiality, an opinion can masquerade as fact. You are unlikely to regard a purportedly empirical assertion with the same suspicion and criticism you would a personal conclusion.[8] For example, we see the primary mission of newspapers as reportage of events and expect them to confine opinions to the editorial columns. Because of this expectation, unwary readers may be "brainwashed" into unquestioningly accepting a normative proposition that the editors have allowed to slip into a lead story.

Judges often strive to maintain fairness by applying legal standards impartially (i.e., empirically), while leaving the normative decisions for the legislature. As popular representatives, legislators have a political mandate to prescribe standards of behavior; judges, on the other hand, are well trained in logic and reasoning. The fun starts when these respective roles become blurred.

Consider the classic negligence rule, which is usually framed like this:

A person is negligent when his or her conduct fails to conform to that which a reasonable person would exercise if placed in like circumstances.

The policy behind this rule is simple. Members of society should, as a normative proposition, be able to expect in their daily lives a certain level of prudent behavior from others. If some oversized clod levels you with a beer keg outside his frat, he pays for the damage after peeling you off the ground. Even if he's sorry and didn't mean it. The negligence rule sets the normative dimension of expected behavior at "reasonable conduct."[9]

But when a judge applies the standard, does she simply effectuate the legislature's stated policy, or come up with one of her own? Does she, detachedly and impartially, compare the

---

7. Senior partners generally have a few normative ideas of their own, of course.
8. The use of logic techniques can similarly mislead, as you'll see in chapter 4.
9. It might just as easily be set at a higher or lower level. When one party owes a special duty to another, as did Yale to poor Dudley Guilford, the level of care expected might be greater. The highest expectations are reserved for relationships of trust. Those who safeguard others' property for a fee (e.g., banks that rent safety deposit boxes to their customers) owe a duty of "extraordinary" care.

defendant's actions with those of a statistically average, standard person? Or does she apply her own idea of what she believes reasonable behavior *ought* to be? The difference is important. Each judge might have a different normative ideal in mind, and conforming to the law shouldn't depend on the idiosyncrasies of a particular person's interpretations. It is to the legislature that we turn for such guidelines.

The potential for normative infiltration increases as the rules become less definitive and acquire meaning only through practical application. This difficulty is discussed below in the specific context of statutory interpretation; keep in mind, however, that in the legal world, the normative/empirical distinction may be relevant almost anywhere.

The Objective/Subjective Debate

Think for a moment about the negligence rule stated above. Everyone, regardless of intelligence or infirmity, is held to the same standard of conduct. The reasonable person speaks for all. This choice introduces a moral dilemma: it seems unfair to place liability on someone acting inculpably and conscientiously simply because his idea of "reasonableness" doesn't measure up. Doesn't one's subjective state of mind count for anything? The answer is that we, as a community, have made a decision—indulgence of the individual must yield to the common security. This choice is normative. It reflects a compromise between competing values that are deeply held and reveals permanent and irreconcilable tensions between the individual and society.

A *subjective* system that examines each case from an individual perspective inevitably produces more personalized justice. But there is no free lunch. The price is sacrifice of predictability and ease of administration. An *objective* system, on the other hand, offers simplicity and coherence. Members of society know what to expect of other members, although this may result in unwanted punishment of the morally blameless.

Now reconsider the solutions to the slippery slope discussed previously . A bright-line rule exemplifies the objective alternative, and its operation holds the greatest potential for harshness. For instance, federal securities law[10] regulates insider trading, the purchase and sale of stock by (among others) knowledgeable corporate personnel. A statutory insider is rigidly defined as any company officer or director, or anyone holding more than 10 percent of the company's stock. If an insider both buys and sells company securities within a six-month period, that person has violated the law and must turn any profit over to the corporation. The purpose of the rule is to prevent those with access to privileged, "inside" information from manipulating the stock market.

But wait a minute. The terms seem wildly underinclusive and overinclusive at the same time: many people possessing inside information remain outside the rule's ambit, while many

---

10. Specifically, §16 of the Securities Exchange Act of 1934.

transactions covered by the rule might be completely innocent. The drafters were not oblivious. They reasoned as follows: first, while the definition is narrow, it covers those individuals whose abuses have in the past been most frequent and outrageous; second, the evil at which the rule is directed appeared sufficiently harmful and widespread to justify a flat prohibition—even if completely innocent transactions occasionally get caught in its broad sweep. The rule is simple and mechanical. No thorny issues of intent are open to dispute. Let those whose steps may lead them across its gaping mouth beware.

Fixed rules are most appropriate where the value of predictability is high and the potential for hardship from unintentional application minimal. The most useful rules operate on easily discernible factual criteria (quantitative definitions like age are often chosen) and are as specific as possible to avoid gross over- and underinclusion. From the point of view of the rule-making authority and its agents charged with enforcement, such clarity yields (1) cheap and relatively unambiguous implementation—you're speeding if the radar reads over 55 mph, and (2) an easily followed guideline to foster voluntary compliance. Those subject to the rule hope the same explicitness will (1) limit the discretion of enforcement personnel to avoid arbitrariness, and (2) provide terms clear enough to enable straightforward adjustment of activity to avoid official sanction.

Sometimes a limiting principle or legal standard can achieve a compromise between clarity and particularity. The legislature, for example, may enact a general rule and leave to the courts its application in particular circumstances. Standards typically contain terms such as "reasonableness," which must be interpreted as well as applied. While such rules are objective, in the sense that the same standard applies to all, their imprecise character leaves room for adaptation. Flexibility is dual-edged, however. Although applying standards on an individual basis clearly avoids much unwanted inclusion, the price paid is a measure of certainty and safety from arbitrariness.

The most subjective approach to regulation is to apply a balancing test to each individual. Because of the completely indeterminate nature of such a regime, as well as the significant administrative time and expense necessary for its implementation, wholly subjective schemes are reserved for instances where the chances of injustice appear high and the consequences of error dire. A good example is the sentencing process of criminal proceedings. While the individual may be protected from an overinclusive rule, discretion remains virtually unlimited and leaves the door wide open for arbitrary decisions. For this reason, drafters of balancing tests strive to preserve some objectivity by listing all factors considered relevant. Maintaining broad flexibility while limiting the scope of discretion frequently proves a very tricky business.

Administrative agencies are unusual in that many can choose whether to take an objective or subjective approach to different situations. An agency can promulgate a set of fixed rules governing a particular activity, first notifying the public that such rules are on their way and soliciting comments on proposed drafts, or it can instead adjudicate on a case-by-case basis like a court. Although unique in their ability to choose regulatory methods, agencies frequently face criticism for making the wrong selection. Such criticism goes with the territory. The tension between objectivity and subjectivity is fundamental, leaving choices that favor one over the other forever open to dispute.

2.4 Understanding Statutes

Many legal controversies center on the interpretation of a law. Practitioners refer to this as statutory construction. The basic problem is this: In an ideal world, a legislature would identify a specific problem to be addressed and mold a snugly fitting provision to deal with the problem completely and unambiguously. Such is, of course, impossible in all but the most narrow contexts. It is up to the courts to apply the legislature's best effort in actual circumstances, and deduce just how the lawmakers intended their handiwork to function in cases they may not have anticipated.

Again, this is only the basic problem. Vast opportunities for uncertainty and misunderstanding present themselves from the time legislators first debate a proposal to the point at which lawyers and judges get hold of it. On the legislative side, representatives must struggle to reach a compromise on the new law's substantive scope. Who will be covered, and who will remain unaffected? Often, differing political interests clash so strongly that the best the legislature can do is enact a deliberately vague measure. In other words, political bargains often result in adoption of generalized formulations, leaving the fine-tuning to the courts (and leaving lawmakers free to mollify angry political constituencies by pointing a dismayed finger at wayward judges' misinterpretations). Even if a broad agenda can be agreed upon, the drafters of novel legislation face the difficult task of producing verbiage robust enough to cover all anticipated applications, resilient enough to withstand the efforts of those determined to avoid its reach (tax provisions tend to generate the most fertile efforts), and explicit enough to avoid gross misinterpretations by the courts.

On the judicial side, the line between interpreting law empirically and actually making it normatively can be lost in the enthusiasm of it all. Of course, the first duty of courts is to the drafters' intentions. But faced with a vague statute capable of producing distasteful results (as the court sees it) or of conflicting with other existing law, or that simply fails to articulate what those folks under the big dome had in mind, judges may have to get creative in a manner that goes beyond merely matching words to cases.[11]

---

11. A good, if somewhat technical, example can be found in bankruptcy law. In this field, much can turn on whether a contract is considered *executory,* meaning that at least some performance remains due on both sides. When you think about it, this definition can be quite difficult to apply to specific cases, and attempts to produce definitive guidelines have repeatedly foundered. Some courts, recognizing the futility even of trying to stick to the statutory text, suggested that they would simply work backward: if calling a contract executory were to appear to further the policies underlying the Bankruptcy Code, the contract would be deemed executory; otherwise, it would not. *See, e.g.,* In re Jolly, 574 F.2d 349, 351 (6th Cir. 1978); In re Richmond Metal Finishers, 34 Bankr. 521, 523 (Bankr. E.D. Va. 1983).

Grappling With Words

The awful truth of the matter is that statutes are just plain difficult to read. Narrow laws must be ruthlessly concise. Even the vague ones are deliberately mechanical, full of legalese repetitions and at least some specificities. Explicit language helps to avoid misinterpretations and misapplications but also forces you to approach statutes very slowly, word by word.

"The first rule of statutory construction," goes an old saw, "is *read on.*" What the first sentence gives, the last may take away. This pattern is not uncommon; it arises from the political process. Instead of tinkering with the guts of a statute or deliberately introducing ambiguity, legislators may work out a compromise by accepting straightforward terms but including specific "cutbacks." These exclude particular political constituencies or restrict the circumstances in which the statute will apply. Such retrenchments usually appear at the end of the text and announce themselves with the telltale phrase "provided, however, that..." In the extreme, the statute says, "You may carve your pound of flesh; provided, however, that you spill not one drop of blood in so doing."[12]

As you read through a statute, try to invent little hypotheticals that explain just why particular words were chosen. What loopholes did the drafter seek to close? In what situations might ambiguity arise? Also, make sure to avoid improper inferences as you read; stick to the statutory language! A common error is to make assumptions that *appear* to follow naturally but in reality expand the statute's intended scope.

For instance, the Copyright Act[13] grants to the owner of a copyright the exclusive right to reproduce, sell reproductions of, display, and/or perform the copyrighted work. Who is the owner? A quick glance at §201, entitled "Ownership of Copyright," indicates that ownership initially rests with the creator unless the work is one made for hire. Well, that seems straightforward enough; if someone pays an author or artist to create something, that someone gets the copyright...right? Wrong! The term *work made for hire* is a term of art, defined at the beginning of the Copyright Act (although you'd never know it from §201). A work is made for hire only if created by an employee in the course of employment, or if it fits within one of a series of technical categories.[14] Ownership of the copyright to works falling outside these categories remains with the work's creator. This scheme often surprises those who commission works of art, and the surprise frequently comes after it's too late. A number of

---

12. Sometimes the exception represents a gift to a particular constituent. The legislature, not wishing to appear corrupt, may employ superficially neutral language that just happens to apply solely to the favored party. Title 35 of the U.S. Code, which deals with patents, contains a provision (§155A) that provides a lengthened term of protection for the manufacturers of Aspartame, the artificial sweetener. Neither Aspartame nor the patent owner is mentioned by name; the terms of the provision are general. However, only those who received particular types of correspondence from the Food and Drug Administration on specific, named dates qualify. Guess how many patentees fit that description?

13. Title 17 of the United States Code.

14. For example, if it's a translation, an instructional text, a test or answer material for a test, an atlas, or part of a motion picture, and so long as the parties agree in writing that the work is made for hire.

lawsuits could have been avoided by greater familiarity with *all* relevant terms of the Copyright Act.

When you read a case that turns on the interpretation of a statute, it's important to avoid automatically regarding the court's conclusions as eternal and self-evident. After all, two sides were urging versions of the statute so different as to justify opposite results. Perhaps the court did identify the better-reasoned reading. To a law student, however, that's a secondary matter. Your paramount objective is the ability to give life to a set of words and make them work in a particular context. Observing how others have done so—whether or not they proved successful in court—will develop your own skills.

To illustrate all of this, consider the following hypothetical situation:

Joe Niceguy is the owner of Uncle Joe's Radio Shoppe, a small electronics store located in a rapidly gentrifying section of town. Joe plans to cash in on the sudden influx of yuppies by ordering a large shipment of portable compact-disc players and hopefully raise enough money to cover his ailing mother's hospital bills. He sends Sleazo Distributors an order at their latest catalogue price. Sleazo does not respond to Joe but places the order on one of their delivery trucks and sends a bill of lading as evidence of the shipment to Joe. Just before the driver leaves, however, Fred Sleazo has Joe's order delivered to his arch competitor, Madman Mort, who wants to drive Joe out of business for good. Mort sells the entire shipment. By then the eighties are over. The yuppies flee to the suburbs or succumb to life-style angst, and Joe's mother needs another operation. Guilt-ridden, Sleazo's driver tells Joe of the switch. Joe humbly comes to you for advice on his rights against Sleazo.

As an experienced commercial lawyer, you immediately realize that the situation falls under §2–206 of your state's version of the Uniform Commercial Code. It says:

(1) Unless otherwise unambiguously indicated by the language or circumstances
  (a) An offer to make a contract shall be construed as inviting acceptance in any manner and by any medium reasonable in the circumstances;
  (b) An order or other offer to buy goods for prompt or current shipment shall be construed as inviting acceptance either by a prompt promise to ship or by the prompt or current shipment of [the goods].
2. Where the beginning of a requested performance is a reasonable mode of acceptance an offeror who is not notified of acceptance within a reasonable time may treat the offer as having lapsed before acceptance.

If we can show that a contract existed between Sleazo and Joe, and that Sleazo breached, Joe will be entitled to damages. Having found a relevant provision (not generally such an easy matter), it is first necessary to apply the statute's definitions to the facts before you. A contract becomes complete when the offeree formally accepts an offer that is still open and available. But who is the offeror, and who the offeree? Sleazo has sent out a catalogue, so perhaps that makes him the offeror. A little legwork by your overworked associate, however, reveals that courts usually view catalogues as solicitations for offers, rather than offers in themselves. By placing an order, Joe presented Sleazo with an offer. Did he accept? Joe would certainly like to think so, but Sleazo will insist otherwise.

Whom does the statute favor? Sleazo can point to §(1)(a), and argue that he never responded to Joe's offer at all. How could Joe possibly infer acceptance from silence?

This is certainly a strong argument. Does Joe have anything on his side? Section (2) does not seem especially relevant to Joe, as he seeks to enforce the contract as an offeror, not to get out of it. Section (1)(b) shows more promise. Acceptance may consist of a promise to ship or shipment itself. It is the word *shipment* that we must zero in on to assess the strength of Joe's case. Was the order "shipped" as soon as it left Sleazo's warehouse? When it was put on the truck? When the bill of lading was issued? When Joe received the bill of lading?

Where do you look for clues to the meaning of words used in a statute? The most direct sources include accompanying legislative materials and cases that discuss its terms explicitly. The UCC is unusual in that its drafters prepared an extensive set of comments to guide future uncertainties. While these are not legally binding on courts, judges generally give them a great deal of deference. The comment to §2–206 says in part:

> "Shipment" . . . does not include the beginning of delivery by the seller's own truck or by messenger. But loading on the seller's own truck might be a beginning of performance under subsection (2).

The first sentence is quite disappointing. It squarely states that placement on the Sleazo truck will not qualify as a shipment and hence cannot be considered an acceptance. Moreover, Sleazo could turn the wording of subsection (2) to his advantage: "Even though I'm not the offeror," Sleazo would say, "the idea of 'reasonable mode of acceptance' should apply to me, too. It's really the same as the requirement of §(1)(b) that any mode of acceptance be 'reasonable under the circumstances.' A contract is supposed to express an agreement between two parties. I never actually accepted. How can my actions at my own private warehouse initiate a joint enterprise against my will? Is this 'reasonable'?"

Strong stuff. Is all lost for Joe? No way! You now direct your attention to the bill of lading. Common carriers typically use these as evidence of a shipment; a seller's own delivery team would have no use for such a document. Therefore, Sleazo might be operating his own freight system as a separate business; in that case, the comment's reference to the "seller's own truck" would probably not apply, since Sleazo's shipping procedures could no longer be considered private. Moreover, the bill of lading might well constitute an "acceptance" in itself. Either way, you would argue, Joe had every right under the statute to *consider* the offer accepted when he received the document, even though Sleazo did not himself *intend* to accept. Shipment now appears as a more reasonable mode of acceptance.

Resolving Ambiguities

As a lawyer, it is crucial to be able to argue effectively for statutory constructions that will support your side. The bottom line, however, is whether a judge will buy it. A lawyer must remain objective enough to evaluate his reasoning the way a court would so the shaky arguments can be weeded out. The next section attempts to offer insight into how judges approach statutes and arguments about them.

Unclear Provisions   Despite legislative attempts at clarity, courts sometimes face a statute whose meaning is elusive, or in which the phraseology can be interpreted several ways. Judges don't like to toss word salads. Instead, they prefer to turn to the lawmakers themselves—or at least to their verbal legacies in the form of legislative histories and committee reports. In these materials judges hope to discover the statute's true soul, from which proper interpretation will naturally follow.

It all sounds quite sensible. Too bad it rarely turns out that way. Unless the lawmakers are the U.S. Congress, legislative history tends to be quite skimpy. And even when evidence of purpose can be ferreted out, it may be too vague to be useful in a particular case. Indeed, Supreme Court Justice Antonin Scalia has repeatedly voiced skepticism over *any* reliance on materials outside the statutory text. What Congress passed and what the President signed, Scalia emphasizes, is the statute itself; lawmakers frequently ignore committee reports altogether. Courts' reliance on such reports invites opportunistic legislators to slip one-sided language into them and thereby suggest an interpretation that lawmakers never approved or even debated.

So, confused courts must often define a policy of their own, and that's asking for trouble. A shortsighted decision can produce unforeseen consequences that last until someone gets around to correcting the problem.

In addition, though statutory construction is most appropriately viewed as an honest endeavor, it must be remembered that courts have engaged in some rather outrageous abuses. Judges occasionally disregard the clear purpose behind a law, or strain to find enough ambiguity in the language, to justify a refusal to enforce it. In the early nineteenth century, for example, Southern courts groped wildly for ways to avoid undermining the slave economy in the face of increasingly permissive and sympathetic legislation. A 1791 North Carolina statute provided:

> And whereas by another act of Assembly passed in the year 1744, the killing a slave [sic], however wanton, cruel and deliberate, is only punishable in the first instance by imprisonment and paying the value thereof to the owner; which distinction of criminality between the murder of a white person and of one who is equally an human creature, but merely of a different complexion, is disgraceful to humanity and degrading in the highest degree to the laws and principles of a free, christian and enlightened country: *Be it enacted by the authority aforesaid,* That if

any person shall hereafter be guilty of willfully and maliciously killing a slave, such offender shall upon the first conviction thereof be adjudged guilty of murder, and shall suffer the same punishment as if he had killed a free man[.]

One might think all this clear enough to prevent any tinkering. No so, decided the North Carolina Court of Conference in 1801. In *State v. Boon*,[15] the court decided that since not all "killings" are criminal, the statute was simply too broad to be workable. The court held that literal interpretation would compel a judge to find guilty of murder even one who had killed in self-defense. Nonsense, you say. The legislature had demonstrated its goal quite amply in the statute's opening sentence. Perhaps, but the court managed to ignore this as well, dismissing it as a "mere preamble," insufficient to assuage its lingering judicial doubt.

An extreme example, to be sure, but one that illustrates the prerogative of a judge to ignore interpretive evidence (even when embedded within the statute itself) in order to advance his own agenda. Judges have also been known to play games when the legislative history is vague. Meager commentary can often be twisted into supporting any interpretation whatever—again, to promote a particular viewpoint rather than to serve the will of the lawmakers. Especially devious efforts seek to extract support from the *absence* of explanation, as in this convenient two-headed coin: "Nothing in the legislative history reveals an intent to preclude/include whatever-it-is we want/don't want."

Most of the time, judges don't cynically subvert the "intent of the drafters." But they do find themselves completely at sea every now and then without the moorings furnished by clear legislative history. And nowhere have judges run adrift more often than in that ocean of arcane mystery, tax law. In 1958, Congress sought to close an embarrassing and costly tax loophole that involved death benefits given to widows by the late husband's employer. Everyone agreed that these often large sums were tax-free gifts as far as the widows were concerned, but for many employers, generosity was not boundless: they were deducting the "gifts" as business expenses.

Congress could not permit such an absurdity to continue and passed Internal Revenue Code §101(b)(2) to ensure a fair degree of altruism on the corporate side. Up to $5,000, the prevailing practice could continue (Congress didn't want to appear too hard-hearted when it came to widows); above this amount, however, someone would have to pay Uncle Sam. If the payment were tax-free to the widow/er, then it would be a nondeductible gift as far as the employer was concerned. If the employer wished to consider the payment a business expense, however, it would constitute taxable income to the recipient.

Alas, that's not the way the courts read the provision. They applied the $5,000 limitation only if the payment was specifically *not* intended as a gift. So all a corporation had to do to avoid §101(b)(2) was simply declare the payment to be a gift, in which case the deduction could be taken freely while the widow paid no tax. This interpretation was the exact opposite

---

15. Taylor's (N.C.) Reps. 246.

of what Congress had intended and was only possible because none of the drafters thought that any court could conceivably allow the employer to deduct a payment that it *admitted* to be a gift. Congress finally plugged the leakage in 1962 with the passage of §274(b)(1). This provision forbids deduction of virtually all business gifts in excess of $25, thus forcing corporations to award death benefits under §101(b)(2) as originally intended.

Techniques of Judicial Construction   Although exactly how a court will ultimately interpret a particular statute is anyone's guess, judges have developed certain styles of construction to lay a more solid foundation for their decisions. This represents an attempt at candor. If the court tells us at the outset how it plans to approach its work, we are less likely to view its outcome as whimsical or idiosyncratic. The polar extremes of this process go by the names *strict* and *loose* construction.

Often, a case that examines a federal statute will begin with homage to the following quotation from *Blue Chip Stamps v. Manor Drug Stores:* "The starting point in every case involving construction of a statute is the language itself."[16] Your response might be, "Well, no kidding." Why would a court waste its judicial breath on a proposition so plainly obvious? The reference serves two purposes. First, it alerts the reader to the fact that the judge is about to perform a *strict* construction of the statutory language. This means that she will not enlarge the scope of the statute beyond its own words and will focus more sharply on the statute's phraseology than on such uncertain concepts as spirit and legislative intent. The second purpose is to justify this approach, making it seem natural and obvious.

Strict construction is an *objective* technique and suffers from the same shortcomings as all attempts at objectivity. Because legislatures cannot conceive all situations at all times, an overly strict construction can choke a statute's clear purpose. The North Carolina court in *State v. Boon* might have considered its analysis a (very) strict construction.

Other courts (or the same court in a different context) may look well beyond the statute's words for an interpretation. *Loose* construction allows overly restrictive language to accommodate novel or changing circumstances. Notwithstanding Justice Scalia's reservations, judges quite often consider legislative history. This is particularly so for statutes that engendered considerable debate, resulting in committee reports that reliably communicate legislative will. When passed, the Copyright Act of 1976 capped twenty-five years of congressional efforts and produced mountains of often-cited legislative materials.

Judges may opt for looseness not only when the legislative history is very abundant, but also when it is hopelessly meager. Poor evidence of the drafters' intent may provoke examination of more general policy goals. If the analysis is too loose, however, it can drop to the ankles like oversized trousers. Vague *subjective* notions of intent and statutory purpose can distort as easily as clarify. People turn first to the text of the statute to assess what behavior is expected of them. The more statutory interpretation departs from the apparent

---

16. 421 U.S. 723, 756 (1975) (Powell, J., concurring).

meaning of the words themselves, the less fair it seems to hold people accountable to such interpretation.

Personality also plays a part. Strict and loose styles of construction can reflect differing judicial temperaments. As the terms of a statute become more general and the legislative history more obscure, the law's particular purpose may seem unclear, the need to enforce that purpose less urgent. A judge will then feel freer to indulge his own philosophy.

Conflicts Among Statutes   The sharpest ambiguity arises when two statutes enacted by the same governing body collide with one another. Sometimes the opposing terms are so inherently contradictory that they simply can't exist side by side, and the court must make a choice. More often, however, an interpretation can found to permit peaceful coexistence. Such was the desire of the Supreme Court in *Harris v. McRae*.[17] Part of the case concerned whether Title XIX of the 1965 Social Security Act (commonly known as the "Medicaid Act")[18] required state funding of medically necessary abortions despite the Hyde Amendment, which made federal funds unavailable. Enacted in 1976, the amendment provides:

> [N]one of the funds provided by this joint resolution shall be used to perform abortions except where the life of the mother would be endangered if the fetus were carried to term; or except for such medical procedures necessary for the victims of rape or incest when such rape or incest has been reported promptly to a law enforcement agency or public health service.

Title XIX and regulations promulgated to administer the statute required Medicaid plans to cover "inpatient hospital services," and to refrain from reducing "the amount, duration or scope of a service...solely because of the diagnosis, type of illness, or condition."

Plaintiff, a New York Medicaid recipient, sought an abortion that she alleged to be medically necessary, although she conceded that its unavailability would not be life-threatening. Her lawyers argued along these lines: (1) Title XIX does not permit a participating state to exclude from its Medicaid plan any medically necessary service solely on the basis of diagnosis or condition, even if federal reimbursement is unobtainable for that service.[19] (2) The Hyde Amendment is merely a limitation on federal funding. (3) Therefore,

---

17. 448 U.S. 297 (1980).

18. Medicaid is a federal undertaking designed to provide certain segments of the indigent population with access to medical care. To be eligible, a recipient must demonstrate that he or she fits within one of six specific categories intended to limit assistance to those whose needs seem most compelling. Funding for physician reimbursement comes from both federal *and* state sources according to federal guidelines, so the program is actually a cooperative endeavor.

19. This reading of the statute was endorsed by the Supreme Court in *Beal v. Doe*, 432 U.S. 438 (1977).

states are still obliged under the original Medicaid Act to provide for medically necessary abortions despite the Hyde cutoff. Any other interpretation would result in direct conflict between Title XIX and the Hyde Amendment.

The federal district court decided that the plaintiff's construction might indeed avoid conflict, but would also undermine the purpose of the Hyde Amendment. Therefore, the original act had to give way.

The Supreme Court concluded that there was a way to permit states to refuse to fund medically necessary abortions but preserve Title XIX intact. The problem, it said, was that the original act was being interpreted too broadly:

> Nothing in Title XIX as originally enacted, or in its legislative history, suggests the Congress intended to require a participating state to assume the full costs of providing any health services in its Medicaid plan. . . . Since the Congress that enacted title XIX did not intend a participating State to assume a unilateral funding obligation for any health service [whatsoever,] it follows that Title XIX does not require a participating State to include in its plan any services for which a subsequent Congress has withheld funding. Title XIX was designed as a cooperative program of shared financial responsibility, not as device for the Federal Government to compel a State to provide services that Congress itself is unwilling to fund.

Did the Court really avoid a conflict, or did it overrule the original Medicaid Act without saying so? Leaving aside the tendentious political aspects of the decision, the Court's reasoning was certainly not whimsical—it did not create a travesty. When statutes threaten to annihilate one another, judges often feel a special obligation to act as conciliators. After all, the lawmakers probably did not mean to overrule themselves without saying so, and preserving both statutes can therefore be seen as faithfulness to legislative intent—even if the effort requires a bit of creativity.

The moral of all this is that conflicts often appear in the eyes of the beholder; much can turn on the result the court wants to achieve. Clever judicial twists may avoid obvious statutory inconsistencies, while what might seem a mere brush between statutes can be elevated into a head-on collision. Again, a little suspicion on your part is often healthy.

We end this chapter as we began, with an example. This apocryphal case of statutory construction actually appeared in a semiofficial Canadian publication,[20] planted there by a prankish editor.

---

20. 8 Criminal Law Quarterly 137 (Toronto, 1965).

* * *

(IN THE SUPREME COURT)

REGINA v. OJIBWAY

BLUE, J.   AUGUST, 1965

BLUE, J.:—This is an appeal by the Crown by way of a stated case from a decision of the magistrate acquitting the accused of a charge under the Small Birds Act, R.S.O., 1960, c. 724, s.2. The facts are not in dispute. Fred Ojibway, an Indian, was riding his pony through Queen's Park on January 2, 1965. Being impoverished, and having been forced to pledge his saddle, he substituted a downy pillow in lieu of the said saddle. On this particular day the accused's misfortune was further heightened by the circumstance of his pony breaking its right foreleg. In accord with Indian custom, the accused then shot the pony to relieve it of its awkwardness.

The accused was then charged with having breached the Small Birds Act, s.2 of which states:

> 2. Anyone maiming, injuring or killing small birds is guilty of an offence and subject to a fine not in excess of two hundred dollars.

The learned magistrate acquitted the accused holding, in fact, that he had killed his horse and not a small bird. With respect, I cannot agree.

In light of the definition section my course is quite clear. Section 1 defines "bird" as "a two-legged animal covered with feathers." There can be no doubt that this case is covered by this section.

Counsel for the accused made several ingenious arguments to which, in fairness, I must address myself. He submitted that the evidence of the expert clearly concluded that the animal in question was a pony and not a bird, but this is not the issue. We are not interested in whether the animal in question is a bird or not in fact but whether it is one in law. Statutory interpretation has forced many a horse to eat birdseed for the rest of its life.

Counsel also contended that the neighing noise emitted by the animal could not possibly be produced by a bird. With respect, the sounds emitted by an animal are irrelevant to its nature, for a bird is no less a bird because it is silent.

Counsel for the accused also argued that since there was evidence to show accused had ridden the animal, this pointed to the fact that it could not be a bird but was actually a pony. Obviously, this avoids the issue. The issue is not whether the animal was ridden or not, but whether it was shot or not, for to ride a pony or a bird is of no offense at all. I believe counsel now sees his mistake.

48

Counsel contends that the iron shoes found on the animal decisively disqualify it from being a bird. I must inform counsel, however, that how an animal dresses is of no concern to this court.

Counsel relied on the decision in *Re Chicadee*, where he contends that in similar circumstances the accused was acquitted. However, this is a horse of a different colour. A close reading of that case indicates that the animal in question there was not a small bird, but, in fact, a midget of a much larger species. Therefore, that case is inapplicable to our facts.

Counsel finally submits that the word "small" in the title Small Birds Act refers not to "Birds" but to "Act", making it The Small Act relating to Birds. With respect, counsel did not do his homework very well, for the Large Birds Act, R.S.O. 1960, c. 725, is just as small. If pressed, I need only to refer to the Small Loans Act R.S.O. 1960, c. 727 which is twice as large as the Large Birds Act.

It remains then to state my reason for judgment which, simply, is as follows: Different things may take on the same meaning for different purposes. For the purpose of the Small Birds Act, all two-legged, feather-covered animals are birds. This, of course, does not imply that only two-legged animals qualify, for the legislative intent is to make two legs merely the minimum requirement. The statute therefore contemplated multi-legged animals with feathers as well. Counsel submits that having regard to the purpose of the statute only small animals "naturally covered" with feathers could have been contemplated. However, had this been the intention of the legislature, I am certain that the phrase "naturally covered" would have been expressly inserted just as "Long" was inserted in the Longshoreman's Act.

Therefore, a horse with feathers on its back must be deemed for the purposes of this Act to be a bird, and *a fortiori*, a pony with feathers on its back is a small bird.

Counsel posed the following rhetorical question: If the pillow had been removed prior to the shooting, would the animal still be a bird? To this let me answer rhetorically: Is a bird any less of a bird without its feathers?

Appeal allowed.

3

Relationships Among Cases

WHEN A LAWYER starts to work on a new project and begins her research, what's she up to as she hunts through the case reporters? If she finds a case precisely on point, does that end the matter? If, on the other hand, the controversy is a fresh one, are all the old cases useless? A variety of principles help connect cases with one another, and they operate on a number of levels. Our intrepid lawyer knows that the *content* of one case may relate to that of another because of their similarities. She collects relevant decisions based on their legal and factual parallels; and when she's done, her hoard consists of similar cases that are "horizontally" related—joined only by their common features.

Reading casebooks—the fat collections of legal opinions and related writings that law professors employ as textbooks—requires the same kind of analysis, only from a different perspective. The casebook editors have thoughtfully assembled a congeries of decisions they believe fairly describes a particular area of law. The mere fact that these cases have been chosen tells us that they're horizontally linked. The question is how.

Judicial decisions can also relate to one another *structurally,* as a consequence of the legal system's organization. When an appellate court overrules a lower court's judgment, both decisions are intimately related to one another because of the hierarchy among courts. A new lower court, facing the same issue, will follow the edict of the appellate court instead of the wayward example of the overruled lower court. Let's call this kind of structural relationship "vertical." Vertical relationships, unlike horizontal ones, arise automatically and according to fixed rules.

In the world of legal research, horizontal similarity determines the *relevance* of a case you've uncovered to the one you're working on. The vertical dimension tells you how much *deference* your court owes to the one that decided the earlier case. So even if your research turns up a case that's identical to the one you're working on (a perfect horizontal match), your judge may disregard it if he feels no particular allegiance to its author. Conversely, all the deference in the world won't persuade a judge to apply a factually irrelevant case.

Understanding how cases—whether assigned as reading by a professor or developed in the course of research—relate to one another is not easy. In fact, the biggest mistake you can make as a first-year law student is to oversimplify such associations. You desperately want those decisions to fit together neatly, like pieces of a quilt, all somehow connected by an elusive—yet discoverable—silver thread. It doesn't work that way. Law is messy. You won't find many untattered quilts.

Instead, think of cases as short stories, and groups of cases as well-chosen anthologies. Somehow, those individual entries reinforce one another on thematic or philosophical grounds. But they don't work together like the chapters of a novel. This particular chapter will show you how to read a set of cases and get a sense of their complex relationships, either as a case-chasing attorney or as a law student trying to make sense out of a casebook.

3.1 Vertical Relationships

Level 1: *Res Judicata*

The Latin term *res judicata* means "a thing adjudged." While its application is fraught with subtlety and technicalities, the principle of res judicata is really the least equivocal form of precedent: you only get your day in court once, so an original judgment binds all parties concerned, permanently. There are no second chances (other than appeals, of course—that's still the same case). So don't darken the courthouse door again; the outcome will be the same. And that's true even if you cleverly attempt to relitigate the same case under a different legal theory. It's still res judicata, and you're still out of luck.

Although it's the most powerful form of vertical authority, res judicata rarely helps with research or casebook reading. That's because as a researcher, you're already familiar with your client's previous litigations. And casebook editors won't make you read the same case twice. But the central idea of res judicata—preventing multiple adjudications of the same controversy—represents the foundation of all vertical relationships.

Level 2: Hierarchy

Application of precedent is *nearly* automatic where a higher court has recently addressed the same legal issue. Assuming similar facts—a horizontal question—the earlier decision is said to "control." Again, the idea is to avoid revisiting the same issues. But why should one court pay attention to the pronouncements of a higher court? Just because the court of appeals reversed Judge Fred on a particular issue, how does Judge Ethel know she'll get the same treatment? No statute forces Judge Ethel to follow the reasoning of her senior colleagues if she thinks they're wrong.

Nevertheless, there are two reasons why she will probably do so: respect and fear. Respect means that disagreeing with those of higher rank doesn't justify defiance. And the appeals judges' respect for one another means that they will most probably make the same decision once again, even though they play golf every week with Judge Ethel. Fear means that if Judge Ethel tempts the gods and gets reversed, she can hurt her career. Judges receive appointments to higher courts based on their esteem in the legal community. A judge's batting record of affirmances and reversals forms part of his or her reputation.[1] Should she choose simply to ignore a clear mandate, Judge Ethel will look like quite the sap. And she may get censured if the practice becomes flagrant.

Level 3: *Stare Decisis*

Respect does have its limits, however. Times change, and an older opinion might outlive its usefulness. In that case, a court will *overrule* its earlier decision. But until then, older opinions remain good law. Courts don't like to depart from their previous edicts; it just confuses everybody. This illustrates the principle of *stare decisis,* "adherence to decided cases."

But stare decisis only operates as a strong suggestion. Courts remain free to do as they please, ignoring the suggestion or dumping their earlier ruling entirely. For this reason, stare decisis is the weakest form of vertical relationship.

What about cases from other jurisdictions? Stare decisis does not apply. One state's judges have no obligation to follow the predilections of their out-of-state colleagues. And since state and federal courts also exist in separate jurisdictions, state judges can ignore the pronouncements of *all* federal courts when it comes to state law and need listen only to the U.S. Supreme Court on matters of federal law. Similarly, federal courts are free to decide federal issues however they please, regardless of the views of state-court judges.[2]

As a practical matter, courts do pay attention to what's going on in other jurisdictions, often voluntarily following nonbinding judgments. What factors might motivate such

---

1. Next time you hear media reports of a judge in a well-publicized criminal trial making rulings that seem biased against the prosecution, ask yourself whether she may simply be trying to avoid reversal on appeal should the jury convict. In a sense, by erring on the side of deference to the defense, the judge helps to strengthen the prosecution's chances of prevailing on appeal.

2. Recall that when it comes to state law, the decisions of a state high court bind both state and federal courts *in a vertical sense* (as long as those decisions don't conflict with federal law).

importation? Once again it's mostly a question of respect, both of the other court and the reasoning that went into its decision. Other considerations include similarities in surrounding areas of law and the perceived need for consistency (as when a "uniform" statutory provision has been adopted in many states).

3.2 Horizontal Relationships

If the legal world were organized vertically only, each court would mechanistically decide whether one of its previous cases "matches" those of a new controversy and then either apply the case or overrule it. Cases are rarely identical, however, and similarity is a subjective judgment. Determining when the old will speak for the new presents both analytical and normative questions. The analytical steps come first—the most relevant cases will be similar both *legally* and *factually.* But even this preliminary analysis is not merely mechanical. As we will see, the normative dimension permits much discretion to infiltrate the comparison and application of precedent. Let's consider the process from the perspective of a judge. Suppose counsel has proffered a case she considers relevant. The judge must now decide the law. How does she go about it?

Comparing Cases

Legal Issues   The first step in analyzing any case is to distill the legal issue by separating holding from superfluous dicta (or positively superfluous obiter dicta). A judge is obliged to resolve the controversy before him, but no more. His holding and the reasoning that got him there[3] have meaning only to the extent they support the actual *judgment.* If a portion of his opinion is not palpably demanded by its outcome, the judge is digressing. He has produced dicta, gratuitous legal or policy analyses, for which he was not asked. They are not part of the "rule" of the case.

Spotting "mere dicta" can prove a tricky and elusive task. What at first seems indispensable might, upon further reflection, appear only marginally relevant, or perhaps even unnecessary. Broad holdings, personal commentary, and far-reaching policy (as opposed to purely legal) analysis all signal the presence of dicta. When the sultan exclaims, "Out of my sight! And may the fleas of a dozen camels follow you to bed each night," the first sentence is holding; the second is just dicta.

The process of paring away dicta takes on particular importance in cases where a judge has used sweeping language to lay down an unnecessarily broad rule. Time may undermine his efforts. Later judges might not be persuaded of the need for an expansive directive when a

---

3. The *ratio decidendi* for Latinists.

narrow one seems adequate to the task. They remain free to confine the earlier rule, applying it only in similar factual circumstances, so that the rule's excessive scope evaporates into dicta. The core holding, then, emerges as the bottom line of any legal decision—all that tomorrow's lawyer can really trust.

Legal rules usually develop in response to repeated run-ins with similar kinds of fact patterns. But not always. Sometimes a judge will decide a case with reference to a completely unrelated legal rule imported exclusively for the occasion. Analogies are common in the law. The court may not always rest its holding on the parallel rule or even acknowledge its presence explicitly—judges don't like to appear revolutionary—but its presence can be instructive both to judge and case reader alike. In *Hawaii Housing Authority v. Midkiff,*[4] the state of Hawaii sought to use its power of eminent domain[5] to lessen the concentration of land ownership. As a consequence of Hawaii's early feudal land tenure system, its legislature found that seventy-two private landowners controlled 47 percent of the land in Hawaii; with the state and federal government owning another 49 percent, only 4 percent remained for all other private owners. In an 8–0 opinion,[6] the U.S. Supreme Court upheld Hawaii's exercise of eminent domain:

> [W]e have no trouble concluding that the Hawaii Act is constitutional. The people of Hawaii have attempted, much as the settlers of the original 13 colonies did, to reduce the perceived social and economic evils of a land oligopoly traceable to their monarchs. The land oligopoly has, according to the Hawaii Legislature, created artificial deterrents to the normal functioning of the State's residential land market[.] Regulating oligopoly and the evils associated with it is a classic exercise of a State's police powers.

Perhaps the court's eminent domain holding seems to have a ring of antitrust law to it, especially in the last sentence of the excerpt. Eminent domain is a property issue; antitrust law involves regulation of trade. Ordinarily, these two areas of law have nothing to do with one another. But Professor Laurence Tribe, who wrote the brief and argued for the state of Hawaii, saw a connection:

> [T]he Act is designed to disperse the extraordinarily concentrated market power of a small oligopoly of landowners in Hawaii, and to increase the bargaining power of lessees in relation to those landowners. Breaking up concentrated economic power so as to enhance competition, efficiency, and the functioning of

---

4. 467 U.S. 229 (1984).

5. *Eminent domain* refers to the state's power to appropriate private property for public use, so long as just compensation is paid to its erstwhile owners.

6. Justice Marshall did not participate.

the market is the classic purpose of the antitrust laws, and the states are clearly empowered to order monopolists or oligopolists to divest their property.[7]

The frequent appearance in legal reasoning of analogies demonstrates the ease with which fundamental legal principles can propagate through wholly distinct fields of law. Often, a judge's inclination to analogize where no judge had analogized before reflects the tandem development of similar principles in unrelated areas, developments whose relevance to one another had previously gone unrecognized.

Factual Issues Some facts are more important than others in determining the outcome of a case. The second step in case analysis requires identification of these significant facts—the ones that bear on the operation of a legal rule. This exercise requires a certain amount of discipline. Unimportant facts always lurk in the background, tempting the reader to stray from the true analytical path. You must resist such blandishments; dalliance with irrelevant facts only hampers understanding and application of the rule.

However, as stated earlier, the world is not neatly divided into significant and insignificant facts. They're all over the place, distributed along a continuum of progressively more useful pieces of information. Cases that involve the same legal issue and feature similar factual patterns are likely to be treated similarly. As the important facts of a precedent begin to diverge from those under consideration, a court will find itself freer to disregard that precedent. How do you pursue the quest for legally significant facts? Where along the continuum should you draw the line? The key is to keep your eye on the legal rule that's at stake. Professor Karl Llewellyn[8] captured well the spirit of this undertaking:

> The plaintiff's name is Atkinson and the defendant's Walpole. The defendant, despite his name, is an Italian by extraction, but the plaintiff's ancestors came over with the Pilgrims. The defendant has a schnautzer-dog named Walter, red hair, and $30,000 worth of life insurance. All these are facts. The case, however, does not deal with life insurance. It is about an auto accident. The defendant's auto was a Buick painted pale magenta. He is married. His wife was in the back seat, an irritable, somewhat faded blonde. She was attempting back-seat driving when the accident occurred. He had turned around to make objection. In the process the car swerved and hit the plaintiff. The sun was shining; there was a rather lovely dappled sky low to the west. The time was late October on a Tuesday. The road was smooth, concrete. It had been put in by the McCarthy Road Work Company.

Any event of human activity spreads out into as many facets as we care to examine. Some are critical to the legal question at stake in a case; others are marginal; still others

---

7. Brief for Appellant at 14. citations omitted.
8. In *The Bramble Bush* (2d ed. 1951).

wholly useless. Precise facts add nothing when they answer the wrong questions, and even facts that are relevant need not be so to the utmost detail. The law is often more concerned with classes and varieties of fact.

It is not the road between Pottsville and Arlington; it is a "highway." It is not a particular pale magenta Buick eight, by number 732507, but…"a vehicle." It is not a turning around to look at Adorée Walpole, but a lapse from the supposedly proper procedure of careful drivers, with which you are concerned.

By focusing attention on the legal rule, you get a sense of the appropriate level of generality at which to assess the facts. If the case turns on the value of an antique automobile, its identity may prove critical; but if, as here, the case deals with driving generally, it becomes necessary to view the defendant's car as a generic vehicle.

Reaching the right level of generality is crucial to developing a case's factual context. But your analysis should then move a step deeper. How complete is the court's factual picture in the first place? This is not an easy question, but one you must consider. As will become clearer in the next chapter, an insurmountable barrier prevents us from knowing the "true" facts of any past event, and surrounds every case with uncertainty. Yet, every appellate opinion has settled on *some* version of the facts, saddling you—the case reader—with this version as you attempt to separate relevant from irrelevant data. Recognize that in doing so, you will not be first in line. The court has already performed its *own* screening and presents readers with its view of what happened.

There is no reason to assume unquestioningly that the court has told the whole story. Actually, the incentive is quite the opposite. A legal mind, whether assuming the role of judge or advocate, will naturally select those facts that best support the conclusion drawn or argument made. Persuasive reasoning involves not only identifying a series of rules that leads to a particular result, but also making those rules seem the most apt in a given situation. Therefore, while the court's facts are no doubt *consistent* with reality, they may not be exhaustive.

It is true, of course, that the reader of a case cannot decide how fair the court has been in its factual exposition. We are stuck with the information we are given. Yet it's important, as you search for the legally significant facts, to recognize this inherent bias and utilize it constructively. Let it make you skeptical. Merely associating the details of a given case with its outcome teaches you very little about the law. Reading into, through, and around the facts will help you evaluate the persuasiveness of a judge's reasoning. It will also enable you to discern the contours of the rule at issue so you can work with it as you encounter new fact patterns. The selection of relevant facts is an exercise performed not only by the author of a particular legal opinion, but also by future authors who later rely on that opinion.

Suppose, for example, that the court in *Atkinson v. Walpole* referred to the Buick merely as "a vehicle" and announced a negligence standard for vehicle drivers. Did the judge really mean automobiles, or was he deliberately vague so his rule would apply to every kind of vehicle? And if the latter, is that broad rule defensible? Should the same standard apply to drivers of large trucks? Of school buses? Of bicycles?

Distinguishing Cases: How and Why

All of which leads to the process of case comparison. Uncovering the holding and sifting out the legally relevant facts produces a case's most obvious meaning, the one we'd expect a future court to attach to it. But the technique of applying precedent is more art than science; our preliminary analysis takes us only to the threshold. Suppose, for the time being at least, that Judge Ethel—recently promoted to the court of appeals for her unflagging respect— must decide how to apply a precedent to a new controversy. That precedent is *State v. Lloyd*. It seems that Lloyd the Bankrobber, while in the process of holding up the First National Bank, shot a teller. Intending merely to scare the teller with his pistol, Lloyd nevertheless killed him. The court of appeals, in affirming the trial court's conviction for murder, remarked as follows:

> A person is responsible for the natural consequences of his or her conduct.
> That Lloyd did not intend to kill the teller as he pulled the trigger is of no moment.
> His act proximately caused death. That is enough for the law.

The current case concerns Floyd the Other Bankrobber. While robbing the Second National Bank, Floyd similarly shot a teller in an unintentional fashion. However, the teller died as a result of medical negligence that occurred during the treatment of his wound. Floyd was convicted of murder. Should Judge Ethel uphold or reverse the conviction? Because *State v. Lloyd* was also decided by the court of appeals, it is binding as stare decisis unless overruled. Judge Ethel now must decide whether to apply the case, overrule it, or distinguish it away on the basis of some legal or factual discrepancy.[9] Floyd's attorney argues that *State v. Lloyd* ought to be distinguished, since the chain of causation was unbroken in that case. Here, he implores Judge Ethel, the doctor's negligence intervened; Floyd could not have proximately caused the teller's death.

The state's attorney responds, "Is this a factual difference that makes a difference? Of course not. After all, Lloyd didn't intend to kill either. But both robbers pulled their triggers, and now two innocent tellers are dead. How can a legal principle turn on whether the criminal or a third party makes the last mistake?"

Clearly, factual analysis takes us only so far. Rarely can the process of comparison, by itself, ordain the applicability or irrelevance of precedent. Judge Ethel considers both

---

9. Since appellate courts ordinarily consist of more than one judge, we're assuming that Ethel's wisdom allows her to speak for all.

arguments and the factual distinction around which they revolve, knowing that a decision either way would be analytically consistent with the *Lloyd* rule. She decides, however, to affirm, and states:

> Defendant urges us to disregard *State v. Lloyd* because of the causation issue. We think, however, that our earlier holding is broad enough to cover the instant case. In employing the expression "natural consequences," we did not intend to confine the inquiry merely to the physical connectedness of act and result. Our words must be interpreted as imposing responsibility on actors for all reasonably foreseeable consequences. That death is a reasonably foreseeable result of a gunshot wound seems beyond question.

The new case didn't fit neatly into the precedential pattern, so a bit of interpretive creativity was necessary. But Judge Ethel did more than simply apply the earlier case. The choice of enlarging the earlier ruling, rather than narrowing it, reflects a normative public-policy decision: she decided that the community's need for security outweighs the added imposition of responsibility on its individual members.

Next week, Judge Ethel is scheduled to hear argument on another case, *State v. Boyd.* Boyd the Bungler, brandishing a pistol, entered the Third National Bank with the intent of robbing it. A frightened elderly teller, seeing the gun, went into cardiac arrest and instantly died. Boyd quickly fled but was apprehended as he slipped on a banana peel. A jury found him guilty of murder. How should Judge Ethel approach this case? Is *State v. Floyd* distinguishable? *Should* it be distinguished, or do we *want* to extend the concept of causation (and hence criminal liability) this far?

Such normative choices attend most applications of precedent. It's the way the common law develops. Distinctions help shape the texture of legal rules, and the process of clarification and refinement permits the law to grow as society changes.

But enough of this philosophical rumination. Now it's time to get cynical. Judge Ethel has just taken up a car-crash case. She knows how she wants to decide this controversy, but an annoying precedent—the one involving Karl Llewellyn's Walpole and Atkinson characters—seems to stand in the way. It appears to her a distraction. Read broadly, the case stands for the proposition that back-seat drivers can be held responsible for the actual driver's negligence. A questionable result, but because of the flood of public sympathy for Atkinson at the conclusion of trial, Judge Ethel is reluctant to overrule the case. She would rather avoid so controversial a decision.

How can she do so? By recognizing that the mechanism of comparing cases is not self-policing. No one can ensure that judges will evaluate past decisions with an earnest view toward their proper development. A less-than-candid Judge Ethel can get rid of her unwelcome precedent by sneaking past it, pretending to distinguish its obvious similarity on the basis of some trivial difference.

Llewellyn's example was replete with legally irrelevant facts, differences that should make no difference whatsoever. If Judge Ethel disregards the case by seizing upon the color of Walpole's automobile or Adorée's hairstyle, she would, of course, strike us as supremely disingenuous. And when a lawyer does find a case so ingloriously discredited, he must recognize that its continued vitality is quite shaky. Perhaps Judge Ethel reached far and wide to distinguish the case only for today's dispute and will not do so again. Perhaps, but who knows? An ill-favored precedent may be crumpled repeatedly before its ultimate demise.

Indeed, Judge Ethel may proceed even further, and make her disdain for the precedent unquestionable, by "confining the case to its facts." That is, henceforth the decision will apply only to disputes identical thereto in all factual respects, trivial and significant—namely, only to redheaded Walpoles in pale magenta Buicks. Such a hyper-narrowing of the precedent is functionally equivalent to discarding it, but the case technically remains in force due to its tiny window of possible relevance.

The practice of torturing precedent to suit present whim is by no means limited to getting rid of past cases. It is equally possible to corral earlier cases that *don't* really seem to apply and characterize them as "precedent" for purposes of a present decision. The line that separates holding from dicta is as indistinct as the one dividing legally relevant facts from those that are not, so it is always possible to read a case for all it is worth—and perhaps a bit more.

So why all the deception? What might induce a judge to approach precedent elliptically, pretending to leave a battered case intact instead of just being honest and overruling (or ignoring) it? The basic motivation is the desire to be (or at least to *appear*) consistent. Judges strive to treat litigants fairly. They don't want to foist any surprises if they can avoid doing so and recognize that the sudden demise of a well-worn precedent can come as quite a shock.[10] Indeed, lawyers would become (*gasp*) useless—and judges vulnerable to criticism—if people were to suspect the law of susceptibility to arbitrary and unpredictable alteration.

Judges therefore fret least about overruling cases that are very old, in which the underlying assumptions have changed demonstrably, or if change has been brewing incrementally for some time (so that the overruling can be seen as merely the final step). But when a questionable precedent falls outside these categories, judges must struggle to resolve the need for predictability with the perceived need for change. Sometimes their resolution of this conflict takes the form of a bit of subterfuge.

At this point you may be asking, Just how common is all this subterfuge? Why bother to learn the rules if they're easily avoided? The answer is that judicial trickery, while always possible, is also pretty rare. In the main, judges read cases fairly. The process of case analysis yields the interpretation *most likely* to be embraced by a contemporary court. The judge *may* deviate from this interpretation, but probably won't, or at least not too much. A lawyer's time researching and analyzing is therefore well-spent; it produces a reasonably good prediction.

---

10. We'll have more to say about such surprises, and how their effects can be blunted, in chapter 5.

59

The point, then, is that any case may be cited for a *range* of propositions, and analyzing a case means getting a feel for that range. Knowing how well the case will hold up as precedent, on the other hand, gives you a sense of how far from the most likely interpretation a judge may choose to deviate; that is, where within the range she's likely to wind up. Acquiring that sense is the subject of the next section.

3.3 Research and Casebooks

So far, this discussion has focused primarily on analytical comparison of one case to another case. Now we proceed to consider groups of decisions involving the same or similar legal issues. Any area of law may be thought of as the collective response of the courts to a certain problem. Were values clear and disputes unknown, there would be no problems requiring such a response. But we know better. That's why we have courts, judges, and lawyers. And as society grows more complex, the problems become ever more vexing and harder to solve. Any legal formulation selected to regulate a particular area or need becomes commensurately less likely to provide an ideal answer. In law, as in life, there are few absolute, clear-cut choices; mostly there are trade-offs. Want greater individual liberties and less police intrusion? The price is a higher crime rate. How about better access to the judicial system for society's vulnerable? Get ready for an increase in baseless litigation and consequent suffering by those unfairly dragged into court; the easier it becomes to sue, the harder it is to avoid getting sued.

Courts face these trade-offs all the time. When two cases that turn on the same legal issue come out differently, don't assume that one must be right and the other wrong. Instead, they probably evince alternative choices—two different points along the spectrum of possible, but imperfect, solutions to the problems they address.

Yes, friends, we're talking spectrums again. Just as facts resolve themselves along a continuum of relevance, so do different judicial approaches to the same problem reflect a blend of competing—and frequently opposing—values. Exactly where a court will come out depends on the relative stress it places on these values. Rarely can one identify the best overall mix with any certainty. Reasonable people may indeed differ, and perceptions change over time. Solutions that seemed the most reasonable a decade ago may now appear intolerable.

Ordering a body of precedent along a progression of choices enables us to see where the law is and where it seems to be heading. We get a sense of the large-scale philosophies at work. Older cases do not disappear but represent fragments in the total quantity of cumulative experience from which new decisions are derived. Mores and habits change with time. Judges decide (and lawyers argue) cases from new perspectives. The trail of earlier choices helps point us to the next stop along the value spectrum.

Of course, the business of the courts is to decide cases, not expound on values. Only rarely will an opinion expressly inform you of the court's philosophical outlook (such as by overruling an earlier decision). But those values lie just beneath the surface and provide the normative context for the way judges approach facts. One court may interpret a precedent expansively; another may confine it to its facts. For example, *State v. Floyd* suggests that Judge Ethel is tough on crime. If so, she may feel inclined to extend its reasoning to cover Boyd's conduct. But her other opinions may suggest a contrary bent. Perhaps her toughness is tempered by reluctance to overextend a criminal statute.

Once you've identified the underlying values in a set of cases, you know what the cases are all about. You have your bearings. But values provide a compass to future decision-making, not a road map. Equally important are the practicalities of analysis. Every area of the law has its own vocabulary, its own paradigmatic fact patterns. Even judges with differing philosophies analyze similar cases in similar ways (although they may ultimately reach different conclusions). Reading a group of related cases tells you how judges go about their business in a particular area of law. What kinds of issues tend to concern them? What classes of fact seem to be most important? Suppose two courts sharing the same values reach contrary results in cases with different fact patterns. *Which* facts caused the divergence in outcome? It's not always easy to decide whether such divergences reflect different values or just different facts. That's why casebook editors force you to read a variety of opinions, and why lawyers spend so much time in library stacks. The more you look, the better you see.

So as you read a set of cases, consider underlying values, consider case facts, and try to see how these work together to produce outcomes. To add one final complication, never forget the power of analogy. As we have seen, whole bodies of legal doctrine often borrow from one another. While the interconnectedness of different legal domains is far less direct than relationships among cases within a domain, the creative legal mind always looks beyond its immediate surroundings. Which other areas of law seem to be undergoing similar evolutions? Where are the underlying values similar?

To be concrete in all of this, let's take a group of cases from a particular segment of law and see what insights we can derive. The "fighting words" doctrine—fertile ground for some good laughs as well as high-minded legal analysis—refers to a branch of First Amendment law that deals with the ability of states to regulate offensive words and speech. The authors of the U.S. Supreme Court opinions synopsized below have attempted to articulate principles that determine whether certain forms of speech will receive First Amendment protection or instead remain subject to state control.[11]

THE FIRST AMENDMENT

Congress shall make no law respecting an establishment of religion, or prohibiting the free exercise thereof; or abridging the freedom of speech, or of the

---

11. Citations have been omitted from all cases, and any emphasis is found in the original.

press; or the right of the people peaceably to assemble, and to petition the Government for a redress of grievances.

CASE I

Chaplinsky v. New Hampshire
315 U.S. 568 (1942)

The defendant,[12] a Jehovah's Witness, was distributing religious literature on the streets of Rochester on a busy Saturday afternoon. He verbally denounced all organized religion as a "racket," prompting several listeners to complain of his irreverence to the city marshal. The marshal warned Chaplinsky that the crowd was "getting restless," but to no avail; Chaplinsky continued his peroration until a harried traffic officer finally led him toward the police station. On the way, they once again encountered the city marshal, "who had been advised that a riot was underway and was therefore hurrying to the scene." Chaplinsky addressed the marshal (he claimed, though the marshal denied, in response to the marshal's curses) as follows: "You are a God damned racketeer" and "a damned Fascist and the whole government of Rochester are Fascists or agents of Fascists." He was convicted of violating the following statute:

No person shall address any offensive, derisive or annoying word to any other person who is lawfully in any street or other public place, nor call him by any offensive or derisive name, nor make any noise or exclamation in his presence and hearing with intent to deride, offend or annoy him, or to prevent him from pursuing his lawful business or occupation.

Justice Murphy, writing for the Supreme Court majority, upheld the conviction, stating:

There are certain well-defined and narrowly limited classes of speech, the prevention and punishment of which have never been thought to raise any Constitutional problem. These include the lewd and obscene, the profane, the libelous, and the insulting or "fighting" words—those which by their very utterance inflict injury or tend to incite an immediate breach of the peace. [S]uch utterances are no essential part of any exposition of ideas, and are of such slight

---

12. You may wonder why the defendant's name appears first, since we usually associate the title *A vs. B* with the idea that A has sued B. On appeal, the names are often switched so that of the *appellant* (the party who lost in the court below) now comes first. The practice is not uniform, however, and it is impossible to tell the parties' posture in litigation without reference to context.

social value as a step to truth that any benefit that may be derived from them is clearly outweighed by the social interest in order and morality.

CASE II

Feiner v. New York
340 U.S. 315 (1951)

The defendant, standing on a large wooden box on the sidewalk of a predominantly black section of Syracuse, New York, was addressing a crowd through a loudspeaker system. Although the purpose of his speech was ostensibly to publicize a local meeting of the Young Progressives of America, Feiner found occasion to refer to then-President Truman as a "bum," to the American Legion as "a Nazi Gestapo," and to the mayor of Syracuse as "a champagne-sipping bum" who "does not speak for the Negro people." Speaking a "loud, high-pitched voice," he "gave the impression that he was endeavoring to arouse the Negro people against the whites, urging that they rise up in arms and fight for equal rights." The statements "stirred up a little excitement," and two police officers "stepped in to prevent . . . a fight." After ignoring two requests to stop speaking, Feiner was arrested and convicted for disorderly conduct.

The Supreme Court affirmed. Chief Justice Vinson wrote:

> [I]t is one thing to say that the police cannot be used as an instrument for the suppression of unpopular views, and another to say that, when as here the speaker passes the bounds of argument or persuasion and undertakes incitement to riot, they are powerless to prevent a breach of the peace. Nor in this case can we condemn the considered judgment of three New York courts approving the means which the police, faced with a crisis, used in the exercise of their power and duty to preserve peace and order.

CASE III

Edwards v. South Carolina
372 U.S. 229 (1963)

In this case, 187 black youths gathered at a church to protest "the present condition of discriminatory actions against Negroes." They marched to the grounds of the state house, where "30 or more law enforcement officers" awaited their arrival. They were told that "they had a right, as a citizen, to go through the State House grounds, as any other citizen has, as long as they were peaceful." This they did, walking in small groups through the grounds in an orderly fashion. A crowd of two to three hundred onlookers collected nearby, but no one actually caused or threatened any trouble. Nevertheless, police authorities advised the protesters that they would be arrested if they did not disperse within fifteen minutes. Instead of dispersing, the youths began to sing, clap their hands, and stamp their feet. After fifteen minutes had passed, all 187 were arrested and carted off to jail. They were subsequently convicted of breach of the peace.

The Supreme Court reversed, Justice Stewart observing:

> [The] circumstances in this case reflect an exercise of [First Amendment] rights in their most pristine and classic form. [Defendants] peacefully assembled at the site of the State Government and there peaceably expressed their grievances. [Only when] told by police officials that they must disperse on pain of arrest did they do more. Even then, they but sang patriotic and religious songs after one of their leaders had delivered a "religious harangue." There was no violence or threat of violence on their part or on the part of any member of the crowd watching them. Police protection was "ample." This, therefore, was a far cry from the situation in *Feiner.* [And] the record is barren of any evidence of "fighting words."

CASE IV

Cohen v. California
403 U.S. 15 (1971)

"On April 26, 1968, defendant was observed in the Los Angeles County Courthouse in the corridor outside of Division 20 of the municipal court wearing a jacket bearing the words 'Fuck the draft' which were plainly visible. There were women and children present in the corridor. The defendant was arrested [and] testified that he wore the jacket...as a means of informing the public of the depth of his feelings against the Vietnam War and the draft.

"The defendant did not engage in, nor threaten to engage in, nor did anyone as a result of his conduct in fact commit or threaten to commit any act of violence. The defendant did not make any loud or unusual noise, nor was there any evidence that he uttered any sound prior to his arrest."

He was convicted of violating a general California disturbing-the-peace statute which in part prohibited "maliciously and willfully disturb[ing] the peace or quiet of any neighborhood or person" by "offensive conduct." The Supreme Court reversed, Justice Harlan delivering the majority opinion:

> The conviction quite clearly rests upon the asserted offensiveness of the *words* Cohen used to convey his message to the public. The only "conduct" which the

State sought to punish is the fact of communication. Thus, we deal here with a conviction resting solely upon "speech," not upon any separately identifiable conduct which allegedly was intended by Cohen to be received by others as expressive of particular views but which, on its face, does not necessarily convey any message[.]

[The issue in this case] is whether California can excise, as "offensive conduct," one particular scurrilous epithet from the public discourse, either upon the theory of the court below that its use is inherently likely to cause violent reaction or upon a more general assertion that the States, acting as guardians of public morality, may properly remove this offensive word from the public vocabulary.

The rationale of the California court is plainly untenable. At most it reflects an undifferentiated fear or apprehension of disturbance [that] is not enough to overcome the right of freedom of expression. We have been shown no evidence that substantial numbers of citizens are standing ready to strike out physically at whoever may assault their sensibilities with execrations like that uttered by Cohen.... The argument amounts to little more than the self-defeating proposition that to avoid physical censorship of one who has not sought to provoke such a response by a hypothetical coterie of the violent and lawless, the States may more appropriately effectuate that censorship themselves.

How might we evaluate these four cases? First, we note that they all occupy the same vertical tier: each was decided by the U.S. Supreme Court. The distance in time between the first and last, however, is a considerable twenty-nine years, so we should expect some intervening change in outlook and philosophy.

What underlying values of policy are at stake throughout all four cases? Plainly, the court is trying to grapple with the First Amendment value of freedom of expression on the one hand, and the legitimate right of states to prevent public violence on the other. This is the essential trade-off. The relative importance attached to each value has changed over time, as manifested by the disparate focal points of the court's inquiries. Each test announced by the court favors a different point on the value scale.

In *Chaplinsky,* the concern centered exclusively on the words themselves and the harm such words were *likely* to cause or might be *capable* of arousing. Plainly, the court was concerned with the sensibilities of bystanders, and treated all "fighting words" as entirely unworthy of utterance. *Feiner* presents a different type of situation. As political discourse, the defendant's speech clearly demands First Amendment protection, but the danger of violence is heightened. Instead of enumerating the words spoken and condemning them as unprotected "fighting words," the court instead directs its attention to the actual *harm* caused by the defendant's behavior in the context of a hostile audience. In other words, the court is now looking at an additional class of fact.

Because the facts of *Feiner* differ so strongly from those in *Chaplinsky*, we cannot be sure whether the court is becoming more or less protective of speech. Are the justices shifting their emphasis from a strict *content* orientation to one that evaluates the *harm* actually caused by the speech in a given context? This would represent a more protective approach. Or have they merely added a new, additional category of unprotected speech, namely, that of otherwise permissible expression in the context of a hostile audience?

Edwards gives us some idea, but does not fully answer this question. The court makes it plain in this case that attempts to suppress speech on a spurious pretext of preventing potential violence won't do. But again, the speech itself was clearly protectable under the First Amendment. We cannot tell whether there remains a category of words which are *per se* outside the First Amendment's ambit. By the time we get to *Cohen*, however, we discover that the inquiry has shifted over entirely to the *context* in which speech takes place. The court explicitly rejects the *Chaplinsky* approach to carving out an exception to the First Amendment for offensive language, and announces a policy of recognizing the "fighting words" doctrine only when the context so demands—situations where the utterance of offensive statements is likely to result in violent confrontation. Protection of speech is therefore maximized within the constraints posed by due regard for public safety. The justices have journeyed from one end of the value spectrum to the other, and in the process shifted their factual focus as well.

Yet despite the significant change in the court's orientation, its progression is both incremental and comprehensible. Shifts in doctrine are best viewed as expressions of continued experimentation with the underlying value equation. It is at this level of generality that topically related cases should be organized and understood. In some instances, a set of decisions will be internally consistent; the *Lloyd, Floyd,* and *Boyd* cases illustrate the development of a single legal rule. Instead of contradicting one another, their sum helps build meaning and resolve ambiguity. At other times, however, decisions may prod and push one another, as was the case in the "fighting words" cases. And in yet other circumstances, developments in unrelated areas of law furnish a useful analogy that can reorient the analysis entirely.

Attempting to find a single principle that will explain disparate cases is inevitably futile—the process is simply not that tidy. There is no silver thread. What connects cases with one another is a broad arc of common underlying values, not a slender filament of logical consistency. Can we pretend that the holding of *Chaplinsky* is still alive after *Cohen*? Is any of the four "fighting words" cases the most logical expression of First Amendment doctrine? The answer to both questions is of course no; value judgments have indeed changed. It is the values themselves—First Amendment freedom of speech versus public safety—which endure.

Identifying these values, translating them into a coherent picture, and fitting cases within this picture are the tasks of case analysis. We've made some headway into this difficult realm, but not as much as you probably think. All we've really done is to sketch the process and provide some operational parameters. You need more. On the purely analytical side, you must be equipped with the intellectual tools necessary to evaluate consistency in the application of legal rules—that is, to circumscribe the permissible range of propositions for which a case may reasonably stand. On the normative side, you need greater familiarity with the values that may motivate a judge to move off-center within this range. You've seen a few already—the need for consistency and objectivity, the importance of public-policy analysis. But understanding patterns of judicial thought requires some additional reference points. Providing you with the necessary grounding, both in terms of analytical tools and jurisprudential values, is the task of the next two chapters.

4

The Logic of the Law

Logic is a lawyer's mental safety net. Legislators and their political ideologies may come and go, theories of law fall in and out of favor, but we can always count on the bedrock principles of logic to deliver objective analysis. Like a clearsighted escort, logic steers us away from questionable reasoning. It guides us through confusing strands of doctrine and keeps us on firm ground when we argue.

Our escort doesn't have all the answers, however. It knows the path but not the destination. Logic can't help us make choices; it can only clarify them. Logic doesn't tell us what we want from life. And our guide is sometimes misquoted. The cynics of the world may rail indignation at trivial or nonexistent reasoning errors. That's called logic chopping. Or they may disguise normative policy decisions in terms that seem merely deductive, telling us they had no choice but to follow logic's strong tow. With its reputation for scientific neutrality and Olympian objectivity, logic can provide an impartial (if unwitting) cover for all sorts of intellectual con artists.

Yet despite these shortcomings, logic has always been critical to legal reasoning. It keeps our thoughts straight. When analyzing a legal question, logic provides the first cut—although not the last word. This chapter will show you how to use logic to compare cases and define the range of possibilities for which a legal rule may legitimately be cited. Logical analysis reveals the kinds of reasoning errors that can lead you (or a judge) to stray outside the proper range. Before making normative appeals or pronouncements, lawyers and judges must initially map out the options realistically available within the constraints imposed by previous decisions or statutory language. Only then may they criticize those options.

Delineating the fair range of choices requires (at least) three separate investigations. The first is pure data gathering: Which cases are relevant to a particular dispute under consideration? The second involves movement from general to particular and back again. Can we infer a single rule from the specific cases we've identified? How broad is this rule? Does it encompass the set of facts before us? And finally, there is the issue of language. What meaning do we ascribe to the words of an opinion—particularly to indeterminate, open-textured terms like *reasonable* or *foreseeable*? If such expressions are to have any meaning at all, they can't be stretched too far beyond everyday understanding.

This short introduction to practical, lawyer's logic will also help you identify poorly reasoned cases. When a judge treads outside the legitimate range of choices without telling us, or commits an error of reasoning, or applies the technique of logic where it is inappropriate, we must not be fooled. Learning to critique a judge's thoughts will help you keep your own on track when it really counts.

If you have no background in philosophy, the terms presented below may seem algorithmic or cumbersome at first; rest assured that they will become dynamic and viable as you think about them, apply them, and play with them. In law-school classes you will encounter their often careless—but invariably pretentious—application by amateur dialecticians who toss logical terms around with abandon. If nothing else, reading this chapter will give you the confidence to roll your eyes in disgust.

4.1 Deductive Reasoning

Think of reasoning as a system of proceeding from one judgment to a second on the basis of consistent principles. The simplest logical inference consists of a proposition, or *premise* (the first judgment); a *conclusion* (the second judgment); and a rationale for the connection. *Inductive* and *deductive* reasoning methods each provide rules for establishing that rationale. Deductive reasoning, the stuff of which judicial decisions are made, refers to the process of working down from a universal or general truth to a special case. The role of this process is analytical only. It maintains consistency between judgments but offers no insight as to their innate truth or falsehood. A deductive conclusion is either valid or invalid; acceptance of the premises leads inescapably to or away from the conclusion.

So much for background. While all that is technically necessary for deductive inference is a premise and a conclusion, meaningful argumentation typically requires combining two premises to derive a third. This form is called a *syllogism*. The proposition of most general scope in a syllogism, the *major premise,* is followed by a narrower *minor premise.* The *middle term* links the two propositions and furnishes the basis for the conclusion. Here's an example:

> Major premise: Lawyers are dull, dull, dull
> Minor premise: Sally is a lawyer
> Conclusion: Therefore, she's seriously dull

The major premise contains the most general term, dullness. Lawyers, the middle term, are a subset of dull people. Sally is the most particular term, and it follows simply by proceeding from general to specific that she, too, is hopelessly dull. Deduction is less a matter of thought than an exercise in classification and identification.

The technical name for this reasoning process is *modus ponens*. The simplest rule of inference, it merely assures us that if we have a major premise and a properly subordinate minor premise, then we can safely draw a conclusion merely by substitution (dull → lawyers → Sally). Judges often announce the successful completion of a syllogism with the expression *a fortiori,* meaning that the greater (lawyers) necessarily includes the lesser (Sally).

All of this undoubtedly appears as an unnecessary formal way of restating the obvious. What is the virtue of structuring an argument this way? As will become clear, organizing the building blocks of reasoning into a syllogism facilitates their systematic analysis. But this form also has special significance for legal purposes because of the way different courts are interrelated.

As you know, state and federal courts are arranged in a hierarchy of two or more tiers, each with certain limitations on what issues it may consider. A typical dispute might involve a legal rule (the major premise), an issue of fact (minor premise), and a conclusion based on whether the rule applies to the particular set of facts. The lowest tribunal on the hierarchy, the trial court, exercises the broadest jurisdiction over the entire controversy. It may hear evidence and draw conclusions about all three components. Appellate courts can only review the record established at trial. Based on that record, appellate courts draw their own conclusions about legal questions and applications of law to fact, but generally defer to the trial court on questions of pure fact—the minor premises of the controversy. After all, the trial judge heard the evidence when it was actually presented. Appellate judges, who author most of the opinions you'll read in law school, preside over the most purely deductive aspects of a case.

To illustrate with two polar examples: whether a law is constitutional represents a legal question, while the credibility of a witness at trial raises an issue of fact. Far subtler distinctions are common, however, and the boundary separating legal issues from factual ones can become quite fuzzy. A trial judge may seek to avoid appellate reversal by characterizing crucial portions of her decision as factual; the court of appeals, indignant at the attempt to deprive them of the pleasure, may recast those portions as applications of law to fact (and hence appropriate fodder for their review). Consider the following example:

The Fourth Amendment assures citizens that they will be secure against unreasonable searches and seizures

FBI agents placed a wiretap on defendant's phone and arrested him based on certain conversations

Defendant claims the procedures followed by the agents violated the Fourth Amendment

Now suppose at trial one of the agents was questioned about the steps taken to comply with the Fourth Amendment; he describes how he obtained a warrant and how he studiously avoided recording irrelevant conversations. Determining whether those procedures did indeed fulfill the requirements of the Fourth Amendment requires application of law to fact, though whether the agent was telling the truth is a question of pure fact. The trial judge, who makes a decision on the entire case, may not care how neatly these issues separate.

But on appeal, the difference affects the permissible subjects of review. Say the trial judge found that the procedures employed satisfied the Fourth Amendment. He characterizes his conclusion as one of fact. If the legal requirements for compliance are very clear and precise, and if the procedures the agent said he followed meet those requirements, then maybe he's right—the issue does seem to turn almost entirely on the agent's credibility. And because such an issue is so quintessentially factual, perhaps the appellate court ought not to second-guess the trial judge, who actually heard the testimony. But if the trial judge must *additionally* decide just what is "reasonable" for Fourth Amendment purposes and what isn't, then we have an issue of pure law in addition to the question of credibility. In that case the appeals court must decide how much of the trial court's decision was factually based, how much depended on legal issues, and whether it even wants to open this can of worms.

The remainder of this section focuses on the syllogism itself, the way an appellate court would. However, try to keep the distinctions just discussed in the back of your mind as a sort of overlay when you read cases. Always ask yourself whether the author of an appellate opinion overstepped his authority or failed to fully and fairly discharge his responsibility. It is important to proper decision-making for judges to maintain their proper roles as well as to get their logic straight.

Technical Reasoning Errors

Many errors of logic can be traced directly to improper maneuvering between premises and conclusions. Some of these admittedly seem quite obvious, but others are insidiously subtle; those are the ones to watch for. The ability to recognize reasoning errors is not something that arises instantaneously, but don't worry: tempting opportunities for practice occur everywhere. You'll soon analyze unconsciously every assertion that dares to cross your path, the same way that learning a foreign language coaxes silent translations of everyday conversation. But watch out when it comes to interpersonal relationships—parents and significant others tend to greet the rigorous application of logic with unappreciative scowls, especially in the midst of hostilities.

Premise Problems   While all improper reasoning involves drawing the wrong (or any) conclusion from the given premises, some errors are rooted in the structure and content of the premises themselves. They seem superficially and semantically related, but in reality do not interact to produce a legitimate conclusion. These errors often result in mischaracterization of statutory language or an attempt to force application of a precedent that really doesn't fit.

A simple example arises when the middle term has two meanings. Unless it is used in the same sense in both premises, no valid conclusion can be drawn.

> Rule: Male corporate lawyers shave their cheeks daily
> Fact: Mike, a corporate lawyer, has a full beard
> Conclusion: The rule doesn't hold for everyone

Unless male corporate lawyers have some pretty odd (and acrobatic) personal habits, the conclusion must be correct: the rule states a generality rather than a universal premise. But then again, maybe we don't really know corporate lawyers all that well...

Does this seem far-removed from the world of cases and statutes? In fact, terms with multiple meanings present an occupational hazard to lawyers, always ready to cause mischief in an endless variety of contexts. In a 1973 case, *Palmore v. United States*,[1] the Supreme Court considered the extent to which Congress is free to create certain nontraditional federal courts called Article I courts. At issue were tribunals set up by Congress to adjudicate cases in the District of Columbia. Because the judges in these tribunals were not given life tenure and salary protection,[2] the courts did not qualify as traditional Article III federal courts. The Supreme Court held in *Palmore* that Congress did indeed have the power to establish Article I courts in the District of Columbia, and went on to state generally that such courts are appropriate "with respect to specialized areas having particularized needs and warranting distinctive treatment."

Barely nine years later, the Supreme Court once again faced the question of congressional power to create Article I tribunals. At issue in the *Northern Pipeline* case[3] were bankruptcy courts. This time, the Supreme Court wasn't so sure of the wisdom of bypassing those Article III requirements. But bankruptcy is certainly a "specialized area" and its procedures highly particularized—so what about *Palmore*?

No problem, said Justice Brennan. "[O]ur reference in *Palmore* to 'specialized areas having particularized needs' referred only to *geographic* areas, such as the District of Columbia or territories outside the States of the Federal Union." A pretty tortured reading of *Palmore*, to be sure, particularly given the rest of that opinion; but it's linguistically consistent with the words of that decision, if not its spirit.

Another premise distortion that can lead to unjustified conclusions occurs when characteristics of a class are interchanged with those of the individuals making up the class.

---

1. 411 U.S. 389 (1973).
2. Recall from chapter 1 that federal judges receive these guarantees to assure their independence.
3. Northern Pipeline Construction Co. v. Marathon Pipe Line Co., 458 U.S. 50 (1982).

No one was seriously injured in the accident
Accident costs vary with the seriousness of the injury
Therefore, the accident was not costly

Or the converse:

The accident was very costly
Accident costs vary with the seriousness of injury
Therefore Laura, a victim of the accident, must have been seriously injured

It is impossible to draw a valid deductive conclusion concerning an individual merely from knowledge about the class to which she belongs, and vice versa. This general idea becomes quite important when evaluating the statistical or economic implications of legal rules. For example, a traditional principle of tort compensation holds a negligent party liable for the total value of the injury inflicted on another, notwithstanding any special vulnerabilities of the victim. This has come to be known rather gruesomely as the "eggshell skull" rule of taking the victim as he is found.

An injurer's lawyer might argue that the rule is unduly harsh. "My client employs thousands," she insists. "Its safety expenditures are necessarily based on harm to average people. Holding my client responsible for the full measure of damages to *any* plaintiff would require it to take absurdly excessive safety measures just to eliminate even the tiniest chance of harming the especially vulnerable. This makes no sense."

The response is that counsel has mistakenly viewed the general rule in terms of individuals rather than groups. In fact, she is correct that her client's outlay for safety should be based on the average person, the term *average* referring to some statistical aggregate. But she has failed to recognize that while an injurer may be forced to compensate a few eggshell-skull victims, it will probably also be spared paying anything at all to a similar number of extra-thickheaded types. That's how insurers calculate premiums.

Perhaps the most dangerously subtle reasoning mistake is attempting to draw a conclusion from two premises having nothing whatever to do with one another despite appearances to the contrary. In such an instance, the mismatched premises support no conclusion whatsoever:

White, elderly women are least likely to become victims of crime
Yet white, elderly women are also most afraid of going out at night
Therefore, white, elderly women exhibit excessive fear

The conclusion is certainly *consistent* with the two preceding propositions, but by no means follows from them. Hence, if your mother is white and elderly, think twice before sending her downtown later tonight. The relative improbability of falling victim to crime may itself be due to a healthy timidity about unsafe areas.

Judges sometimes fall prey to this reasoning pitfall when they attempt to state broad rules without sufficient policy justifications for the support of precedent. The result reached is certainly *consistent* with whatever normative factors have been mustered, but is just not convincingly required by them. Often, a dissenter is considerate enough to rip the effort to shreds, just to make sure no one is fooled. Such analyses should be read carefully. The best critique of a case may lie in a thoughtful dissent or the majority's deft resistance to its opposition. Not long ago the Supreme Court considered the scope of presidential immunity in *Nixon v. Fitzgerald.*[4] The issue proved to be quite contentious, and the brethren slugged it out to a 5–4 decision in favor of the former President. Justice Powell, writing for the majority, began by canvassing the "singular importance of the President's duties":

[T]he officeholder must make the most sensitive and far-reaching decisions entrusted to any official under our constitutional system. Nor can the sheer prominence of the President's office be ignored. In view of the visibility of his office and the effect of his actions on countless people, the President would be an easily identifiable target for suits for civil damages. Cognizance of this personal vulnerability frequently could distract a President from his public duties, to the detriment not only of the President and his office but also the Nation that the Presidency was designed to serve. . . . In view of the special nature of the President's constitutional office and functions, we think it appropriate to recognize absolute Presidential immunity from damages liability for acts within the "outer perimeter" of his official responsibility.

Four other justices didn't buy it:

First, the majority informs us that the President occupies a "unique position in the constitutional scheme[.]" True as this may be, it says nothing about why a "unique" rule of immunity should apply to the President. The President's unique role may indeed encompass functions for which he is entitled to a claim of absolute immunity. It does not follow from that, however, that he is entitled to absolute immunity either in general or in this case in particular.

Is either side obviously right? In terms of policy, the issue is open to discussion. But in terms of logic, the dissenters plainly thought the majority's conclusion did not follow as freely from its premises as the majority thought. Rarely is the logic of a situation so clear-cut as to

---

4. 457 U.S. 800 (1982).

permit only one point of view; its value lies in exposing the legitimacy of different—but consistent—points of view.

Unjustified Conclusions Getting the premises right doesn't guarantee a valid argument. Premises may fit properly together in form and still suggest all sorts of unwarranted conclusions. If you misinterpret the *scope* of the premises, you'll wind up with a conclusion that's broader or narrower than it should be. Of course, defining the fair range of a premise requires judgment, and errors of scope can therefore remain open to debate. The conclusion may be right according to one interpretation but not another. Judges make such interpretive choices every time they are asked to apply precedent to new situations. What to one judge may seem an unwarranted extension of an earlier case's holding may appear perfectly acceptable to another.

One of the most popular examples, at least among professors who teach this sort of thing, involves drawing particular conclusions from bare generalities. To wit:

> A law-school graduate will get the job
> Norman is a law-school graduate
> Therefore, Norman will get the job

Being a law-school graduate is a *necessary but insufficient condition* for receiving the job. There is no guarantee that Norman is the particular law-school graduate the job offerors seek, and other possible criteria of importance go unmentioned. A valid conclusion from these premises would be that Norman falls within the category of eligible applicants. Likewise, the above conclusion would be correct if the major premise read, "*Any* law-school graduate will get the job."

This reasoning error can proceed in the opposite direction as well. Attempting to reason backward from a particular case to find an overarching legal principle that explains several holdings presents the danger of "proving too much"; that is, the rule successfully predicts the results correctly but is too broad to be workable or would mandate results that are impermissible for other reasons. Rules that prove too much send us down the slippery slope. It would be wrong, for example, to conclude that because law-school graduate Norman got a particular job, *any* new juris doctor will get a similar job, or that a legal degree is an absolute prerequisite for such a job. Generalizing from particular cases invites just this sort of excess.

A related mistake is confusion of a general statement with a universal statement. Universal propositions apply to the entire set of whatever is being described without exception, while general descriptions merely typify. Hence:

> College seniors are beer drinkers
> Myron is a college senior

Therefore, Myron drinks beer

The major premise is not a universal proposition, as would be true if it read "*All* college seniors are beer drinkers." Despite the best efforts of those who brew the golden elixir, such is still not the case.

If someone is really trying to pull a fast one, she might attempt to dodge the issue entirely by drawing a conclusion that simply has nothing whatsoever to do with the premises. Such bold and desperate groping, in the grandest tradition of pounding the table and yelling when the facts go the wrong way, is sometimes so artfully worded that it appears a rabbit has been cunningly pulled from an empty hat. It's all sleight of hand, though, so you've got to keep your eye on the premises.

In a controversial corporate tax case,[5] the Supreme Court had some trouble refuting the taxpayer's assertion that an adverse decision would result in treating different forms of the same transaction inconsistently:

> Taxpayer strongly argues that to treat the redemption involved here as essentially equivalent to a dividend is to elevate form over substance. Thus, taxpayer argues, had he [reached the same result by formally different means] he could have gotten back his $25,000 with favorable tax treatment. However, the difference between form and substance in the tax law is largely problematical...

It doesn't really bother us that this decision results in inconsistency, say the court. Heck, lots of tax cases have permitted inconsistencies, so why are you so upset?

If all else fails, the forlorn reasoner might resort to *argumentum ad hominem,* whereby the inability to refute convincingly the opponent's argument is resolved by calling him a jerk or making fun of his bow tie.

Circularity Circular reasoning is a difficult error to identify for the same reason that unjustified conclusions prove elusive: subtle judgment is necessary to discern whether a problem even exists. The easier form of circularity to recognize is "question begging," a misconception of what is needed to establish the conclusion. Here the conclusion has crept into the premises, so what is offered as proof is actually the thing to be proved. This kind of circular reasoning proves the existence of God by citing the Bible. And question-begging can get even simpler than that. Sometimes it takes the form of *tautology,* which merely restates. Tautology tries to convince you that $2 + 2 = 4$ because $4 = 2 + 2$. For a less mathematically rigorous example, we turn to the Code of Professional Responsibility, which governs lawyers' conduct in many states.[6] In order to decide whether someone is practicing

---

5. United States v. Davis, 397 U.S. 301 (1970).

6. Many states have adopted or are working toward adopting the newer Model Rules which, like the Model Code, were authored by the American Bar Association.

law without a license, first you have to know what the practice of law is. Here is the Code's definition (Canon 3):

> ...the practice of law [involves] the rendition of services for others that call for the professional judgment of a lawyer.

Doesn't really help answer the question, does it?

Here is a more subtle example. The *Willow River* case[7] involved a suit by a power company against the United States government. The power company operated a hydroelectric plant, and the government constructed a dam about thirty miles downstream. This caused a rise in the water level at the plant, diminishing the amount of power that could be generated. Willow claimed this constituted a taking of property without just compensation. The Supreme Court, in rejecting the argument, had this to say:

> It is clear, of course, that a head of water has value and that the Company has an economic interest in keeping the St. Croix at the lower level. But not all economic interests are "property rights"; only those economic advantages are "rights" which have the law back of them, and only when they are so recognized may courts compel others to forbear from interfering with them or to compensate for their invasion.

Well, that's for sure. But so what? Whether the property interest is legally protected is precisely what the parties have come to court to determine. By framing the issue this way, the court could justify any conclusion it wished to reach, since such a decision either puts the law "back of" the plaintiff or refrains from doing so.[8]

The second and more deceptive form of circularity consists of introducing an unwarranted proposition; that is, taking for a premise a proposition whose truth needs to be proven first. The argument is circular because it *assumes* its conclusion. It can be difficult to identify because whether a proposition appears unwarranted depends on how sympathetic you are toward it.

In order to appreciate the context in which this type of circularity arises most often, it is necessary to introduce another entrant in the parade of logic characters, the *enthymeme*. Often a syllogistic argument is phrased in such a manner that it appears to lack one of the necessary components. It is a syllogism nonetheless, and you should not be fooled into thinking otherwise. The following enthymemes are all technically equivalent to the initial syllogism:

---

7. United States v. Willow River Power Co., 324 U.S. 499 (1945).

8. In fairness, the opinion did indeed go on to consider a variety of factors that might aid in categorizing an interest as "legally protected." This was certainly not compelled, however, by its initial formulation.

Syllogism:

Courts in all common-law countries consider precedent before fashioning law
The United States is a common-law country
Therefore, United States courts consider precedent before fashioning new law

Enthymemes:

1) Because the United States is a common-law country, its courts consider precedent before fashioning new law
2) United States courts consider precedent before fashioning new law because all common-law courts do so
3) All common-law courts consider precedent before fashioning new law; and the United States is a common-law country

Assertions resembling (1) or (2), though especially (1), are capable of disguising circularity because a crucial premise is missing. If that premise is unwarranted, its omission may deflect attention from this fact. The reason that (1), where the major premise is left out, presents a less obvious error than (2) (which omits the minor premise) is simple: Once a major premise is stated, an inconsistent minor term will often reveal itself conspicuously. Deleting the major premise, however, is like telling a bigger lie. The rest of the argument is so completely dependent on the validity of the major premise that its absence may not be questioned—especially if the source carries authority and the language is assertive. A Boston judge once partook of the technique when responding to some rather strident criticism over his release of an attempted-murder suspect on five hundred dollars' bail. His reply was, "Attempted-murder charges are not that big a deal around here. It's sad to have to say that, but it's true."

Are you convinced? His argument, as stated, is this:

Common crimes merit low bail
Attempted murder is a common crime
Therefore, low bail is appropriate for an attempted-murder suspect

The major premise, which was omitted, is a bare general assertion. No reason for this dubious proposition is advanced. Indeed, if relative frequency of a crime's occurrence were sufficient to ensure low bail, wouldn't criminals feel encouraged to step up their illegal activities? Some other justification may exist, of course; overcrowding of jails, low incidence of rearrest of similar suspects free on bail, or a defendant's particular characteristics might persuade us that five hundred dollars was appropriate under the circumstances. But the judge has offered no such considerations, and there is no way to know whether he contemplated any. His reasoning is circular because the conclusion depends on a loaded assumption.

The second enthymeme exposes the ease with which it is possible to slip from the general to the particular without fully considering whether the facts of the minor premise fully meet the requirements stated in the major premise. Omission of the minor premise is a fairly common reasoning error and can take far subtler forms than that of (2) above. Suppose that Judge Ethel has now decided *State v. Boyd.* Her opinion includes the following observations:

> In our recent *Floyd* decision, we unequivocally held foreseeability to be the touchstone of criminal liability. This rule embraces Boyd's conduct just as surely as it does that of Floyd. Indeed, were we to decide differently we would shrink from our duty to punish the guilty and protect society from their wrongful acts.

Judge Ethel has told us what the foreseeability rule is and why it's such a terrific precept to live by. But she offers us no clue as to why it should be held to cover Boyd's conduct.

Because it concludes nothing, the third enthymeme never gets us anywhere. This is the easiest error of circularity to recognize, since it leaves us asking, "Yeah...so?"

Formal Reasoning Errors

Though the fallacies described above might seem like rather technical dissections of the syllogistic form, they are actually considered *material,* as opposed to *formal,* deductive errors. Formal errors occur when the precise rules for creating logically proper syllogisms are violated. These errors are less common than the technical problems just presented, but you should have at least passing familiarity with them.

In order to describe the possible fallacies that arise as a consequence of the syllogistic form, we must first define the three types of syllogisms and the rules for constructing them. The variety with which we have been concerned so far is the *categorical* syllogism, whose premises are straightforward categorical propositions. The following rules govern:

1. At least one premise must be universal.
2. At least one premise must be affirmative.
3. If one premise is particular, then the conclusion can only be particular.
4. If one premise is negative, the conclusion must be negative.

Violation of any rule results in a formal reasoning error. For instance:

> No doctors make house calls

John does not make house calls
Therefore, John is a doctor

Violating rule 2 can never produce a valid conclusion, because two negatives cannot imply an affirmative.

A syllogism may also be *conditional,* the truth of the conclusion depending on the fulfillment of some prerequisite. In that case, the minor premise must either affirm the condition (the "if" clause) or deny the consequent (the "then" clause).

If it is cloudy, there will be no dew tonight
There was no dew
Therefore, it must have been cloudy

Can't get away with that, because affirming the consequent does not imply the truth of the condition. That's a variety of erroneously inferring causation merely from correlation. Nor will denying the condition refute the consequent:

If the temperature is 25 degrees, then the lake is frozen
The temperature is not 25 degrees
Therefore, the lake is not frozen

A *disjunctive* syllogism presents two alternatives as a major premise. A valid conclusion may only be drawn when the minor premise affirms or denies one of the given alternatives. For example,

The defendant is either innocent or he is guilty
The defendant is not innocent
Therefore, he's guilty

Logic Operators

Logic operators are analytical tools used to wiggle propositions in order to explore their boundaries. If the wiggle produces a result equivalent to (or different from) the original proposition, we have learned something more about the scope of that proposition. Judges and law professors frequently apply these tools in evaluating the contours of a legal rule. It is important to be familiar with them both to understand their analyses and to perform your own.

The simplest operator is the *obverse,* in which an affirmative proposition is doubly negated. For example:

Proposition:
I will go for a walk if the sun is shining

Obverse:
I will not go for a walk if the sun is not shining

While the obverse is always *consistent* with the proposition, verification of its truth tells us something we could not legitimately infer from the proposition alone. Now we understand more about the speaker's intentions, namely, what will happen if the stated condition goes unfulfilled.

To obtain a proposition's *converse,* you "convert" it by transposing subject and predicate. Thus:

Proposition:
Those with licenses may practice law

Converse:
Those who may practice law have licenses

The converse of a proposition may always be made to express the same judgment as long as we're careful to quantify each term. In the example above, we cannot be certain of equivalence because the proposition does not inform us whether some others *without* licenses may practice law as well. We could correct this by changing the proposition to "*Only* those with licenses may practice law," or qualifying the converse to "*At least some of* those who may practice law have licenses." Judges occasionally confuse the two operators just discussed, promising a converse and proceeding to obvert. That's not terribly important. What is important is avoiding hidden assumptions. Don't argue a proposition (those practicing law have licenses) if you're really trying to prove the converse (*only* those with licenses may practice law), since one does not automatically follow from the other.

The third operator, the *contrapositive,* is a bit less commonplace. It involves obverting the proposition followed by conversion:

Proposition:
If it is sunny, I'll go for a walk

Contrapositive:
If I didn't go for a walk, it wasn't sunny

The contrapositive is the only operator that always produces a proposition equivalent to the root proposition. For this reason, it is of limited analytical usefulness.

4.2 Inductive Reasoning

As discussed above, the process of deductive inference operates mechanically on a set of facts to produce a conclusion. But so far, we've left something out: the existence of a unique set of facts itself presupposes a special type of logical inquiry. How does a trial judge or jury arrive at the factual picture upon which judgment will be based? By introduction of evidence, of course. But moving from evidence to facts involves a key leap of faith. Even assuming perfect evidence and reliable observations, how can we be sure that what we saw gives us a true account of what actually *happened*? The events are past, gone forever, but the trial is today. The finder of fact must infer backward from the evidence and arrive at its own picture of what occurred.

The reasoning process used to do this is *inductive,* reaching beyond the premises—that is, the evidence—to extend this existing knowledge into new knowledge. What is the basis upon which this "inductive leap" is made? All we have is a range of intuitions based on past experience. We have learned to associate certain observations with particular events. But how accurate is this intuition, and how far can it take us?

As you know, a deductive conclusion follows automatically from acceptance of the premises. An inductive conclusion, in contrast, must be based on probability alone. Bertrand Russell[9] put it this way: how can we know that the sun will rise tomorrow? Because it has always risen, for one thing. But we can do better than that. The sun will rise tomorrow because of the physical laws of planetary motion. Yet why should we assume these laws will continue to operate tomorrow as they always have? "[T]he real question is: Do *any* number of cases of a law being fulfilled in the past afford evidence that it will be fulfilled in the future?"

As a matter of deductive logic, the answer is no. Yet the courtroom process assumes just this sort of connection between observations and expectation. The judge or jury forms a picture of what happened from the evidence it hears. It accepts this picture, for purposes of making a decision, as a surrogate for unknowable reality. That's the best we can do. Trials are not about truth; they're about evidence and proof.[10] The gap between evidence and actual events is unbridgeable. Each side wants the court to imagine a different picture, to leap across the gap in a different way.

How trustworthy, then, are our expectations? How likely is it for the picture the evidence draws to resemble what really occurred? Underlying every inductive conclusion is an implied relationship based on experience. The value of a piece of evidence in reaching an inductive conclusion cannot exceed the credibility of this relationship. Consider the major premises assumed in the following conclusions:

---

9. "On Induction," in *The Problems of Philosophy* (1912).

10. A trial answers the following question: has the plaintiff carried his burden of proof? In a criminal proceeding, the state must convince a group of (hopefully) fair-minded citizens that the defendant is guilty beyond a reasonable doubt. A civil plaintiff shoulders a much lighter burden: she must merely demonstrate that liability is more likely than not.

1. I watched the assailant, Tim, pull the trigger on his gun aimed at the victim, and saw the victim drop. Conclusion: Tim shot victim.
2. Tim is known to have shot three other victims in the same manner on the same day. Conclusion: Tim shot victim.
3. Tim has a nasty disposition. Conclusion: Tim shot victim.

As to the first conclusion, assuming accurate observation, the evidence seems convincing beyond reasonable doubt. Of course, there can always be *some* doubt. Maybe Tim's gun was loaded with blanks and the shot came from elsewhere. Maybe it was all done with mirrors. Who knows? We can nevertheless feel pretty secure in relying on the extremely high probability that physical laws will operate as usual, and that a lead pellet discharged at high velocity from a pistol will inflict injury on its target.

The second conclusion requires a much broader leap. The connection is more tenuous, possibly not conclusive to the point of certainty we might desire, but still highly relevant. We want to know more. Where was Tim on the night of February 17...

The third conclusion seems so extravagant that we are tempted to completely disregard it. Perhaps the conclusion is unjustified, but does that mean the observation is wholly irrelevant? It certainly places Tim in a class of people more likely to commit assault than the average person, and is therefore *logically* relevant to the question of Tim's guilt or innocence. But logical relevance, while *necessary*, is not *sufficient* to guarantee the admissibility of evidence in court. There must be more. Rules of evidence have been drafted to ensure not only relevance, but overall fairness in the fact-finding process—that is, to keep questionable inferences to a minimum. To be admissible in court, information must be more than merely useful. Its value as evidence must outweigh any unfair, prejudicial implications. A jury may all too easily develop a dislike for Tim based on evidence of his nasty disposition and judge him guilty as an expression of this dislike, rather than on the evidence of the crime itself.

In chapter 3 we observed that the facts of a case, as transmitted to the case reader through a judge's opinion, have undergone a filtering process—the judge decides which facts will and will not be reported in the opinion. Rules of evidence and the limits of inductive reasoning further distance us from what actually happened. Every lawyer deals with these distancing mechanisms every day. As she reads cases, she must remain aware that the entire story may not have been told and watch for gaps that bear relevance to her own set of facts. As trial advocate, she must organize and present her evidence in a way that will portray her version of the facts convincingly, but also remain solidly within the rules of evidence. And she must approach clients with the same degree of skepticism she reserves for case analysis, since anyone's memory can become selective under the press of self-interest. It can be all too easy for a client to adopt the manner of Baron von Münchhausen, countering the lawyer's doubts with a sly, "Were you there, Charlie?"

5

Thinking About the Law

SUPPOSE LAW were totally logical. Suppose we could decide every case merely by applying neutral principle, so all those thorny normative issues wouldn't dare disturb our well-reasoned repose. What a safe, passionless world that would be—a place many lawyers and judges might mistake for heaven. Just think of all the enticements a purely objective system offers. Chapter 2 introduced you to two of them, predictability and coherence. People have a right to know what the law expects from them; even small changes, if unannounced, can come as big surprises.

Objectivity can also mean avoiding the heat for controversial decisions. "Hey, look, I'm just doing what the law says I have to," says the detached jurist. "If you want change, write to your representatives." And avoiding the heat means skirting the difficult policy questions. Judges who live in the land of logic can stay serenely aloof from the messy side of law—its impact on the litigants before them and the rest of the world at large.

In these senses, then, adopting an objective viewpoint represents a normative choice in itself, a decision not to decide that elevates the value of consistency over every other value. Most judges are too smart and too aware of their surroundings to take such an easy way out. They remain acutely cognizant of the public-policy considerations that swirl around important controversies, yet also recognize the limitations of their office; ours is a democracy with common-law traditions, where legislators make law and judges must respect their handiwork as well as the opinions of earlier judges.

So what's a judge to do? When sitting down to write an opinion, how does he balance these competing priorities? And how do lawyers argue a case within the framework of this balancing act? There is more to the process than simply trumpeting the virtues of objectivity when your client likes the law as written and reversing this stand to stress normative values when he doesn't. For over a century, legal minds have fought over the values judges should and should not bring to bear on their decisions. These "metalegal" debates go a step beyond ordinary legal analysis. The debaters are thinking *about* the law rather than within it, practicing the art of something called *jurisprudence.*

Surely you thirst with anticipation at this point, desperate to know more. Calm down, it's not *that* exciting. But you will find well-reasoned criticisms of matters legal both interesting and refreshing. Really. The important critics don't just look at specific cases. They have tossed aside decades of musty historical baggage to expose fundamental tensions and predict trends. Sometimes their opinions are controversial, politically tendentious, or just plain offbeat, but schools of legal thought have opened new horizons for appreciating the unstated assumptions behind judicial decisions.

Law professors expect you to understand some elementary jurisprudence. That's because principled criticism of a case requires more than disagreement with its outcome, and jurisprudence—like logic—provides us with a set of critical principles. But watch out. Jurisprudence and politics are more than just friends. In criticizing a case, you may inadvertently tap into an entire school of thought, one that comes complete with a set of political perspectives. This chapter will introduce you to the business of jurisprudence and help you recognize how various bundles of ideology have become associated with different approaches to legal criticism.

5.1 The Emergence of Formalism

> A foolish consistency is the hobgoblin of little minds, adored by little statesmen and philosophers and divines.
> —Ralph Waldo Emerson, *Self-Reliance*

Long, long ago, in a legal universe far removed from our own, Christopher Columbus Langdell, venerable president of Harvard Law School, hit on the idea of teaching legal doctrine by subjecting students to reams of past decisions. He figured that these cases, if well-chosen, could map out the features of an area of law and impart a sense of the underlying principles that had motivated their authors. This style of instruction was cleverly designated the case method, and generations of law students have come to know (and not always love) its virtues.

When the case method first caught on, however, it was more than a pedagogical tool—it reflected a way of life as well. During much of the nineteenth century, legal scholars viewed their discipline as science. They felt that law could be reduced to fixed parameters and determinate, predictable outcomes. To find the answer to a legal problem, the competent juristic scientist needed only to visit his laboratory (the library) and probe the body of the law with proper analytical instruments (legal training) to extract specimens (relevant cases) that would contain the unique answer. Somewhere in the body of law, a case precedent could be found to "match" any new set of circumstances; the key lay in turning the right stone.

All in all, you might say, a supremely objective, logical approach to law. Of course, in such a contrived universe, judges had very little to say about what the law should be. Sure, they could help the law crystallize through repeated examination and clarification. But rewrite established doctrine? Might as well commit treason. Rules could be discovered and occasionally fine-tuned, but never trampled. This was the universe of formalism.

How far could such reasoning go? An 1878 Supreme Court case[1] established the rule that jurisdiction over parties to a civil lawsuit could not reach beyond a state's borders. Case closed. If the defendant built his house in New York, five feet past the Massachusetts line, there was no way anyone on the other side could get him into a Massachusetts court as long as he remained across the border—no matter how ghastly a tort he may have committed while in Massachusetts.

All kinds of clever absurdities were concocted to overcome this artificial territorial limitation. One was "constructive consent." In legalese, the word *constructive* usually means "let's pretend." So the Massachusetts legislature passed a law that said anyone operating a motor vehicle in Massachusetts will be *deemed* to have "constructively" consented to local jurisdiction over matters involving the automobile—whether he likes it or not.[2] Taking an even more creative approach, some enterprising Arkansas litigants successfully initiated suit by serving an airborne summons as the defendant's nonstop flight from Memphis, Tennessee, to Dallas, Texas, passed over the Eastern District of Arkansas.[3]

In the formalist universe, the matrix of rules becomes self-supporting as the principles on which they were built fade into the background.

5.2 Conceptualism and the Art of Analogy

There is no expedient to which a man will not resort to avoid the real labor of thinking.

—Sir Joshua Reynolds

1. Pennoyer v. Neff, 95 U.S. 714 (1878).
2. The Supreme Court upheld this approach. Hess v. Pawloski, 274 U.S. 352 (1927).
3. Grace v. MacArthur, 170 F.Supp. 442 (E.D. Ark. 1959).

And legal thinking can demand quite a bit of labor. Each year, a new crop of law students learns how legal doctrine can often twist and meander into a gnarled, confusing mess. This unfortunate reality has not escaped the attention of judges, either, who sometimes find welcome relief in the form of a clever model or metaphor that seems to squeeze all those awful complexities into an easy-to-use package. This type of "conceptualist" reasoning is really just an applied version of formalism; whereas formalism traffics in rules, conceptualism offers mental shortcuts. The conceptualist model, perhaps appropriate as a mnemonic device, itself becomes an immanent and immutable source of law.

Conceptualism need not announce itself boldly. After all, conceptualism is analogy, lawyers learn to think by analogy, and analogy is essential to consistent patterns of reasoning. So reasonable lawyers may differ: what appears to one a useful tool for spotting functionally identical phenomena might seem like a conceptualist straightjacket to another. And different contexts may merit dissimilar treatment. Reasoning by strict analogy can be quite helpful in achieving equal tax treatment of two economically equivalent financial transactions. However, when applied to matters of social policy or individual rights, such an approach appears decidedly artificial—a way of avoiding the really tough issues.

In 1922, the Supreme Court decided the famous *Coronado* case.[4] The issue it confronted was whether an employer could sue a labor union for harm suffered during a strike, or if it had to go after striking union members on an individual basis. Commercial entities like corporations face liability for injuries caused by their employees; looser associations such as partnerships do not automatically face this type of extended accountability.

If you were a Supreme Court justice, how would you decide whether or not to hold the labor union liable as an entity? You might start by examining why "enterprise liability" exists at all; that is, why is it applied to some businesses and not to others? One reason, you would find, is ability to supervise: because employers stand in the best position to control the activities of those under their charge, the threat of liability provides considerable incentive for prudent oversight. Another reason stems from the difficulty and expense of locating numerous individual defendants and initiating multiple lawsuits. So you might well inquire, as a deciding justice, whether these criteria apply to labor unions.

Your attentions might then turn to the broader social impact of a decision either way. If liability seems appropriate based on the foregoing facts, would the financial burden nevertheless cripple labor unions? Do labor unions serve a vital function in modern industrial society? Or do they already have too much power and need to be reined in?

The *Coronado* court, slaves to conceptualism, would have none of these normative considerations. The real justices confined their inquiry to a purely analytical question: does a labor union *look* more like a corporation or a loose association? They concluded that "[a]

---

4. United Mine Workers v. Coronado Coal Co., 259 U.S. 344 (1922).

labor union can be sued because it is, in essential aspects, a person, a quasi-corporation." As justification for this result, the court cited several findings of fact: (1) unions have been recognized as lawful by antitrust laws; (2) the Transportation Act of 1920 provides for labor union participation in rate setting; and (3) periodical publications issued by unions are treated as second-class mail matter.

Obviously, this approach is artificial. Who cares what kind of entity a labor union resembles most closely in appearance? Such an analysis plainly ignores the underlying policies that give rise to liability in some cases but not others.

In fact, problems with the court's reasoning go even deeper. The justices appear to have engaged in a subtle form of circular reasoning. Legal "personhood" is an abstract, metaphysical notion. We can no more look at an entity and deduce, solely from observation, whether it is a person or nonperson any better than we can determine how many angels might dance on the head of a pin. Are any of the three factors cited by the court really convincing? It's all a matter of conjecture. And this very indeterminacy allows either result to be reached with minimal effort. Should labor unions be forced to pay for the wrongs of their members? Well, then, of course a union is a person. Anyone can see that. Should they be relieved of enterprise liability? Then there is no person involved. Only a fool would say otherwise.

Sometimes, conceptualism emerges from the confinement of language. The law operates through classification; definitions and categories separate acceptable behavior from illegal conduct and help us to understand relationships. As discussed in chapter 3, the category to which a fact belongs—a car as a "vehicle" or as an "antique"—can determine the legal significance of that fact. But because of the subtle ability of words to overtake thought, lawyers and judges sometimes forget their responsibility to evaluate facts fully and slip into the mechanical process of pigeonholing. Instead of analyzing, they search for the convenient label and, when it is found, sigh with satisfaction and abandon further thought. Once again, circular reasoning takes hold to justify the label's suitability.

Remember the *Willow River* case mentioned a chapter ago? That decision turned on whether the label "property" could be placed on the height of a power company's water table. A similar issue confronted the Supreme Court in *International News Service v. Associated Press,*[5] where AP tried to put a stop to pirating of its news messages during their transmission. Does information collected by a news-gathering agency qualify as property? Justice Brandeis agreed that the process of assembling such information requires labor and money, and that others are willing to pay for the agency's efforts.

But he disagreed with the majority's willingness to rule in favor of AP on this basis. Brandeis refused to be hoodwinked into circular reasoning, concluding that merely because something gives off the odor of property does not mean courts should treat it as property. That's a public-policy issue, one that judges might do better leaving in the hands of others:

5. 248 U.S. 215 (1918).

[W]ith the increasing complexity of society, the public interest tends to become omnipresent; and the problems presented by new demands for justice cease to be simple. Then the creation or recognition by courts of a new private right may work serious injury to the general public, unless the boundaries of the right are definitely established and wisely guarded....Courts are ill-equipped to make the investigations which should precede a determination of the limitations which should be set upon any property right[.]

Occasionally, the conceptualist metaphor acquires such veneration that ridiculous efforts must be made to preserve it in the face of changing realities. What started as a means of avoiding complexity can become a wellspring for the intricate and arcane. To give you a glimpse of such progressive entanglement, we take a brief journey through the minefields of sovereign immunity. This legal concept protects state and federal governments from lawsuits arising from the conduct of their officials. The idea behind sovereign immunity originated from this medieval aphorism: The King Can Do No Wrong, So You Can't Sue The King (without his consent, anyway).

Of course, governments are free to waive sovereign immunity and consent to suit, just like the king. And in many cases they routinely do. Ever notice those signs along the side of a thoroughfare that say something like "Road legally closed—pass at your own risk"? These mean that the government entity in charge of the road's upkeep *refuses* to waive its claim of sovereign immunity in this instance; but in the absence of such a warning, hapless motorists injured by negligent highway maintenance can probably sue the (ir)responsible government.

The doctrine of sovereign immunity found its way into postrevolutionary American law to protect the states' fledgling economies. Rather than permitting potentially enormous damage actions to deplete state treasuries, state courts just said No and refused even to entertain actions in which the state was defendant. Federal courts followed this lead by way of an expansive reading of the Eleventh Amendment, and for a while states were completely immune from all types of lawsuits in every court.

While the conceptualism of the king doing no wrong is certainly succinct, effortless, and effective in protecting state coffers, as a legal rule it "proves too much": if legal liability is strictly precluded, then why play by any rules?[6] Permitting no one to be above the law requires that everyone be subject to the law's ultimate supremacy, regardless of uniform or title. And that means somehow forcing states and their officials to accept legal responsibility for their actions.

Instead of simply recognizing these two competing objectives and somehow hammering

---

6. Even in England, where sovereign immunity originated, no one really imagined that the ruler could get away with anything he or she pleased and disregard the rule of law at whim. Rather, the doctrine was employed to deflect embarrassment away from the monarch and find some minister or other to take the blame. If this were impossible, the ruler would often consent to suit.

out a reconciliation, courts instead stuck to the easy nostrum that the king can do no wrong. So to preserve this metaphor but still do justice, the courts had to invent ways of enforcing the law without admitting wrongdoing by the king. The result? A mess.

First, courts held that the Eleventh Amendment did not apply to *local* governments and municipalities. This senseless result actually worked against the original pocket-protecting rationale of sovereign immunity, since of all governmental entities, local treasuries have the least to give away. Moreover, most municipalities receive state subsidies anyway. But local governments are not the king.

Then, in *Ex Parte Young*,[7] the Supreme Court decided that the Eleventh Amendment did not bar prospective, injunctive relief[8] against a state official. The theory was that such action would not actually extract funds from the state fisc, and the courts would obtain at least some control over unlawful state acts without unduly upsetting the existing pattern of sovereign immunity law: the king may be restrained from doing harm in the future, although his past acts will remain unquestioned.

The prospective/retrospective distinction seemed like a good idea at the time, but amidst the enthusiasm someone forgot that even prospectivity would not guarantee protection of state treasuries. For example, the rule of *Ex Parte Young* could prevent a state from collecting revenues, since that's a future act. In fact, the Supreme court even went as far as to order the state of Michigan to pay money to provide for future payments in a school desegregation case,[9] reasoning that anything involving the future is fair game under *Young*. But when the state of Illinois was held to have wrongfully withheld welfare payments, the Supreme Court declared itself without power to compel payment because ... well, gee, that's retrospective, isn't it?[10] And more recently, state universities have been allowed to get away with copyright[11] and patent[12] infringement for the same reason.

Perhaps protecting the size of the state wallet is no longer important. But then what conceivable purpose does the retrospectivity bar serve? Indeed, what purpose does the whole of sovereign immunity law serve? Here we see desperate, groping attempts to reach around the law's obstacles as they have developed and to impose accountability where it appears warranted. But in order to avoid sacrificing the conceptualism and addressing the underlying issues, the law of sovereign immunity has progressed haphazardly and illogically, untrue to the original rationale for its adoption and indirectly sustaining the very priorities it refuses to face.

---

7. 269 U.S. 123 (1908).

8. That is, an order to refrain from doing something in the future.

9. Milliken v. Bradley ("Milliken II"), 433 U.S. 267 (1977).

10. Edelman v. Jordan, 415 U.S. 651 (1974).

11. BV Engineering v. UCLA, 858 F.2d 1394 (9th Cir. 1988). A 1990 federal statute reversed this and similar decisions. States can't get away with copyright infringement anymore—the king has consented to suit.

12. Chew v. California, 893 F.2d 331 (Fed. Cir. 1990).

5.3 The Realist Assault

> "That is no excuse," replied Mr. Brownlow..."in the eye of the law; for the
> law supposes that your wife acts under your direction."
> "If the law supposes that," said Mr. Bumble..."the law is a ass—a idiot."
> —Charles Dickens, *Oliver Twist*

Criticism of formalist reasoning reached a crescendo in the 1920s and early 1930s. Sophisticated scholarly analyses urged an end not merely to formalism and its disingenuous fabrications, but to the entire regime of legal thought that depicted law as somehow sacrosanct. These "legal realists" maintained that no law can be applied in isolation from the social effects it creates. Mechanistic applications merely dodge such issues.

The full dimension of realist philosophy is difficult to appreciate because legal realists were (and their progeny continue to be) a rather hereogeneous bunch. There is no single set of beliefs that fully characterizes the movement, and its various strains are deeply anchored in political and social philosophies. Mainstream adherents have tended to de-emphasize the more divisive political aspects. The proponents of more controversial versions, however, draw heavily from leftist ideologies. One contingent that has attracted recent attention is Critical Legal Studies, a modern reformist movement. Much of its intellectual foundation shares a common heritage with that of the more radical realists, and CLS is frequently described as a form of realist resurgence.

Though legal realism is a multifarious subject, each segment along the realist spectrum often proclaims itself the true and sole exponent of its principles. To develop an appreciation for the basic values common to all interpretations and obtain some idea of how these values can shift, let's quietly join a cocktail party in which three advocates are engaged in discussion. Any of them might be one of your professors. The first is somewhat conservative and rather apolitical, but understands and appreciates the realists' contribution; call him the Enlightened Traditionalist. The Moderate Realist is more skeptical politically, but not nearly so much as the radical Heavy-Duty Realist.

The traditionalist, dressed in a suit and wearing a tie that doesn't match, gulps down the last of his hamburger and says, "I don't understand why you two always dwell on politics. The end of formalist reasoning is the product of one simple realization: law is a functional tool and not a treasure hunt. Way back when, the legal community thought of prevailing law was something eternal and fundamental, commandments from on high. Then people started to realize that it's not enough to tell someone, 'Sorry, you lose. Why? Oh, because that's the law.' The consequences produced by a particular law are not side effects; they're the main event. When we have added together all the effects, good and bad, we must ask the bottom-line normative question: Is this law something we want? Or do its costs outweigh benefits? It was this normative dimension that had been missing from formalist reasoning, and the realists forced its recognition. But that doesn't require political motivations. Judges still follow rules. They have to. The values supporting the rules are just as legitimate as those calling for change.

"Take *Pennoyer v. Neff.* Was setting the jurisdictional boundary at state lines some kind of political conspiracy to maintain the distribution of wealth? I think not. But it probably made some kind of pragmatic sense in an earlier day when interstate commerce was scant and travel between states tremendously inconvenient. Unfortunately, it became enshrined by courts as a clear and unassailable postulate, despite changed circumstances that rendered it obsolete. So courts began opening their eyes and fashioning newer, more realistic formations. In *International Shoe Co. v. Washington,*[13] the Supreme Court held that a state's jurisdiction may indeed protrude beyond its borders so long as the defendant has had enough contact with that state to render jurisdiction consistent with 'traditional notions of fair play and substantial justice.' Get it? This is just traditional common-law development. The old test didn't work anymore. Something new was needed. Nothing political involved.

"What my radical friend here is really saying is that the rule of law does not even exist. Each time a judge decides a case, he writes on a *tabula rasa,* unencumbered by the past, to achieve whatever result he wants. And since each judge acts as a one-person legislature anyway, he ought at least to act truthfully by outlining the social implications of the decision. I completely disagree with any such notion. It ignores our system's rigid separation of judiciary and legislature. It implies that judges either care only about the rich or shape their opinions around the latest fancies of sociologists and psychologists. This is not the system I know. The way I see things, judges simply retain the distinction between interpretation, for which they get paid, and lawmaking, where they have no business."

To which the moderate, after scooping up the chunk of Brie she just dropped on her Liz Claiborne skirt, replies, "First of all, tuck in your shirt. Now I agree with most of your analysis, but you're naïve to think you've told the whole story. Let's dig a little deeper into your explanation for the value placed on precedent. You say it's homage to the past and judges' respect for their proper role. But I'll bet there's some selfish motivation in there as well. Both lawyers and judges have strong personal interests in stable laws: if the rules are fixed, you don't have to learn new rules. Understanding and applying new provisions can be quite difficult, especially after you've spent years unraveling the earlier set.

"Second, I think judges like to endow the law with a certain magnificence and mystery. This supports the idea that the system is one of law, not of influential people. If a judge contaminates the system's purity with her own normative, personal values, she undermines respect for the law as a majestic spirit. Hey, the law's very complexity reinforces its aura of mystery. The legal system has maintained its own language of arcana, using Latin terms where English would do just as well or ungainly English words that might as well be Latin.

"Add it all up and the conclusion you reach is this: the bar has always had a big stake in

---

13. 326 U.S. 310 (1945).

the status quo. But attempts to keep things the way they are, while politically undesirable, need not always reflect a specific political agenda. The tradition of judicial restraint really owes its origin to judicial self-interest.

"The realists taught us that passivity is not necessarily value-neutral. *Any* legal decision produces social consequences, even if that decision simply leaves things as they are. So when you suggest that a judge's job is periodically to resurrect the principles behind a formalist rule and then tweak the rule to serve those principles better, you're still advocating an essentially passive mode. And that's not enough for me. We must not be afraid to subject the entire framework—rules, principles, values—to constant reevaluation. There is no room for notions of sacredness; law, as the primary engine of societal organization, must bear ultimate responsibility for societal inequity. A world of judicial restraint, masquerading in the respectable guise of reverence for the rule of law, can no longer be tolerated."

The radical's face is red. He's sucked the life out of two packs of clove cigarettes and fidgets uncontrollably with his goatee. "Fools! Liars! Hypocrites!" he exclaims at last. "How can you possibly think that these judges are somehow on a quest for the truth? We've seen identical cases distinguished on the slenderest factual discrepancies, completely irrelevant cases tortured to fit any context, and references to the 'will of the legislature' employed to subvert a statute's plain meaning. While I've always hated the traditionalist's taste in both clothes and viewpoint, you, my moderate amigo, really disappoint me. You're the one being naïve by viewing the legal profession's rapture with the status quo as deriving solely from its own self-interest. Don't you see that the alliance among lawyers, judges, and the privileged class is no accident? Nineteenth-century jurists were aggressive social Darwinists, believers in laissez-faire policy. They considered capital growth essential to continued industrial expansion and placed their faith in the fairness of the market. The result was a concerted effort to shape the legal system in the best interest of business. Industrial enterprise needed what objectivity had to offer. How, after all, could large-scale commercial transactions take place in an uncertain environment?

"This goal was insidiously pursued in a number of ways. In tort law, for example, the negligence rule emerged as the predominant test of liability. This meant that '[i]f, in the prosecution of a lawful act, a casualty purely accidental arises, no action can be supported for an injury arising therefrom.'[14] The negligence rule relieved heavy industries like railroads and steel mills from financial responsibility for the harm they caused, as long as the injuries were inflicted 'accidentally.' And fault was pretty hard to prove if a defendant adhered to even minimal safety standards.

"While the negligence standard has a certain moral appeal—one that eases its acceptance by the unwitting masses—its logic is only appropriate in a homespun setting. Sure, it may seem unfair to saddle someone with responsibility for mishap that occurs in spite

---

14. Brown v. Kendall, 60 Mass. (6. Cush.) 292, 296 (1850). This case is one of the first to endorse widespread use of the negligence standard.

of reasonable precautions. But what about a railroad that develops a switching system which is reliable 98 percent of the time? Trains will nearly always be diverted onto the proper tracks as they pass the switching station. Once in a while, however, the mechanics go awry and the train proceeds along the wrong set of tracks, possibly causing injury. No one knows *when* this will happen, but happen it will. When the probability of accidents approaches statistical certainty, a negligence standard shields the railroad from liability for what is properly a cost of doing business."

"Now hang on a minute," interjects the traditionalist. "Why does a negligence-based system necessarily indicate some kind of political conspiracy to foster the growth of industry? The case you quoted, *Brown v. Kendall,* involved two men engaged in the undistinguished task of separating their fighting dogs. Doesn't it seem more reasonable to conclude that the negligence standard gained acceptance because of the very moral appeal you describe, but later gave way to stricter forms of liability in cases where it no longer reflected social and economic reality? The world changed, the social costs of industry changed, and the judiciary recognized the negligence rule's obsolescence by modifying it. And by the way, did your mother dress you in that linen jacket and Philippine shirt?"

"Oh, grow up," comes the radical's reply, "and leave my mother out of this. Of course the effects of the negligence rule were deliberate. Its moral attractiveness merely provided a handy smokescreen—a conceptualism—for rationalizing those effects. In fact, many courts were quite honest about their objectives. In *Losee v. Buchanan,*[15] the New York high court put it this way:

> We must have factories, machinery, dams, canals and railroads. They are demanded by the manifold wants of mankind, and lay at the basis of all our civilization. If I have any of these upon my lands, and they are not a nuisance and are not so managed as to become such, I am not responsible for any damage they accidentally and unavoidably do my neighbor. He receives his compensation for such damage by the general good, in which he shares, and the right which he has to place the same things upon his lands.

"Nor does tort law furnish the only example. The formalisms of consideration and liberty of contract were used to 'presume' equality of bargaining power between impoverished laborers and their profit-obsessed employers.[16] Broad conceptualist notions of 'property' allowed the same employers to discriminate against unions and break strikes. So formalism was a vehicle that allowed courts to subordinate actual conditions to legal abstractions. Judges could then implement their own social policy free from accusations of

---

15. 51 N.Y. 476, 484-85 (1873).

16. In Adair v. United States, 208 U.S. 161, 175 (1908), the Supreme Court said: "The right of a person to sell his labor upon such terms as he deems proper, is in its essence the same as the right of the purchaser of labor to prescribe the conditions upon which he will accept such labor from the person offering to sell it. . . . In all such particulars the employer and the employee have equality of right[.]"

playing politics. By showing how legal questions actually reduce to choices about social management, the realists exposed the lies of the orthodoxy.

"My moderate friend obviously doesn't recognize that judicial restraint need not be conservative, nor judicial activism progressive. Each may reflect a studied and forceful attempt to keep things the way they are. In the infamous case of *Lochner v. New York*,[17] an activist Supreme Court struck down forward-thinking legislation aimed at preventing excessive work hours."

"All right, all right, I've had enough abuse," the moderate cuts in. "Have you noticed that every case you cite was decided many decades ago? The realists have had their effect. Judges have become more socially aware and know they can't advance a political agenda like they used to. Too many of us are watching. I teach my students about legal realism not because there is something fundamentally wrong with the world, but because they need to evaluate objectivity in law against the background of realist critique. To you, objectivity means entrenchment of the privileged class. To me, it means an easy way out. I'll concede that in an earlier day, judges were freer to pursue their own social agendas. And I expect my students to appreciate this political dimension of formalism. But today? I think that viewing current decisions through Marxist lenses distorts rather than clarifies, and suggests that you're just pursuing an agenda of your own—one that criticizes but proposes no alternatives."

"You just don't get it," sighs the radical.

"Well, kids, I'm outta here," says the traditionalist. "Going home to study the rules. When I understand them, I'll try to identify underlying values so I can decide whether they're good rules. That's a full enough plate for me without worrying about conspiracies."

5.4 Other Schools of Legal Thought

The main triumph of legal realism was to expose the mass of mechanically applied rules as a dead, unresponsive hulk, and to bring these rules back to life by leavening them with nonobjective values. The early realists stressed values involving social-policy concerns, such as inequality of bargaining power and excessively broad notions of property. There are obviously other values that permeate legal decision-making and other currents of thought regarding objectivity. Newer forms of jurisprudence emphasize values of contemporary concern.

Law and Economics   One recent approach to law involves measuring the effects of legal rules using an economist's yardstick. Not that the law is any stranger to economics. Areas such as antitrust, trade regulation, taxes, and public utilities by their very nature

---

17. 198 U.S. 45 (1905).

demand financial as well as legal analysis. But the Law and Economics proponents go further; they feel that economic principles can both explain historical legal developments and suggest proper rules of law in areas as diverse as torts, property, environmental regulation, contracts, and even questions involving due process.

These adherents insist on separating efficiency from notions of equity. In their lexicon, efficiency refers to the least wasteful approach to a problem, so that the size of society's economic pie is maximized. The best legal rule produces the most efficient outcome, leaving the larger community better off; the issue of who, in fairness, should bear the burden of supporting that rule remains a separate matter.

Another way of expressing this outlook is that the party who can most cheaply avoid the adverse consequences of an activity is the one who should take action; maybe he shouldn't pay, but at least he should act. Suppose a factory pollutes the surrounding air, with the result that five residential neighbors must constantly repaint their houses. Suppose further that the factory can eliminate its pollution by installing an electrostatic precipitator at a cost of $100,000, and that the residents can avoid the need to repaint by installing attractive aluminum siding that resists particulate buildup at a cost of $10,000 per home.

The economically-efficient result is achieved if the homeowners buy the siding; they are the cheapest cost avoiders, since society is $50,000 better off if they take corrective action instead of the factory. Now we can talk about equity. The residents will claim that the factory is a "nuisance," in the sense discussed in chapter 2 with respect to Arnold's Pig Farm. A court will weigh the gravity of the residents' harm against the utility of the factory's conduct. But from an economic perspective, the outcome of the court's balancing should determine only the party who pays—not the action that is taken. Regardless of who actually shells out the money, the economic view dictates that the residents should side their houses.

Now, this is a simplistic example, and simplistic examples tend to generate obvious problems. First, is it really possible to assign a dollar value to every harm? We have assumed that the only harm suffered by the residents relates to their houses' exterior appearances. In reality, this might be the least of their problems. If they can't enjoy their backyards because of the stench of pollution, and if their rate of pollution-related disease such as cancer increases, pretty houses recede into unimportance. Is it possible to determine the costs associated with these more subjective harms? Is it fair to assume that everyone attaches the same value to a particular type of harm? If not, it may not be so easy to identify the cheapest cost avoider.

Another question is whether wealth can easily be redistributed. Suppose that instead of five houses there are many, and each suffers varying degrees of harm. It may cost quite a bit to investigate each case and determine an appropriate level of compensation. In trying to identify the cheapest cost avoider, these transaction costs of assessing harm must be added to the dollar value of the harm itself, and this aggregated figure compared with the price of the pollution-control measure.

These kinds of imperfections limit the ability to formulate an easy economic solution. Law and Economics adherents recognize these limitations and have therefore suggested more elaborate approaches to accommodate the complexity of the real world. For example, if it is impossible to identify the cheapest cost avoider, one might place the burden of action on the party having the ability to make a correction with the lowest transaction costs. In the above hypothetical, it's a fair assumption that it would be easier for the factory to approach its neighbors with the hope of "buying them out" than for the neighbors to organize themselves and buy the factory an electrostatic precipitator. In other words, the factory can take action with smaller transaction costs than those the residents would face. Let's say a court, unable to quantify the harm to the residents, orders the factory to close down or install an electrostatic precipitator.

Let's also suppose that, were we only omniscient enough to realize it, the cost of the pollution-control measure turns out to be higher than the fair amount of compensation for the residents—that is, the residents are the cheapest cost avoiders. The court seems to have put the onus on the wrong party. But at least the factory can still attempt to buy out the residents. If the factory had turned out to be the cheapest cost avoider and the court had made the opposite decision, it may have been nearly impossible for the residents to force the economically-efficient result by purchasing the electrostatic precipitator. By finding for the party having the lowest transaction costs, the court has maximized the chances that the economically-efficient result—taking transaction costs into account—will ultimately be reached.

Natural Law   Throughout the confirmation hearings of Justice Clarence Thomas and the media storm that preceded them, Thomas was repeatedly questioned about his views on natural law. Some of his writings suggested support for the concept, and high-minded commentators were aghast. Many urged his disqualification on this ground alone. Sure, they admitted, the Declaration of Independence repeatedly stresses natural law, speaking eloquently of "the Laws of Nature and of Nature's God." But hadn't the notion of an irrefutable source of moral values gone out of fashion with three-cornered hats and musket balls?

Advocates (and there still are a few) of just such a notion believe that some ethical principles are so universal, so fundamental to civilized society, that their truth cannot even be questioned. The problem, of course, comes when you try to identify a specific set of these "natural" laws. Beyond such quasi-biblical injunctions as "be kind" or "do not needlessly inflict suffering," how many moral precepts are all of us really prepared to embrace without question? Can vague maxims of the "be kind" variety really help us decide controversial public-policy issues?

As an argumentative device, however, resort to natural law has some appeal. It can be deployed in support of virtually any position. But its versatility is also its undoing: if natural law can be used to justify anything, it can *convincingly* justify virtually nothing. The advocate who appeals to natural law risks appearing decidedly disingenuous or even downright mischievous. His audience may well feel he is sidestepping rather than arguing.

And even when sincerity is not an issue, the fact remains that principles touted as somehow "fundamental" are generally either too vague to be useful or too specific to claim universal acceptance.

But why all the fuss? Why do critics get their hackles up at the mere suggestion of a natural law? History provides the answer. In 1872, the Supreme Court denied a woman's application to be a lawyer, stating, "The paramount destiny and mission of woman are to fulfill the noble and benign office of wife and mother. This is the law of the Creator."[18] The court later employed similar reasoning to justify racial segregation.[19] Critics of natural law are quick to cite these and other examples. They feel, often quite strongly, that the concept is too easy to misuse and too rarely appropriate. And they fear the prospect of overturning the decisions of elected representatives based on ideas of morality which at best rest on shifting sands, and at worst can be employed to justify the otherwise unjustifiable.

Law and Feminism   Recognizing that so much legal doctrine has traditionally been shaped by men, a growing number of scholars have attempted to reevaluate certain fundamental legal assumptions and values through female eyes. These scholars explore both ways in which the legal system fails adequately to address women's concerns and, from a philosophical viewpoint, how that system might change if reorganized around women's experiences and perspectives.

Some Law and Feminism scholars focus on purely practical notions of equality between the sexes and work within the system to redress familiar forms of discrimination in familiar ways—advocating legal change to advance women's positions in the workplace, in divorce proceedings, and in society generally. Such efforts have led, for example, to recognition of sexual harassment as an actionable offense, and criminalization of previously tolerated forms of rape (e.g., marital and date rape).

But many adherents of this school go much further, extending their examinations into political theory and value differences. For example, some studies indicate that men, tending to advocate such qualities as autonomy and hierarchy, emphasize moral ideals of right and wrong, while women maintain more communitarian values that stress inclusion, care, and nurturance. A number of Law and Feminism proponents see gender-based differences in outlook translating into highly dissimilar codes of conduct. For example, they point toward harsh, individualistic rules—such as the traditional precept absolving a passerby from the duty to rescue a drowning person even where no risk is involved—as characteristically (and excessively) male-oriented.

Law and Feminism, therefore, questions the values associated with objectivity from a new perspective. Its supporters observe that preoccupation with such rigid notions can rob the law of the ability to foster reciprocity and diminish suffering. Furthermore, where competing

---

18. Bradwell v. Illinois, 16 Wall. 130, 141 (1872) (Bradley, J., concurring).
19. Plessy v. Ferguson, 163 U.S. 537, 544 (1896).

values are at stake, it may be all too easy to support the ones that are most easily quantified or objectively determined. Thus, a feminist perspective might criticize the economist's insistence on putting efficiency before equity, since that order of approaching things may implicitly give too much attention to the size of the pie at the expense of the way it is split up—in other words, elevating concerns about society generally over the interests of individuals.

5.5 Problems of Retrospectivity

> Don't stop thinking about tomorrow . . . yesterday's gone, yesterday's gone.
> —Fleetwood Mac, "Don't Stop," 1977.

The typical exercise of judicial power is retrospective. A judge's decision binds the parties to the original lawsuit as well as future parties caught in the same situation. This is inescapable if courts are to decide disputes after they have arisen. Two opposing litigants present their cases, and The Law is deemed to favor one over the other. One side's conduct has been consistent with The Law, while the other has violated it. The judge, in making his choice, has implicitly told the loser that a bit more prudent attention to The Law might have avoided this whole mess. After all, the guidelines were there all along; the loser deliberately or inattentively failed to adhere to them.

Is this characterization always fair? Of course not! The law is frequently less than crystal clear, and it can be impossible to know in advance how a particular court will ultimately view today's behavior. But because of the retrospective nature of judicial decision-making, potential defendants must constantly take chances. And the greater one's ability to predict the law, the easier it is to evaluate the risks. The harshness of retrospectivity, then, is one factor favoring objectivity and changelessness in law.

One way of getting around all of this, of course, is for judges simply to act prospectively, exempting the actual litigants before them from the effect of court decisions. After all, legislatures do this all the time when they enact statutes,[20] and so do regulatory agencies when they promulgate rules. The Supreme Court has established a set of criteria for determining when a judge should apply a decision of statutory interpretation *in futuro*:

1. The decision must establish a new principle of law, either by overruling clear past precedent or by deciding an issue of first impression whose resolution was not clearly foreshadowed.

---

20. In fact, retrospective or ex post facto criminal laws are prohibited by Article I, Section 9 of the Constitution.

2. A court must decide whether retroactivity will further or retard operation of the statute. The central statutory purpose must not be undermined.

3. Retroactive application would impose some substantially inequitable result.[21]

While this test sanctions prospective rulings, it certainly does not encourage them. Why not? Well, think about the effect on the private law system if prospective judgments were to become commonplace. Plaintiffs do not file (and lawyers do not litigate) suits out of cerebral interest in the development of the law. The plaintiff sues because he wants to WIN! And if the plaintiff WINS, the defendant knows he is going to LOSE! Therein lies the incentive for digging through piles of facts, marshaling the strongest possible arguments, and ultimately presenting the most cogent case. Diligent preparation by each side assures the judge that her decision will be informed by sound advocacy and that she will not overlook any important aspects of the case. Society, in turn, can be sure that its legal system constantly operates in high gear.

It is apparent from the *Chevron Oil* test that retrospectivity produces its harshest effects when courts announce new law. The loser in a case is told that his behavior might have been consistent with earlier law, but from now on, the law will be different—starting with him. Such cases cry out for prospective treatment. But in less extreme situations, this unfairness must bow to the need for competitive litigation. Potential defendants must either take risks or steer clear of the law's outer margins.

Yet because the aversion to unfairness runs so deep, courts and legislatures have developed ways of blunting the abruptness and dislocation that retrospective decisions can cause without limiting themselves to prospective rulings, and also without creating a completely objective world of ossified laws where prospectivity isn't even necessary. The *declaratory judgment* is one such approach, providing a potential defendant with the means to effect a preemptive strike against those she fears might later sue her. Suppose, for example, that the manufacturer of a new type of semiconductor material fears that although the material is quite new and different, a large competitor seeking to create expense and disrupt production may sue for patent infringement. A declaratory judgment allows the manufacturer to eliminate the possibility of future suit by firmly establishing whether or not its technology is covered by the competitor's patent. In such an action, the parties on each side of the *v.* are reversed; the party fearful of becoming a defendant, rather than an aggrieved plaintiff, is the one who initiates suit.

Administrative agencies often provide *advisory opinions* to potential subjects of enforcement proceedings. A corporation contemplating a complex reorganization might ask the Internal Revenue Service for a *revenue ruling* that the proposed transaction will not produce adverse tax consequences, and also request that the Securities and Exchange Commission issue a *no action letter* assuring the corporation that the SEC does not object

---

21. Chevron Oil Co. v. Huson, 404 U.S. 97, 105-09 (1971).

either. Both forms of advisory opinion are informational only; they simply tell the recipient whether or not the agency reserves its right to take action. Thus, the recipient of an unfavorable IRS or SEC advisory opinion may go ahead anyway, in the hope that the agency will ultimately decide not to pursue the matter or, if it does, that a court will disagree with the agency's ultimate ruling.

As noted in chapter 1, state courts will occasionally issue advisory options—federal courts can never do so—but these are by no means commonplace.

Courts may also drop hints that they are prepared to overrule an earlier decision before actually doing so. For nearly a century, Massachusetts law prevented a noncompetition agreement between landowners from binding subsequent purchasers of one of the properties. This fixed rule was announced in *Norcross v. James,*[22] ostensibly to prevent restraint of trade. In 1967, the Massachusetts Supreme Judicial Court declared its dissatisfaction with the *Norcross* restriction, and suggested that a case-by-case approach would be more appropriate.[23] After waiting twelve years, the SJC decided it had found an "appropriate case" and overruled *Norcross.*[24] Sound like a sneaky way of creating a prospective ruling? That's for you to decide.

22. 140 Mass. 188 (1885).
23. Shell Oil Co. v. Henry Ouellette & Sons, 227 N.E.2d 509 (Mass. 1967).
24. Whitinsville Plaza, Inc. v. Kotseas, 390 N.E.2d 243 (Mass. 1979).

PART TWO

Learning the Ropes

6

Coping Strategies

6.1 The Lay of the Land

So, you grumble after reading the last five chapters, now I have a sense of how lawyers think, but what's law school like? Well, at least during the first year, you'll find yourself mystified, intimidated, sometimes overwhelmed, occasionally alienated. But that's also when you learn the foundations of legal analysis. In fact, the first year pretty much teaches you *how* to think; the rest of law school seems more like college, where you take the courses you want to take and already have some idea how to approach them.

Law school usually begins with a running start. You arrive to find that assignments for the first day of classes have already been posted. A faculty member or administrator may welcome you with some words of encouragement, but don't expect to be led through orientation by the hand of a kindhearted dean. You're pretty much left to your own devices from the outset. This may seem harsh, given the novelty of the material and the experience, but you're in *graduate* school now; universities just don't have the resources to coddle new law students as if they were freshmen.

Your professors won't coddle you, either. You will probably have an assigned seat in every class, enabling your professors to use their seating charts like cruise-missile guidance systems—homing in on you when you're most addled and least prepared. As promised earlier, many will employ the Socratic teaching method, forcing unlucky subjects to run a gauntlet of progressively more difficult questions until...what? Its when you look up from your notes and begin asking yourself "what?" that you can be sure you've reached your first law-school crisis point. Congratulate yourself. It happens to everyone. You suddenly realize that you've diligently cracked your thick casebooks every night, carefully read the ten to thirty mind-bending pages of daily assigned reading for each of your courses, and shown up for classes with the sense that you understand what's going on; yet you inevitably leave those same classes feeling as if you've been mugged of your confidence. You walk in cautiously enlightened; you leave feeling baffled. What gives?

Your sense of bewilderment is compounded by the few obnoxious dweebs who just love to hear themselves talk in class. They don't answer questions; they deliver monologues. "Ah, professor, I find the judge's construction of the facts overly cynical. Back at Oxford, when I was a Rhodes scholar..."

Don't let them fool you. They're just as confused as you are.

Naturally enough, most first-year students blame their professors for all of this confusion. You may feel that the man or woman in front of the class is hiding the ball. When you read them the night before, the cases seemed clear enough. It's only under the glare of the professor's questioning that you begin to discover ambiguity. And yet Socratic dialogue leaves that newfound ambiguity unresolved! Strange as it may seem, your professors are not hiding balls (although they're not waving any around, either). Ambiguity is part of the message: there aren't many absolute rights and wrongs in this world. Your professors use questions to map out the possibilities. Only they're not telling you how these possibilities fit together or which are the most persuasive. That's for you to figure out, and that's also what chapter 3 was all about—remember? Soon you'll see how to apply, in a practical way, the principles you already know to make sense out of a law-school course.

The other part of your professor's message is the need to develop toughness under questioning. You must learn to think on your feet. And when you've arrived at an opinion you must defend it as best you can. So how do you gird yourself, intellectually and emotionally, for this battle of wits? First, by being prepared; that's what the rest of this chapter is about. Second, by accepting the inevitable. You're not going to beat your professor to an intellectual pulp. She knows the law, you don't, end of story. You may resent her repeated questioning. You may feel like you're being cross-examined. So what? Classes are a joint enterprise, everyone else is getting the same treatment, and a bit of ego-toughening is a healthy thing. Third, if you're reading this before you begin law school, you'll walk into class prepared for some of your professors' favorite intellectual traps. You'll recognize when you're being pushed down a slippery slope. You already understand the tensions between objective and subjective approaches to law.

Finally, approach classes realistically and constructively. With few exceptions, your professors are decent people who recognize what you're going through. They may be tough in class, but they're available after class or during office hours to answer your questions. After a night's reading, you'll probably have several. Class discussion frequently raises a few more.

Try to isolate the source of your confusion; if you put your mind to it, what at first appears a dense fog often resolves itself into specific areas of uncertainty. Take these uncertainties to your professor, who's probably more approachable than her classroom demeanor suggests.

By your second year, you'll be asking these questions in class. The dweebs who dominated first-year class discussions with their pretentious commentaries will have disappeared, drowned out by exchanges among curious students just trying to learn the material. And your professors will seem more candid, too. Satisfied that you've absorbed the rudiments of legal thinking, they're more likely just to explain the law and tell you how they feel about it.

6.2 Case Briefs

Briefing a case involves shaking loose the important elements from long, often verbose judicial opinions, and then writing them down in an easily accessible format. We touched on all these elements previously in section 2.2. When you're done, you've got a thumbnail sketch that you can scan during class or while studying for exams. Just about everyone starts out briefing cases and just about everyone also stops at some point. After producing enough actual briefs, law students begin to instinctively recognize the key components of a case as they read, and the briefs turn into margin notes.

But don't be too eager to abandon the formal exercise! It's part of the learning process. Teasing the necessary information out of a case takes practice. Committing it to memory for class discussion or subsequent study takes discipline. And the only reliable way to acquire these skills is to train yourself, right at the outset, to gather the proper information and *write it down*.

A good brief enables you to recall, with a glance, the *facts* of a case, the *law,* the way the court *applied* the law to the facts, and the *policies* underlying the law. Sometimes a diagram belongs in the brief to help you understand the facts. The following are two sample briefs, one of *Guilford v. Yale University* and the other relating to a case you can find on page 132. We've used the following heading abbreviations:

Plaintiff (P)	Defendant (D)
Procedural Facts (PF)	Substantive Facts (SF)
Issue (I)	Holding (H)
Reasoning (R)	Dissent (Ds)

Guilford v. Yale University
128 Conn. 449, 23 A.2d 917 (1942)

PF: Case filed in superior court, which found for P; D appealed to Connecticut high court

SF: P injured on D's property during class reunion, to which D had invited him

I: What is the duty of care owed by D to P as a reunion invitee? Did D breach that duty?

H: P is a business invitee; D breached duty

R: D's invitation involved at least some hope of financial gain; P did not exceed scope of invitation; injury was foreseeable. POLICY: no clear underlying policy.

World-Wide Volkswagen Corp. v. Woodson
444 U.S. 286 (1980)

PF: Products-liability suit filed in *state* district court; "writ of prohibition" denied by state high court; certiorari granted by U.S. Supreme Court

SF: P injured in Okl. while riding in an Audi purchased in NY from D; D is NY corporation with principal place of business in NY; D does no business in Okl.

I: May P assert personal jurisdiction over D in Okl. based on foreseeability of car's use in Okl.?

H: "Minimum contacts" test not satisfied; no jurisdiction

R: D's conduct and connection with forum state must be such that D should reasonably anticipate being hauled into court. POLICY: fairness to D.

Ds: Court focuses too narrowly on contacts; should consider forum state's interest in case and inconvenience to D

The best repository for a brief is a sheet of looseleaf paper with a margin line that runs down the middle of the page. Your law school's bookstore is probably the only place you'll find this strange papyrus. Write your brief on the right side of the page, leaving the left side free for class notes.

How long should you continue to brief cases? For at least a semester, and probably longer. By the second half of your first year, the cases grow more complex but you begin to run out of steam; briefing cases forces you to stay alert. In fact, many students maintain their briefing habits long after their first year, largely because the process becomes much easier over time. Your briefs will become shorter as you learn which procedural facts are important and you begin to concentrate on the heart of the holdings. When the elements begin to enter your mind routinely and without effort, you may want to consider abandoning case briefs and devoting the time to development of your personal outline (a topic we'll get to soon). But don't stop writing in those margins, and definitely don't stop briefing until you're sure it's time.

6.3 Studying: Alone or Together?

A revered technique for learning the law involves a team effort among several students. Sometimes the group directs its attentions to a single class, but more commonly a gaggle of first-year students gets together and tackles the entire curriculum. The group usually produces a set of outlines for use by its members and meets periodically (perhaps nearly continuously as exams approach) to discuss class material.

The study-group experience can range from exhilarating to disastrous. Law school is a funny place. On one hand, your fellow students have all passed twice through the sieve of scholastic admissions screening, so they probably represent a smarter class than the one you went to college with. Discussions with talented classmates can produce tremendous intellectual synergy, opening doors to understanding you could never have passed through on your own. Sometimes the very act of verbalizing your thoughts results in deeper comprehension. And in a world where fellowship is often sacrificed to diligence, guiltless opportunities for social interaction can be quite welcome.

But law school is also highly competitive. Some law students will stop at nothing to get ahead, even if that means sabotaging the efforts of others. Others promise more than they can (or will) deliver. You'll meet students who buckle under the pressure of law school, as well as those who deny such pressures by pretending they're not subject to them. None of these people make particularly attractive study mates. In a group environment it's easy to make commitments of time and assistance, but far easier not to live up to them. It's also tempting to seek psychological support from study buddies and turn review sessions into exercises in collective commiseration.

These are the basic pleasures and dangers of study groups. Should you join one? It depends on your prospective cohorts and the degree to which you feel you can benefit from group dynamics. You give something up when you study with others—the prerogative to direct your attention exclusively at the problems that vex you most. In return for aid with the objects of your confusion, you agree to spend time helping to relieve the confusions of others. Those who work best on their own will feel shackled by group discussions. Evening students may have difficulty adhering to a rigid schedule. Think about it before you blindly hop on the study-group bandwagon. Once you obligate yourself, you must be prepared to follow through.

To organize a study group, you obviously need to identify like-minded partners whom you trust to make a commitment. Then you need some ground rules. The first rule is that everyone participates and contributes equally. Other rules involve administration. How often will you meet? For how long? How will you organize the group's outline? The most common approach is to divide up the class syllabi and assign each group member an equal portion. Set deadlines. When are all contributions due? Agree on a basic format. Most study-group outlines resembles condensed versions of case briefs, with insights gained during class thrown in for good measure.

You'll also need to approach your regular meetings with a certain amount of discipline. Contrary to what you might think, excessive socializing isn't what ruins study groups. People sense when the group begins to sink into kaffeeklatsch digressions, and they get antsy. So long as you have a clear agenda for each meeting, *some*one will say *some*thing when the discussion starts to drift. The real pitfall is inefficiency. First-year law students tend to dissect ferociously even the most insignificant aspects of law. You'll be moving along, going over the prior week's material and, bang, someone suddenly identifies a dark legal corner no one else has seen. Adrenaline levels begin to rise. No case has considered the issue! It's a perfect exam question! AND NO ONE UNDERSTANDS IT!

Relax. Take a breath, get a grip. How far have you strayed from the subject you're studying? Obsession over details and metaphysical reveries can go on indefinitely. Step back when things get intense, and try to evaluate the importance of the issue you're stuck on. If it's really significant, designate someone to speak with the professor, *and then move on*. As Justice Holmes once put it, certain limits are simply "a concession to the shortness of life."

6.4 Outlines

Law students prepare and use various kinds of personal—as opposed to commercial[1]—outlines to help manage reams of course materials, casebook pages, and class notes. A veritable culture of greed and heartlessness has grown up around them, and often they are traded with the briskness of Big Board stocks. Study groups prepare outlines. Occasionally

---

1. We'll talk about commercial outlines in the next chapter.

whole classes collaborate on an outline. And individual students often go it alone and digest their notes and cases into a readily accessible outline form. Such efforts are jealously guarded. However, their proprietary value completely disappears at the conclusion of the exam. Student broker-dealers usually trade in *last year's* outlines, since these are the ones most likely to be available.

The useful life of an outline is generally about two to four years—professors do occasionally change their syllabi and teaching styles, after all. For study purposes such outlines will prove far more useful than commercial aids, since they're tailored to the course you're actually taking. It's well worth getting your hands on one if you can. But a couple of caveats are in order. First, know your sources. Don't rely heedlessly on the efforts of others. The most frequent shortcoming of student outlines is not inaccuracy, but incompleteness. Take pains to compare such outlines with your notes to identify omissions and root out whatever inaccuracies may exist.

Second, use these outlines only as a supplement to your own study efforts, rather than as a replacement. Exams test your ability to reason as well as remember. Merely reading outlines won't teach you how to analyze legal problems any more than reading fitness magazines will turn you into a bodybuilder.

Outlines prepared by your study group reflect both collective discussions and individual writing efforts, and therefore serve as better study devices. But the best outlines are the ones you create yourself. The chief advantage of a solo opus is flexibility. An individual's outline can vary widely in size, format, and method of preparation. You're free to create diagrams, charts, and graphs to your heart's content. Your primary goal in preparing such an outline is to reorganize course materials into a more natural format. Casebook editors may order cases to reflect historical development or statutory organization, while law professors sometimes present topics along lines of increasing difficulty. None of these approaches is particularly conducive to studying. You want to parse each course from a different angle, the one that reflects the most logical organization of the legal concepts you've learned.

When you're done, you'll have a ready reference to use during open-book exams (contrary to what you hear, you *will* have time—though by no means leisured amounts—to skim through a well-organized outline) and a comprehensible review to precede closed-book exams.

The simplest effort is merely a map to other sources. For example, let's say you have a clear set of notes and an outline you wrote with your study group. Try preparing an index, organized by course topic, that references different subtopics to the locations of explanations in the outline and in your notes. Since it won't take much time, you can compose such an index during the reading period that precedes exams. A better idea, however, is to write it continuously over the semester. This will force you to think constantly about how the course is organized; and since organization reflects understanding, you'll be developing a sense of what the course is all about even as you progress.

If you're not committed to a study group (or if you're very ambitious), you may want to

111

produce a more comprehensive personal outline. Such efforts obviously require the continuous approach. Contribute new material to your outline after each class. Constantly think about how the cases should be organized to reflect their thematic relationships. But don't stop there. The law is full of interrelationships, and no one organization can reflect all of them. The choice of any particular set of subject headings inevitably scatters related material. That means you'll either have to cross-reference or create additional subject headings that repeat (or cross-reference) the same cases. Either approach is fine, but too many headings can lead your outline out of control.

As example of all this, suppose you're currently taking Tax, and begin to notice that several transactions have taken place in a divorce context. Or that sale-and-leaseback devices have come up more than once. First decide on overall organization. Does your professor's approach express the most natural presentation? Or would "Divorce" and "Sale-and-Leaseback" headings be more sensible? Make a choice and cross-reference, or avoid the choice by adding subject headings to organize the cases both ways. And while you're at it, cross-reference to your notes, to other outlines, and to pages in the casebook.

Don't get too attached to your initial organization. Remember, you're learning as you go along. The classifications that appear intuitively satisfying today may seem awkward or cumbersome by the time the semester ends. Don't be afraid to retype or rewrite! You need not do so every week; make editing notes in your outline as you progress, and produce a new version only when the one you've got turns into a hopeless mess. Obviously, it helps if you can type, and it helps even more if you've got a word processor. You don't have to own a computer. Most universities (and many law schools) provide banks of word-processor terminals for use by their students at no charge or for a small hourly fee. And if you can't type, write. Plenty of sturdy-wristed law students compose their outlines with pen alone.

Now to the mechanics of your personal outline. Brevity and conciseness are critical; the most useful outline triggers maximum recall with the fewest words. Try to follow each subject heading with a short description of the competing values that are at stake, or the legal framework that guides decision-making. This will help you see how different courts have approached the underlying value equation. But remember, tracking the migration of judicial philosophy is only part of the story. You must also learn the ways in which courts apply their philosophies to actual facts. So after you sketch the framework, add brief observations about each case that indicate both how they fit in and which facts were important.

As an example, the outline that follows summarizes the fighting-words cases from chapter 3. It would form the basis of one topic under the heading of First Amendment law, which is itself one of many subjects covered in a Constitutional Law class. The competing values at stake involve protection of speech, on one hand, and avoiding violence on the other. These underlying values find expression in the spectrum of approaches courts have taken in fighting-words cases, ranging from concern solely with the words themselves to emphasis on the context in which the words are spoken. In the outline, this spectrum is represented as "Content ↔ Harm ↔ Context". The shift in the Supreme Court's orientation from content to context, representing increasing protection of speech, is indicated beneath with another arrow.

Make sure you draw up a table of contents. Not only will it save page-turning time during an open-book exam, but it's also your checklist. Remember, law-school exams test your creativity. Their more subtle features may involve application of a seemingly irrelevant area of law to an odd set of facts. Systematically scanning your table of contents is far more likely to trigger the association than a fortuitous leap of imagination. And don't discard your outlines when you graduate from law school. They provide maps to tremendous amounts of disparate material in subject areas you'll return to again and again during the first few years of practice. Those outlines will come in handy more often than you may now think.

In the outline excerpt that follows, cases have been reduced to their barest essence. The descriptions include only those facts crucial to the decision and the development of the law. We've used the following abbreviations:

N.nn	=	reference to page nn of class notes
O.nn	=	reference to page nn of class outline
CB.nn	=	reference to page nn of casebook
CR.nn	=	cross-reference to page nn of this outline
FWs	=	fighting words
sp	=	speech
SC	=	Supreme Court
( )	=	(Supreme Court Justice, year)

FIRST AMENDMENT

A. Fighting Words
   (1) FRAMEWORK
       a. Values: protection of sp v. avoiding violence
       b. Content ↔ Harm ↔ Context
           1. Content = FWs bad, period
           2. Harm = evaluate harm to listeners
           3. Context = FWs unprotected only when likely to provoke violence, directed at specific person
       c. Content → context orientation of SC
           1. Early: content
           2. Up until *Cohen:* harm
              —protectible sp + hostile audience = no 1st Am. protection
           3. *Cohen*: all sp protectible in *absence* of hostile audience
           4. Related topic: hostile audience doctrine, CR.13
   (2) *Chaplinsky* (Murphy 1942)
       a. Enumerated categories of unprotected sp
       b. FWs = "by very utterance inflict injury or tend to incite breech of the peace." CB.1038
           1. Content, not context oriented
           2. Deference to legislative judgment as to danger. CR.12, 28
   (3) *Feiner* (Vinson 1951)
       a. Context of hostile audience
       b. Even if sp permissible, may police stop speaker when crowd becomes riotous?
           1. Do best to protect speaker but state has interest in stopping riot
           2. Intent of speaker, refusal to desist, effort by police
       c. In some contexts, otherwise protected sp will be unprotected. N.35
       d. But uncertain whether more or less protective of sp than *Chaplinsky*
   (4) *Edwards* (Stewart 1963)
       a. Clarifies *Feiner:* uncertain threat not enough. 0.49
       b. Fear of adverse audience reaction by police not enough. N.36
   (5) *Cohen* (Harlan 1971)
       a. Pure sp, no potential for riot
       b. Very protective of sp
           1. "Offensive language" rejected as category of unprotected sp
           2. FWs narrowed: not directed to particular person = not a FW issue
           3. Definition of obscenity narrowed as well. N.38, CR.17

┌─────────┐
│   7   │
└─────────┘

Commercial Study Aids

LAW-SCHOOL SUPPORT DEVICES are everywhere. The publishers of commercial study aids—books, outlines, flow charts, prewritten briefs, and cassette tapes—beckon you constantly with testimonials and attractive covers. Most of these tools can be useful, to varying degrees, if used correctly. Some are better than others. None is especially cheap.

This chapter will give you an idea of what's out there and which occasions call for which tool. Don't settle on a single type of study aid and stick with it exclusively; nor should you opt for the shotgun approach, where you buy everything in sight and ultimately land yourself in a rest home for bleary-eyed, bankrupt insomniacs. You might consider abstaining altogether. All study aids are backups, not required reading for success. Many law students routinely turn up their noses at these device; others don't leave home without them.

****

Type of Study Aid: Hornbooks

Publishers: West Publishing Company
Foundation Press
Little, Brown & Co.

Price Range: Paperback—$15–$20
Hardcover—$23–$40 (per volume)

****

115

Hornbooks, whose very name evokes images of elementary learning in a little red schoolhouse, are textbooks that describe a particular field of law. Their authors hail from the ranks of outstanding law professors, who often produce hornbooks by condensing much larger treatises. A comprehensive, well-written hornbook provides an overview of the law and discussions of all the important cases. The presentation tends to maintain a consistent level of depth, while your courses at law school will vary from class to class. Hornbooks put cases in doctrinal context. They may help you get a sense of the underlying themes and changing judicial priorities.

But each represents the views of a single author. Your professor's approach to the subject matter may differ dramatically. She might emphasize specific areas in such detail as to render the hornbook discussion superficial and largely useless, while ignoring subjects that occupy much of the hornbook's bulk. Reading a hornbook can also add quite a bit to the time you devote to studying (unless you use the hornbook as a substitute for the assigned reading—a practice you'll regret).

You should buy a hornbook only when none of that really matters. Subject matter that is sufficiently and uniformly difficult may require frequent reference to the guideposts a hornbook provides; having wriggled free of utter confusion, you can focus clearheaded attention on your professor's more esoteric points.

While hornbooks are written to be accessible to law students, practitioners represent a huge market for these publications. If you plan on practicing in a particular area, purchase of a hornbook can be an investment that will yield returns long after the exam. But if you're just looking to solve a few isolated mysteries, a better approach might be to consult your library's hornbook collection or, better yet, have a look at the leading treatise in the area.

Recommendations

White and Summers, *The Uniform Commercial Code*. One of the best hornbooks available, it's also the only clear and comprehensive guide to a very complex world of arcane transactions and confusing statutes. This hornbook is published in a single volume for law students, while a more exhaustive two-volume set awaits practitioners and judges. Despite their thoroughness, the books are written with a refreshingly light hand.

Chirelstein, *Federal Income Taxation*. Taxation is a highly mathematical subject with a host of intricate, interrelated statutory provisions that can be nearly impossible to understand. Some sort of escort through this minefield is essential. Unfortunately, your casebook probably offers little beyond cases and questions. Enter Chirelstein, a noted scholar in areas of law involving business and finance, to lead the way with this descriptive overview. His acute awareness of matters financial is reflected in the book's paperback format.

Prosser and Keeton, *Hornbook on Torts*. No two torts professors teach the same course. Some stress legal doctrine, others pure theory, still others economics. Prosser has long reigned as the undisputed authority in the field of torts, and this volume is notable for its range of topics. Although the authors don't stray too far into the world of economics, they do an admirable job covering both the policy goals of a private compensation system and the black-letter elements of the various torts.

Clark, *Corporate Law.* Robert Clark, dean of Harvard Law School and a renowned authority on matters corporate, has produced a masterful and readable volume covering the practical and theoretical sides of the corporate enterprise. Clark introduces topics (which include financing, corporation operation, duties to creditors and shareholders, and an introduction to securities regulation) with original examples and case holdings. If nothing else, this text will introduce you to Clark's method of representing complex fact patterns with elegant, understandable diagrams.

Lilly, *An Introduction to the Law of Evidence.* Plan on doing some litigation in the future? This book will prove a worthwhile resource down the road, and in the meantime provides a clear, readable introduction to an area of law that contains plenty of subtlety. The book is printed in unusually small dimensions, fitting nicely in your backpack as well as your budget. It contains not only case citations, but also references to the larger hornbook on evidence by McCormick.

****

Type of Study Aid: Nutshell Series

Publishers: West Publishing Company

Price Range: $15–$20

****

Distill a hornbook down to its bones and you have a Nutshell. These little volumes canvass entire fields of law with considerable breadth, but little depth. That's perfect in a number of contexts. If a professor's course presentation is diffuse, focusing on specific topics without integrating them, read the Nutshell. It will tell you what the course is *really* all about without miring you in technicalities. If you feel yourself lost in the swirl of rules of a complex statutory field—commercial paper, secured transactions, sales—read the Nutshell to get a basic sense of how the rules work together. And in areas of law that stress concepts over technicalities, read the Nutshell for an overview of important topics.

The usefulness of Nutshells does not disappear when you graduate; if anything, it increases. Should you suddenly acquire responsibility for an area of law you know nothing about, read the Nutshell and soon you'll be able to speak the language. Also, Nutshells can quickly and efficiently clear the cobwebs from your memory and reacquaint you with a field of law you haven't thought about in years.

Nutshells give you readily accessible, quickly grasped descriptions of legal topics. The range of Nutshell topics is quite broad and includes emerging or narrow areas of law—sex discrimination, architecture and engineering law, AIDS law—that haven't spawned hornbooks (yet). But Nutshells just aren't that big. Don't delude yourself into thinking you're an expert merely because you've read the Nutshell. Short overviews are necessarily incomplete, and they can only skim the surface of the topics they do cover. Although they tend to be revised more frequently than hornbooks, Nutshells can still become outdated. Important developments may have occurred since publication of the latest edition.

Recommendations

The *Administrative Law and Process, Consumer Law, Labor Law,* and *Intellectual Property* titles are well-suited to their respective areas, since concepts loom large and the rules are broad. At the other end of the spectrum, Nutshells confined to narrow, technical areas deliver concise explanations of how the rules work together. Consider the *Securities Regulation, Commercial Paper, Secured Transactions,* and *Sales* volumes.

———————

****

Type of Study Aid: Substantive Outlines

Publishers: Gilbert Law Summaries (Harcourt Brace Jovanovich)
Emanuel Law Outlines
Sum & Substance (Josephson/Kluwer)
Black Letter Series (West)
Casenote Law Outlines
Legalines
Finals Law School Exam Series
Examples & Explanations (Little, Brown & Co.)
Socratutor

Price Range: $20–$30

****

Substantive outlines of course material have become enormously popular in the last decade or so. Well-organized and comprehensive, they represent the most straightforward effort to structure legal doctrine in a form easily digestible by law students. Although a number of publishers with differing approaches market this kind of study aid, all those listed above share certain features. Substantive outlines concentrate unabashedly on the grit of legal doctrine. You won't find overview statements or analysis of policy considerations.

The format, a highly methodical arrangement of subject headings and concise text entries, proves quite convenient for pinpointing specific areas of interest. The authors maintain constant awareness of law students' inexperience by providing frequent hypotheticals and illustrations. Case analyses tend to be far more self-contained and explicit than those found in hornbooks, and usually cover all but the most recent cases your professors assign. In courses that involve lots of technical rules, substantive outlines do the opposite of Nutshells: they provide precise explanations and interpretations of each and every rule. In courses that emphasize concepts over rules, outlines summarize all the important holdings.

Substantive outlines are so prevalent in law school that it almost requires will power to keep away from them. Keep in mind, as you shop, that their greatest strengths may also pose serious weaknesses. A highly structured organization can make it difficult to see the big picture. Uniformly detailed presentations may distract your attention from the areas most important to your professor. For example, as we've noted, many professors downplay the significance of doctrine and use assigned cases as stepping-off points for theoretical analysis. Outlines don't help much here. On the other hand, a few professors dwell on theory all right, but test you on doctrine as well—assuming you've somehow picked it up along the way. In these relatively rare instances, a substantive outline is required reading.

Don't put too much stock in the practice exams included in some outlines. These usually represent nothing more than recapitulations of segments of the outline phrased as answers to questions. They rarely convey a sense of the subtleties so dear to law professors. And don't think for a minute that commercial outlines can substitute for group or personal outlines. They can't. The devices you buy are resources, not oracles; they won't teach you how to think.

Gilbert outlines are the best-selling outlines in the country. This is no accident; they are well-written, complete, and frequently updated. Only rarely will you encounter a case or rule of law not covered somewhere in the Gilbert summary. In addition to the text, Gilbert outlines also feature condensed "capsule" outlines that may prove helpful as exams approach, and correlation tables that relate the various chapters to sections of major casebooks. The thoroughness of Gilbert outlines makes them especially useful when a course demands mastery of a broad and specialized vocabulary; property and procedure courses are examples.

Sum & Substance outlines are also well-written. They tend to provide the most ample explanations (by way of patient verbal descriptions, diagrams, and other illustrations) of difficult topics. Sum & Substance summaries also have capsule outlines and correlation tables. But because of the way the paragraphs are numbered and organized, Sum & Substance titles are somewhat harder to follow than their Gilbert counterparts, and tend to cover (or at least seem to cover) fewer legal topics.

Examples & Explanations titles attempt to bridge the gap between hornbooks and outlines. Written by law professors, these weighty books contain discussions of legal topics followed by questions and answers. The questions aren't really like exams; instead, they're supposed to help teach the material, varying what would otherwise be long stretches of text. Reading one of these requires a substantial time investment, and they don't coordinate with casebooks. Stick with a hornbook if it's reference and enlightenment you're after; otherwise, get yourself an outline.

Entries in the **Black Letter Series** try to describe the law as a series of black-letter rules and definitions, each of which is followed by a discussion and some examples. Cases are rarely mentioned by name. While this approach has some appeal in terms of verbal economy, it also lacks depth and frequently seems artificial. Relatively useless review questions and practice exams occupy much of the volumes. If it's succinctness you're after, better to buy the Nutshell.

Emanuel outlines include the Emanuel Law Outline series, which cover basic legal topics and are written primarily by Emanuel's founder; the Smith's Review series, written by law professors; and Siegel's Essay & Multiple Choice Q&A Series. Compared with, say, Gilbert outlines, the Emanuel entries tend to have larger type and more *italicized,* **boldfaced** text, as well as a looser organization. Some may prefer this format; to others, it's just harder to follow. Like any commercial exam-preparation device, the Siegel's guides cannot substitute for reviews of previous exams actually given by your professors.

Legalines outlines take a different approach to organization, coordinating directly with particular casebooks. The problem is that most of your professors do not. You'll find that law professors tend to teach somewhat personalized courses, and frequent deviations from the casebook's organization render a coordination feature superfluous. One advantage to Legalines outlines is the frequency of updates; since they must keep pace with casebooks, Legalines are updated just as often (typically annually). But Gilbert titles tend to cover more topics and just seem to answer more questions.

The **Finals Law School Exam Series** covers the legal subjects you'll encounter on the multistate portion of the bar exam. The presentation, as well as the copious review-question sets, are keyed to the multistate format. Unfortunately, and once again, most of your law-school courses are not.

The computer has finally insinuated itself into the world of legal study aids. It was just a matter of time. For the price of a paper outline, the **Socratutor** gives you a complete electronic version and lets you customize it on the screen, with word-processing software included in the package. You can "zoom" among varying levels of detail—from a table of contents to an outline to text. You can "highlight" text with yellow shading. You can search for key words. You can print out your work in whole or in part. There are a lot of features here for those fortunate enough to own a computer and who know how to use it.

Recommendations

Which publisher you choose to patronize is obviously a matter of taste, but the courses that tend to benefit most from outlines are Property, Evidence, Corporations, Civil Procedure, Taxation, Antitrust, and Constitutional Law. Of these, you may want to consider Gilbert for technical areas of law and Sum & Substance for courses that present difficult theoretical issues.

For example, the Gilbert *Commercial Paper* or *Secured Transactions* outlines will give you complete summaries and explanations of the rules (in contrast to, for example, the gestalt approach of a Nutshell). The Sum & Substance *Antitrust* outline not only summarizes the important legal topics, but also explains basic economic and patent-law concepts to help give you a proper introductory foundation. For tax courses, annual updates are critical since the law is always changing; buy nothing but an absolutely current outline.

The Socratutor series is perfect for those whose reaction to the personal outline on page 114 was, "He's nuts." It can be hard just to get started on an outline. The editorial skills needed to cluster and group topics may seem more the domain of librarians than of lawyers. For those who get lost in the intricacies of indentation and paragraph numbering, a basic structure might be just what you need. That's fine. But don't forget that the Socratutor provides only a foundation; it can't substitute for the real work of rearranging what you learn and building a useful framework. You should experience genuine guilt if you're not constantly rethinking the outline's organization, adding cross-references to your class notes, casebook, and class outline, and inserting your own annotations.

———————

****

Type of Study Aid: Topical Outlines and Flash Cards

Publishers: Essential Principle (Josephson/Kluwer)
Foldeez Law Outlines
Law Mate Series (Little, Brown & Co.)
Flowlex Law Charts
BarCharts
Flashers
Cram Cards (Josephson/Kluwer)
Law in a Flash

Price Range: $5–$35

****

The term *topical outline* is employed here in a generic sense to refer to study aids whose presentation is more visual than substantive. They attempt to provide maximum condensation by offering methods of organization instead of explanations. Beyond the obviously question-able value of devices whose main selling point is their *lack* of information, topical outlines should be avoided for another reason: your mind must remain independent at the level of course organization. Synthesizing concepts into an overall picture represents a crucial phase of the learning process. Another is developing an appreciation for your professors' priorities. Topical outlines purport to replace all of these intellectual exercises, and they simply cannot.

Flash cards are the most recent innovation to make the study-aid scene. For generations now, flash cards have claimed a devoted following who extol their virtues with near-religious fervor. Members of this cult can now continue their exaltations in law school and on their computer screens. It's difficult to see what all the fuss is about. Few legal topics can be distilled to the kinds of question-and-answer word bites that fit comfortably on 3×5 cards, and memorization will only take you so far in law school. But you flash-card devotees know who you are, and you're not listening anyway.

———————

****

Type of Study Aid: Prepared Briefs

Publishers: Casenotes
Cambridge Law Study Aids
Blond's Law Guides

Numina Case Briefs (for personal computers)

Price Range: $15–$25

****

Because reading cases can be tedious, and because subsequently writing case briefs is even more tedious, a few people got the bright idea of doing all the work for you. These materials offer summaries of all the cases in your casebook, arranged in the traditional "brief" format. Professors absolutely detest them. They view canned briefs as an excuse for laziness, a sidestep around the mental effort necessary to develop a legal mind. Law students buy them by the dozen. They have either learned to utilize these study aids constructively or are actively proving their professors' misgivings true.

The only legitimate use of prepared briefs is to further the goal of efficiency in case reading, and nothing more. Judges are often shabby writers. Their factual descriptions can be involuted enough to confuse Mr. Spock, and issues may lie buried in a mass of pronouns and *heretofores.* Your time and attention are better spent wrestling with legal issues than struggling through turgid prose. A prepared brief may clarify the facts, enabling you to proceed to substance before giving up with a frustrated slam of the casebook cover.

But words of caution are in order. Canned briefs have been known to contain inaccuracies, and even accurate briefs may emphasize the wrong aspects of the court's holding. You probably shouldn't think others' thoughts at this level anyway, but if you do, be careful. Use these tools sparingly, and in difficult or theoretical courses like Federal Courts and Constitutional Law, stay away entirely.

Of the publishers listed above, the Blond's series may be preferable for its inclusion of helpful mnemonics.

****

Type of Study Aid: Cassette Tapes

Publishers: Sum & Substance (Josephson/Kluwer)
Gilbert Law Summaries (Harcourt Brace Jovanovich)

Price Range: $30–$60

****

Who would have thought that spoken communication, perhaps the least efficient form of information transfer, could possibly provide an effective study aid? Even a six-hour set of cassettes can provide only a general overview of a field of law. Nevertheless, those who have tried one of these tapes often purchase additional titles. The lecturers are effective speakers, and their presentations do not have a "scripted" sound to them.

For the visually impaired, their value is obvious. And while playing them as you sleep may not transform you into Clarence Darrow by the next morning, those who commute to law school—and especially evening students who also commute to work—may find taped presentations helpful. They are obviously not for everyone. One must have the time, money, and some special reason for preferring an oration to the printed word.

8

The Marks of Distinction

8.1 The Stuff of Résumés

Law school is competitive because the practice of law is competitive. The need to prove yourself begins with your first class. You'll find that prospective employers care about all of your personal qualifications, but they care most about academic performance. Those at the top of the class receive more offers than they know what to do with; those not so fortunate have a much harder time. Just how high in the rankings must you be to attract the interests of prominent law firms, large corporations, or judges seeking law clerks? That depends, quite frankly, on the prestige associated with your law school.

But don't expect any hard and fast rules. The amount of hiring going on in a particular year, your law school's stature in the marketplace (which can also vary from year to year), and the personal biases of the individuals who do the hiring all enter the equation. Your school's placement counselor can help you arrive at a realistic assessment. If you're still shopping for a law school, be sure to do some investigation before you commit. Visit the campuses, drop in on placement offices, and ask a few questions. What kinds of help does each office provide to students? Do they have some recent hiring statistics you can look at?

The pronounced relationship between law-school grades and employment prospects encourages an attitude toward classes you're probably not used to. Academic satisfaction is secondary; performance on exams becomes your overriding concern. In fact, sometimes you'll feel as if the entire semester is nothing more than an extended period of test preparation. This reality often prompts despair among new students, who succeeded in college because they actually *enjoyed* classes. Don't despair. Educational satisfaction just comes a little later in law school. By the time you reach your second year, you'll enjoy being able to think like a lawyer. And you'll also have the freedom to select courses directly related to your long-term goals.

Of course, the obsession with grades would seem a lot less pernicious—and maybe even constructive—if exams could provide a consistently reliable measure of your potential as a lawyer. Your objective in going to law school is to enter a profession, right? So what if the price of knowing how well you will do in that profession is a little obsession?

Like so many arguments, the problem with that one lies in the premise. Law-school grades do not—cannot—always reflect your abilities or level of knowledge. In general, your entire grade in a class will be based solely on a single final exam (with perhaps some credit for class participation). How can professors design tests that fully represent the prodigious amount of material you've been exposed to, yet which you can complete in a reasonable length of time? The answer is that they can't. By their very nature, exams can probe only a relatively few class topics. And when you're done, your professors must discriminate among the efforts of a fearfully large group of bright, dedicated students, each of whom grappled with an identical exercise. The distinctions they must make are often quite fine. From your own perspective, it's a straightforward matter to walk into the exam, have a terrifically lousy day, and totally miss what your professor was after.

One reason it's so easy to screw up is that classes and case reading do little to prepare you for exams. The kinds of questions law professors ask bear little resemblance to anything you've seen before. A classic exam-question format is known as the issue spotter. It reads like a story, relating a complicated series of events, facts, people, and places. The final sentence asks you to pretend you're an associate or law clerk, and to write a memo that identifies and analyzes lurking legal issues. The facts are subtly intertwined and touch on a number of legal topics. Professors love issue spotters because they test your knowledge of several areas at once, and also bear strong resemblance to the way lawyers approach new problems. But you don't learn issue-spotting skills from classroom discussion or your reading assignments. These, unfortunately, focus on issues that courts have *already* spotted and analyzed.

Because of this, you finish your exams with virtually no idea how well you've done. And you won't find out until two or three agonizing months later, when a grade sheet finally makes its way into your terrified hands. As you peruse this heartless missive, you may find more than mere letters. Many law schools rank their students, by number or percentile, according to grade-point average. That's when you enter the icy realm of statistics, where numbers and letters threaten to chart the course of your entire professional existence. Great grades mean a good summer position that leads to numerous offers of permanent employment; mediocre grades relegate you to the endless hunt for stray positions.

...Right? Well, not necessarily. Statistics, while powerful, are not invincible. By the time you finish law school, first-year grades represent only a minor portion of your transcript. Legal employers evaluate how well you improved throughout the course of your education. They also look at your entire résumé, not just your GPA.

Start building that résumé early. If you want a prestige legal position but find yourself among the 95 percent of law students who aren't in the top 5 percent of their classes, you must simply find ways to distinguish yourself academically other than (or in addition to) your grades. That means getting involved in cocurricular or extracurricular activities. It also means approaching such activities quite differently from the way you did in college. You ply them primarily for what they can do for your résumé, not out of intellectual curiosity. Naturally enough, the most powerful résumé-building pursuits require more than participation; they're the ones that produce winners and losers. At first you may approach these activities with trepidation and resentment, angry at the sacrifice of your precious free time for even more competitive pressures. Rest assured that your attitude will change as you become more involved. You'll soon recognize the value of the experience and enjoy collaborating with your classmates in new ways.

Perhaps the most elite activity of all is something called law review. That hoary institution, with historical roots reaching down into the early days of legal education, publishes a scholarly journal packed with scholarly legal articles written by, and for, those scholarly inclined. Students compete for the privilege of editing the journal. Although the editing itself tends to be quite technical and dry, law-review members screen cutting-edge articles written by famous law professors, judges, and lawyers; they also have fun summarily rejecting the work of such luminaries or hacking it to pieces with editorial revisions. Each member also receives the opportunity to publish her own "note" or "comment"—a (relatively) short examination of a recent decision or particular area of law.

Because editorial spots are limited, highly prized, and awarded competitively, potential employers just love to see "law review" on a résumé. And one source of the trauma surrounding first-year grades is their traditional place as door-openers to membership. Fortunately for the bottom 95 percent of the class, law-review selection criteria have broadened in recent years. Students usually must take part in a writing competition, the results of which are considered by the current board of editors either along with or, in some cases, entirely in lieu of first-year grades. The exact procedure varies from school to school and from year to year. For example, some reviews offer half their editorial positions based on grades, half based on results of the writing competition, and may also temper their decisions by considering such factors as affirmative-action goals.

Many law schools support several legal journals, but one invariably maintains a higher stature than the others and commands the most competitive selection procedure. That review also requires the most work from its editors, up to forty hours per week. No wonder second- and third-year class attendance suffers a drop among law-review members! If you fail to qualify for a top-gun journal, by all means consider participating in another. Alternative law reviews generally publish articles only within a limited domain—law and technology, family law, international law, to name a few possibilities. One of them might be directly in tune with your personal interests. You'll find writing your own note to be challenging and rewarding, the editorial atmosphere congenial and supportive, and the impact on your résumé suitably impressive.

Another path to academic distinction is moot court. Virtually all law schools require first-year students to tackle a legal problem by doing research, writing an appellate brief, and presenting oral argument before faculty or guest judges. But most schools also offer a voluntary, competitive equivalent that begins some time after the required exercise ends. See how you feel after your first moot-court experience. Up for more? The competitive version takes you through a series of rounds that winnows the field to a single team, which then competes regionally and perhaps nationally with winners from other law schools. Your school may offer other competitive undertakings involving mock trials, negotiations, mediations—you name it.

Consider entering writing contests. Many schools award prizes in recognition of distinguished authorship efforts. Legal journals and periodicals often sponsor similar contests, with winners seeing their accomplishments published (and possibly receiving some always-welcome cash). Your school's placement office can give you information about these. You might also consider joining the American Bar Association and its Law Student Division. This nationwide organization provides its members with numerous benefits, among which is *Student Lawyer* magazine. *Student Lawyer* not only makes interesting reading, but also accepts unsolicited manuscripts for publication and frequently advertises writing competitions.

And if you felt particularly stimulated by one of your classes, see if the professor needs research assistance. As a reward you'll receive both monetary compensation and an acknowledgment in publications related to your efforts.

8.2 A Head Start on Experience

In today's legal market, the right experience can give you a very powerful advantage. It's because of clients. They have plenty of work for their lawyers, but insist on streamlined costs and capped fee arrangements. Gone are the days when young associates could earn their keep carrying their superiors' bags, learning by watching, acquiring skills gradually. Overhead is too high and clients' wallets are too lean. Today law firms, rather than their clients, subsidize the cost of associate training. Hiring a fresh law-school grad means years of investment. Is it any wonder that legal recruiters are doing a brisk business filling associate slots with more seasoned practitioners?

Experience, then, is a form of hard currency. Candidates with skills they can put directly to work for a potential employer have already paid part of their apprenticeship tuition. They are certified self-starters. As a result, they have a tremendous leg up on their peers. Consider the avenues you might pursue outside the classroom to get a jump on the learning curve. It could make the difference between you and 125 others with similar academic credentials.

Begin by deciding, as early as possible, where you hope to direct your career. Not that you should choose a life-long specialty before the ink is even dry on your first-semester transcript. But start to think about the role you see yourself growing toward. A few broad themes pervade the lives of lawyers. Acting as *advocates,* lawyers smite the enemy, defend the innocent, and otherwise earn a living arguing before judges, juries, agency boards, government panels, and legislative bodies. As *advisers,* lawyers counsel their clients about the limits of the law and help them navigate through seas of juristic arcana—how to structure that license agreement to avoid antitrust or tax problems, what a fair divorce settlement looks like, why it may not be such a good idea to hire that competitor's employee just yet. And as *facilitators*, lawyers get deals done. They oversee public offerings and real-estate closings, they negotiate corporate mergers and insolvency workouts, they draft the documents that redraw business landscapes.

Although particular practice areas and specialties tend to be closely identified with one of these roles over the others, the truth is that most lawyers frequently straddle these lines. Avowed litigators hammer out settlement agreements. Reclusive tax lawyers pound tables in Tax Court. Bearing this in mind, where do you see yourself?

If you're interested in being an advocate, think about participating in mediation projects with local courts, clinical programs that allow you to represent real clients under the supervision of a faculty member or legal-aid staff attorney, or counseling networks that provide advice to indigent members of the local community. Not only do these programs enable you to make a genuine contribution to the public good; they place you in authentic situations that create experience—that show prospective employers you know your way around a courtroom. You can also check with the legal offices of the federal, state, or even county or municipal government. Lawyers work at all levels of public administration. The U.S. attorney, district attorney, public defender, and counsel to state and federal agencies all have more work than they can handle, and many maintain organized volunteer programs (particularly during the summer months, but don't let the absence of a formal structure stop you). Some entrepreneurial law students have recently organized part-time legal research squads that offer their services to local firms, who pay by the hour to have law students sift through cases and statutes. Consider signing on (or organizing one at your school); it's not very glamorous, but fast, diligent work and a little networking skill might impress someone with clout.

See yourself as a dealmaker or an adviser? Try for an internship in a government agency about which lawyers are frequently consulted. Again, remember how many federal functions are duplicated at the state and local level. The SEC or the IRS may not have any openings, but what about the securities division of the secretary of state's office, or the state department of revenue? Call the bankruptcy court or the office of the U.S. Trustee; see if the judges are hiring law students as clerks (some of them have ridiculous dockets and really need the help). Check with zoning boards and departments of environmental protection if you see real-estate practice in your future. And check out the Internet. We'll have more to say about finding your way around this gargantuan resource in chapter 12, but more and more internships and job listings—including those for which law students might be eligible—are getting posted to Internet sites. Poke around. You never know what you'll find.

8.3 Facing the Inevitable: Exams and Examsmanship

What would a book about law school be without advice on handling exams? Although exam questions most commonly take the form of issue spotters, as discussed above, professors don't confine themselves to a single method of sampling your brain. They may hit you with a traditional essay question, calling for recapitulation and discussion of a particular slice of legal doctrine or theoretical analysis; a multiple-choice section; or a long series of short-answer questions that initially appear simple but actually implicate several topics at once, like mini-issue spotters.

Regardless of your professor's exam-writing predilections, your general approach to studying should be the same. The first step is outlining, a topic we've already covered at length. Go to any class review sessions prepared to ask those inevitable nagging questions. Then find out whether the exam is closed-book or open-book. Neither form is harder or easier than the other, although each requires a different approach to studying. Open-book exams tend to feature more involved questions that place a premium on your ability to recognize interrelated issues. After all, you've got the law right in front of you, so why should your professor give you credit merely for setting out the six elements of fraud? To meet this challenge, you must develop fluency in using your outline(s). That's why a table of contents is so important. Time is truly short, and ideas must come to you fast. Let your index guide both your fingers and your thoughts.

Closed-book exams (as well as the bar exam you'll take when you graduate) require memorization of black-letter doctrine. Devise mnemonics to ease recall of those technical definitions. For example, the important property notion of *adverse possession* (known outside the law as "squatters' rights") prevents a landowner from ejecting someone from his property if he waits too long. But the squatter must fulfill a number of conditions: her possession of that little corner of the world must be continuous for a certain period of time (usually twenty years), open and notorious, consistent with a claim of right to the land, and hostile in the sense that she lacks the owner's permission to be there. Hence the mnemonic CONCH:

C ontinuous
O pen
N otorious
C laim of right
H ostile

Now dig through past exams. Your school's library probably maintains a file of them, perhaps going back decades. What kinds of questions does your professor like to ask? Are they picky or deceptively subtle?

As you sit in the exam room, waiting for the proctors to distribute the test, try to relax (easy to say, hard to do). Read the instructions carefully when you receive the booklet. See how your professor has allocated credit among the different questions, and try to pace yourself accordingly. Read each question more than once.

That's the basic approach. Of course, advice on exams would seem pretty vacant without a few practical examples. You've been expecting them. So here.

The following represent an attempt to distill the most important features of issue-spotter questions into an abbreviated form, one you can tackle without previous experience. In real life (if law school bears any resemblance to real life) an exam will confront you with a considerable amount of information that produces mutually dependent, multilayered legal issues. You will also have read quite a number of relevant cases and statutes. The ensuing examples are factually confined and can be answered clearly from a limited string of cases, but require a typically detailed legal analysis. They involve personal jurisdiction, a topic you encountered in chapter 5.

Definition

A *tort* is a legal wrong committed upon person or property involving: (1) a legal duty, (2) breach of that duty by the defendant, and (3) injury as a proximate result.

Statute

In order for a plaintiff to haul an out-of-state defendant into a local court, his state must have a *long-arm* statute capable of extending jurisdiction beyond state borders. The exercise of jurisdiction must fit within the terms of the statute, as well as satisfy the requirements of the Due Process Clause of the Fourteenth Amendment to the federal Constitution. The East Carolina[1] long-arm statute reads as follows:

A court may exercise personal jurisdiction over a person, who acts directly or by an agent, as to a cause of acting arising from the person's
1. transacting any business in this state;
2. contracting to supply services or things in this state;
3. causing tortious injury by an act or omission in this state; or
4. causing tortious injury by an act or omission outside this state, if he regularly does or solicits business, or engages in any other persistent course of conduct, in this state.

CASE I

Pennoyer v. Neff
95 U.S. 714 (1878)

This is an action to recover the possession of a tract of land, of the alleged value of $15,000, situated in the State of Oregon.... The defendant claims to have acquired the premises under a sheriff's deed, made upon a sale of the property on execution issued upon a judgment in one of the circuit courts of the state. The case turns upon the validity of this judgment.

* * *

---

1. Forgive the pitiful state names. Law professors invent fictitious jurisdictions for their exams to emphasize that they're not testing you on the law of any particular state.

The several States of the Union...possess and exercise the authority of independent States, and the principles of public law are applicable to them. One of these principles is, that every State possesses exclusive jurisdiction and sovereignty over persons and property within its territory.... [N]o state can exercise direct jurisdiction and authority over persons or property without its territory.

* * *

It follows from the views expressed that the personal judgment recovered in the State Court of Oregon against the plaintiff herein, then a nonresident of the State, was without any validity, and did not authorize a sale of the property in controversy.

CASE II

International Shoe Co. v. Washington
326 U.S. 310 (1945)

[One question presented to the Court is] whether, within the limitations of the Due Process Clause of the Fourteenth Amendment, [defendant], a Delaware corporation, has by its activities in the State of Washington rendered itself amenable to proceedings in the courts of that state[.]

[Plaintiff, the state of Washington, seeks to recover unpaid contributions to the state unemployment compensation fund as provided by state statute. Defendant] is a Delaware corporation, having its principal place of business in St. Louis, Missouri,[2] and is engaged in the manufacture and sale of shoes and other footwear. It maintains places of business in several states, other than Washington, at which its manufacturing is carried on and from which its merchandise is distributed interstate through several sales units or branches located outside the State of Washington.

[Defendant] has no office in Washington and makes no contracts either for sale or purchase of merchandise there. It maintains no stock of merchandise in that state and makes there no deliveries of goods in interstate commerce. During the years from 1937 to 1940, now in question, [defendant] employed eleven to thirteen salesmen under direct supervision and control of sales managers located in St. Louis. These salesmen resided in Washington; their principal activities were confined to that state; and they were compensated by commissions based upon the amount of their sales. The commissions for each year totaled more than $31,000. [Defendant] supplies its salesmen with a line of samples, each consisting of one shoe of a pair, which they display to prospective purchasers. On occasion they rent permanent sample rooms, for exhibiting samples, in business buildings, or rent rooms in hotels or business buildings temporarily for that purpose. The cost of such rentals is reimbursed by [defendant].

---

2. [This makes the defendant a citizen of both Missouri and Delaware. The plaintiff wishes to sue in neither of these states.]

The authority of the salesmen is limited to exhibiting their samples and soliciting orders from prospective buyers, at prices and on terms fixed by [defendant]. The salesmen transmit the orders to [defendant's] office in St. Louis for acceptance or rejection, and when accepted the merchandise for filling the orders is shipped f.o.b. from points outside Washington to the purchasers within the state. All the merchandise shipped into Washington is invoiced at the place of shipment from which collections are made. No salesmen has authority to enter into contracts or to make collections.

* * *

Historically the [personal] jurisdiction of the courts...is grounded on their de facto power over the defendant's person. Hence his presence within the territorial jurisdiction of a court was prerequisite to its rendition of a judgment personally binding on him. *Pennoyer v. Neff.* But now that [this requirement] has given way to personal service of summons or other form of notice, due process requires only that in order to subject a defendant to a [personally binding] judgment...if he be not present within the territory of the forum, he have certain minimum contacts with it such that the maintenance of the suit does not offend "traditional notions of fair play and substantial justice."

Presence [in a state] has never been doubted when the activities of the corporation there have not only been continuous and systematic, but also give rise to the liabilities sued on, even though no consent to be sued or authorization to an agent to accept service of process has been given.... [T]here have [also] been instances in which the continuous corporate operations within a state were thought so substantial and of such a nature as to justify suit against it on causes of action arising from dealings entirely distinct from those activities.... Conversely it has been generally recognized that the casual presence of the corporate agent or even his conduct of single or isolated items of activities in a state in the corporation's behalf are not enough to subject it to suit on causes of action unconnected with the activities there. To require the corporation in such circumstances to defend the suit away from its home or other jurisdiction where it carries on more substantial activities has been thought to lay too great and unreasonable a burden on the corporation to comport with due process.

* * *

Applying these standards, the activities carried on in behalf of [defendant] in the State of Washington were neither irregular nor casual. They were systematic and continuous throughout the years in question. They resulted in a large volume of interstate business, in the course of which [defendant] received the benefits and protection of the laws of the state[.] The obligation which is here sued upon arose out of those very activities. It is evident that these operations establish sufficient contacts or ties with the state of the forum to make it reasonable and just, according to our traditional conception of fair play and substantial justice, to permit the state to enforce the obligations which [defendant] has incurred there. Hence we cannot say that the maintenance of the present suit in the State of Washington involves an unreasonable or undue procedure.

CASE III

Hanson v. Denckla
357 U.S. 235 (1958)

[The facts of this case are a mess. Suffice it to say that Denckla sought to assert personal jurisdiction in Florida over a Delaware trustee.]

[Denckla urges] that the circumstances of this case amount to sufficient affiliation with the State of Florida to empower its courts to exercise personal jurisdiction over this nonresident defendant. Principle reliance is placed upon *McGee v. International Life Ins. Co.* In *McGee* the Court noted the trend of expanding personal jurisdiction over nonresidents. As technological progress has increased the flow of commerce between States, the need for jurisdiction over nonresidents has undergone a similar increase. At the same time, progress in communications and transportation has made the defense of a suit in a foreign tribunal less burdensome. In response to these changes, the requirements for personal jurisdiction over nonresidents has evolved from the rigid rule of *Pennoyer v. Neff* to the flexible standard of *International Shoe Co. v. Washington*. But it is a mistake to assume that this trend heralds the eventual demise of all restrictions on the personal jurisdiction of state courts. Those restrictions are more than a guarantee of immunity from inconvenient or distant litigation. They are a consequence of territorial limitations on the power of the respective States. However minimal the burden of defending in a foreign tribunal, a defendant may not be called upon to do so unless he has had the "minimal contacts" with that State that are a prerequisite to its exercise of power over him.

We fail to find such contacts in the circumstances of this case. The defendant trust company has no office in Florida, and transacts no business there. None of the trust assets has ever been held or administered in Florida, and the record discloses no solicitation of business in that State either in person or by mail.

* * *

The unilateral activity of those who claim some relationship with a nonresident defendant cannot satisfy the requirement of contact with the forum State. The application of that rule will vary with the quality and nature of the defendant's activity, but it is essential in each case that there be some act by which the defendant purposefully avails itself of the privilege of conducting activities within the forum State, thus invoking the benefits and protections of its laws.

CASE IV

World-Wide Volkswagen Corp. v. Woodson
444 U.S. 286 (1980)

MR. JUSTICE WHITE delivered the opinion of the court.

[Plaintiffs] Harry and Kay Robinson purchased a new Audi automobile from [defendant] Seaway Volkswagen, Inc. (Seaway) in Massena, N.Y., in 1976. The following year the Robinson family, who resided in New York, left that state for a new home in Arizona. As they passed through the State of Oklahoma, another car struck their Audi in the rear, causing a fire which severely burned Kay Robinson and her two children.

The Robinsons subsequently brought a products liability action in the District Court for Creek County, Okla.,[3] claiming that their injuries resulted from defective design and placement of the Audi's gas tank and fuel system. They joined as defendants the automobile's manufacturer[;] its importer[;] its regional distributor, [defendant] World-Wide Volkswagen Corporation (World-Wide); and its retail dealer [Seaway]. Seaway and World-Wide [claimed] that Oklahoma's exercise of jurisdiction over them would offend the limitations on the State's jurisdiction imposed by the Due Process Clause of the Fourteenth Amendment.

The facts presented to the District Court showed that World-Wide is incorporated and has its business office in New York. It distributes vehicles, parts, and accessories, under contract with Volkswagen, to retail dealers in New York, New Jersey, and Connecticut. Seaway, one of these retail dealers, is incorporated and has its place of business in New York. Insofar as the record reveals, Seaway and World-Wide are fully independent corporations whose relations with each other and with Volkswagen and Audi are contractual only. [Plaintiffs] adduced no evidence that either World-Wide or Seaway does any business in Oklahoma, ships or sells any products to or in that State, has an agent to receive process there, or purchases advertisements in any media calculated to reach Oklahoma. In fact, as [plaintiffs'] counsel conceded at oral argument, there was no showing that any automobile sold by World-Wide or Seaway has ever entered Oklahoma with the single exception of the vehicle involved in the present case.

Despite the apparent paucity of contacts between [defendants] and Oklahoma, the District Court rejected their constitutional claim [and held that jurisdiction was proper. It stated:]

> In the case before us, the product being sold and distributed by the [defendants] is by its very design and purpose so mobile that [defendants] can foresee its possible use in Oklahoma.... The evidence presented below demonstrated that goods sold and distributed by the [defendants] were used in the State of Oklahoma, and under the facts we believe it reasonable to infer, given the retail value of the automobile, that the [defendants] derive substantial income from automobiles which from time to time are used in the State of Oklahoma. This being the case, we hold that under the facts presented, the trial court was justified in concluding that the [defendants] derive substantial revenue from goods used or consumed in this State.

* * *

---

3. [Note that this is a state trial court, not a federal district court.]

We granted certiorari to consider an important constitutional question with respect to state-court jurisdiction and to resolve a conflict between the Supreme Court of Oklahoma and the highest courts of at least four other States. We reverse.

*   *   *

It is argued...that because an automobile is mobile by its very design and purpose it was "foreseeable" that the Robinsons' Audi would cause injury in Oklahoma. Yet "foreseeability" alone has never been a sufficient benchmark for personal jurisdiction under the Due Process Clause....This is not to say, of course, that foreseeability is wholly irrelevant. But the foreseeability that is critical to due process analysis is not the mere likelihood that a product will find its way into the forum State. Rather, it is that the defendant's conduct and connection with the forum State are such that he should reasonably anticipate being haled into court there. The Due Process Clause, by ensuring the "orderly administration of the laws" gives a degree of predictability to the legal system that allows potential defendants to structure their primary conduct with some minimum assurance as to where that conduct will and will not render them liable to suit.

*   *   *

MR. JUSTICE BRENNAN, dissenting.

The Court's [majority focuses] tightly on the existence of contacts between the forum and the defendant. In so doing, they accord too little weight to the strength of the forum State's interest in the case and fail to explore whether there would be any actual inconvenience to the defendant....I would find that the forum State has an interest in permitting the litigation to go forward, the litigation is connected to the forum, the defendant is linked to the forum, and the burden of defending is not unreasonable. Accordingly, I would hold that it is neither unfair nor unreasonable to require these defendants to defend in the forum State.

EXAM 1

Theftech Corporation is a West Coast producer and seller of computer software. Until recently a sole proprietorship of Fred Sleazo, the company is now incorporated in the state of West Dakota. Experience has taught Theftech that the most lucrative form of marketing for its software products is through solicitation of mail orders. It currently does business solely by mail. While its total volume of sales is modest, Theftech has sent its products to all fifty states.

Symplex, Inc. is an East Carolina corporation. It, too, produces and markets computer software, and has achieved far more success than Theftech. Its most recent accomplishment is a program called SHYSTER. Based on artificial-intelligence programming techniques, SHYSTER is a legal "expert system" which Symplex believes will drastically reduce the need for lawyers in the future. Symplex has learned that Theftech recently introduced a program it advertises as performing the same functions as SHYSTER. Suspecting, among other things, copyright infringement, Symplex ordered a copy of Theftech's program. Sure enough, the computer code is virtually identical to that of SHYSTER.

Symplex proceeded to file suit in the East Carolina federal district court. Theftech has moved to dismiss the case for lack of personal jurisdiction. A partner in your law firm, which represents Symplex, has assigned you, her faithful associate, to write a memo discussing two questions:

1. Does the East Carolina statute cover this case?
2. If so, would its application be constitutional?

The partner has provided you with the following information:

1. Theftech's sporadic East Carolina sales accounted for 2 percent of its gross revenues last year. However, Theftech has not sold any copies of the program in question in East Carolina (aside from the one ordered by Symplex).
2. Theftech retains an East Carolina advertising agency, and has advertised in several local publications. It also maintains an East Carolina 1-800 telephone listing.

Of what significance is it that you have been cast as an associate in a law firm? The answer is, of no significance whatever! The first rule of examsmanship is not to be fooled by your designated relationship to one of the parties in the question. Always, always, always fully analyze both sides of any argument. Remain objective unless the question explicitly tells you otherwise.

So how are you supposed to approach this issue spotter? The second rule of examsmanship is an agenda for efficient analysis.

1. *Identify issues.* Read through the question *twice,* making margin notes. Stick to the facts you are given. Occasionally a question will appear to omit an important factual element; you can discuss the effect of this omission, and how your analysis would change if it were present. But *don't* consider facts contrary to those set out in the question. Your professor is lord of his exam. Respect that.

What are the issues in our case above? If you weren't going to law school, you might simply compare these facts to those of the above cases and decide whether any of them fit. But we know law school is tougher than that. Let's start with the statutory question and consider constitutional validity as a secondary matter, since the latter is a moot point if the long-arm statute doesn't even afford a basis for service of process. Does the East Carolina statute apply to our set of facts?

Working backward, the most general section is §4. If Theftech's contacts with East Carolina are "regular" or "persistent," we needn't worry about all those tricky linguistic issues buried in §§1 through 3. But neither logic nor analysis of the statutory language helps us much here. Theftech's contacts are ongoing but weak.

Section 4 also requires a "tortious injury." Is Theftech's alleged infraction a tort? Sure it is, you can see that. The issue is raised just to emphasize that you should hesitate to take anything for granted.

Moving on to §3, that provision also requires a tortious injury, but one that occurs *within* East Carolina. Did Theftech's "act or omission" occur "in this state"? Symplex could argue that it suffers injury at its East Carolina home office—where it keeps its corporate pocketbook. It might analogize Theftech to a gunman standing on one side of a state border who shoots someone on the other side. The act of pulling the trigger may occur where the gunman stands, but doesn't it seem strained to separate an act from the effects that render that act legally significant? Theftech, however, has a ready defense. The statute may literally support jurisdiction, but the Constitution requires more. Theftech's complete lack of East Carolina sales must count for something in the constitutional world.

Section 2 of the statute may be disregarded on its face, once again because Theftech has not sold the program in East Carolina. Finally, we reach another general provision, §1. Unlike §4, §1 requires the *cause of action* to arise from the in-state business upon which the claim of jurisdiction is based. Theftech, of course, will loudly argue that the charge of copyright infringement is completely *unrelated* to its sales in East Carolina and, therefore, that these contacts ought not to count toward any statutory or constitutional minimum. Moreover, Theftech will add, its total volume of business in East Carolina is pathetically puny.

Symplex might respond that Theftech is being overly technical, reading the facts too narrowly. Remember from chapter 3 the way in which facts can be approached at varying levels of generality. Suppose an automobile dealer sells all Chevrolet models except Camaros—or better yet, *blue* Camaros—in the forum state. Should the dealer be immune from jurisdiction because the lawsuit happens to involve a blue Camaro? It is the sale of *cars*, not Camaros, that is relevant, and Symplex would argue that §1 of the statute is concerned with Theftech's sales of *all* its computer programs in East Carolina.

2. *Next, locate relevant cases.* Here we've stacked the deck in your favor by feeding you only the useful decisions. That won't happen on a real exam, where dozens of other cases compete for your attention. But to keep things simple, first we'll assume that you've previously studied the subject matter thoroughly, and that the above cases provide a fair cross-section. What have your ruminations taught you? First, that the cases reflect the Supreme Court's attempt to measure state sovereignty and fairness to defendants against the interest of the forum state in resolving disputes. These are the underlying values. Second, that the formalistic rule of *Pennoyer v. Neff* entered the dustheap of history when the court decided *International Shoe.* Yet we can discern no obvious shift in the court's emphasis throughout the remaining three modern-era cases. While the *International Shoe* court found jurisdiction, the plaintiff's cause of action stemmed directly from the defendant's in-state activity. That connection was present neither in *Hanson* nor in *World-Wide,* where the court refused to uphold jurisdiction.

Since the court has been rather consistent lately, it is the *facts* of a case (rather than the court's current state of mind) that will most strongly determine its outcome. This exam question requires you to apply the reasoning of the decisions you've studied to a new set of facts. So now we'll assume that you've gone through your index, scavenged your outline, and culled the four cases set out above. How is each relevant?

We've identified §§1, 3 and 4 as the potentially relevant statutory provisions. The cases bear on the constitutional issue, but obviously guide our analysis of the statutory language as well. Let's work backward once again. The facts leave us up in the air with respect to §4, since they're weak but not absurdly so. In *International Shoe,* however, the Supreme Court seemed to indicate that "general" jurisdiction—where the defendant's contacts with the forum state are so widespread that we need not worry whether the cause of action relates to the defendant's in-state business—would have to be supported by fairly unequivocal facts. Our facts are far from unequivocal. Therefore, this case weighs against Symplex's ability to rely on the general jurisdiction provision of §4.

Do any cases help us determine whether, for purposes of §3, Symplex's injury occurred within East Carolina? The issue turns on the distinction between act and injury, since these have occurred in different places. But the test in *World-Wide*—reasonable anticipation of being haled into court—seems to cast these kinds of distinctions into irrelevance. In *World-Wide,* the personal and economic consequences of injury would have been felt most strongly in the state where the plaintiffs were hospitalized when they brought suit. But this was held insufficient without a more direct connection, and such a connection seems absent here.

Now, this discussion may have made the applicability of *World-Wide* seem obvious. It was not. As you know, any case may be cited for a variety of propositions. Law-school exams are difficult because they force you not only to identify relevant cases, but also to determine the *reading* of such cases that makes them relevant. Here, the *World-Wide* court's analysis of act and injury proved useful; the case might also be cited as rejecting a foreseeability criterion for personal jurisdiction, or simply for limiting the geographical areas within which defendants can be vulnerable to lawsuits. To succeed on exams you need to remember cases in a kind of soft focus, keeping an open enough mind to let them wrap around your facts. That's how lawyers build legal theories.

Returning finally to §1, what facts and cases do we know of that bear on the applicability of this provision? First, we've been told that Theftech is a small company—only recently a one-man operation. Symplex could argue that drawing a distinction between sales of different products might make sense for a large conglomerate, but a small company's activities are more interrelated; therefore, all of Theftech's sales should count toward §1.

On the constitutional side, *Hanson* speaks in terms of "purposefulness" and intent. While its East Carolina sales volume may be small, Theftech has gone to the trouble of recruiting an advertising agent and conducting an ad campaign, Symplex would argue that this constitutes purposeful involvement in the commerce of the state. Finally, *International Shoe* precludes jurisdiction in cases of "isolated" transactions. How long has Theftech been making sales in East Carolina? Since its inception? We do not know, but we'd certainly like to.

3. *Be sure you understand the gray areas.* The grayest region in this case is the relationship between act and injury.

4. *Think about policy.* Now that you've staked out the doctrinal boundaries, give some thought to policy issues. Remember, courts are no longer formalist; judges (and professors) want normative reasons why one view should prevail over another.

Consider §3 again. Theftech might suggest a slippery slope problem, arguing that if it is subject to jurisdiction, no one is safe. Every plaintiff ultimately suffers injury in its domiciliary state. Where would one draw the line? If territorial limitations are to mean anything, the "minimum contacts" test must have some teeth. On the other hand, from Symplex's perspective deterring copyright violations is also a worthy policy objective. Given the ease with which computer programs can be copied and sold by mail nationwide, perhaps a broader view of jurisdiction is appropriate. One party or other must bear the expenses of litigation, and federal copyright protection becomes meaningless if the protected must exhaust their resources chasing after the violators.

But Theftech has a response: That argument cuts both ways. If the traditional requirements of jurisdiction were to be watered down, small software developers could be subject to limitless suits for copyright infringement. Competitors might initiate frivolous actions in remote areas, knowing that distant litigation of an entire copyright case would financially devastate the little guy.

5. *Organize your answer.* What is the most natural way to present the above analysis? The section-by-section approach seems to make the most sense. It was also helpful to recognize that statutory interpretation logically precedes the constitutional analysis. Organizing your thoughts before you start to write will help you avoid tripping over your own presentation, backtracking and duplicating, wasting time as well as sapping the strength from your analysis.

The third rule of examsmanship is to write persuasively (after you've organized your answer, of course). That's what being a lawyer is all about. Approach each issue like a syllogism. First set out the major premise. This can involve a rule of law, or one or more definitions. In fact, many professors expect you to rigorously define your terms throughout your answer or even in a prefatory "definitions" section. Don't spend too much time defining obvious expressions, but make sure the reader will be convinced you know what you're writing about.

Now state the minor premises—those important factual elements—as tersely as the facts themselves allow. At this point you've set the stage for your analysis, in which you set forth the legal and policy arguments both ways. Your task is to explain. Don't just regurgitate doctrine or gush the issues you've spotted. Finally, draw a conclusion. Who has the better argument? Your professor wants your opinion.

EXAM 2

Same facts, except that Theftech has sold several copies of its infringing program in East Carolina.

This simple addition changes the entire analysis. It probably has the least impact on §4, since we haven't been led to believe that these sales greatly magnify Theftech's East Carolina business.

But now there are three places where the §3 "act" may have occurred. Theftech seemed rather successful, in the previous situation, refuting one of them—the site of injury, Symplex's headquarters—as the proper location. There remain Theftech's offices, where the unlawful copying would actually have happened, and the East Carolina customer sites. Theftech, of course, will argue for the former. It could characterize the word "act" as implying the core element of misconduct, namely, copying. But from Symplex's point of view, infringement sales are acts every bit as unlawful as copying. Indeed, the copying itself is almost unimportant without the commercial exploitation that produces injury.

Section 2 may now be relevant. Theftech has had commercial dealings involving the program with customers in East Carolina. But applicability of this section would require acceptance of two premises: (1) that mail-order solicitations constitute a "contract" within the meaning of the statute; and (2) that the statute was meant to apply to a third party (Symplex) injured as a result of the contract but not directly involved as a participant. The statutory text does not supply an answer, but would any policy objective be served by allowing only the contracting parties themselves to assert the statute?

As a matter of logic, the applicability of §2 may be irrelevant in view of §1. For purposes of this exam, §1 functions as a generalized version of §2, and doesn't bog us down in the contractual issues just discussed. The change in facts bears most heavily on our analysis of this section, since Theftech cannot now complain that the cause of action fails to grow out of its East Carolina business. Theftech might contend that the expression "transacting business" was not meant to include mail-order solicitations, but is this argument convincing?

Exam 3

None of the disputed programs has been sold in East Carolina, but Symplex and Theftech have been collaborating on a joint venture to produce a new type of software package for the chemical industry. All of the negotiations and agreements between the parties were consummated in East Carolina.

The issue now is whether the parties' collaboration relates to the suit for jurisdictional purposes. Theftech will argue that the statutory words "arising from" mean what they say. Why should the joint-venture activity enter into the analysis at all? What does this have to do with infringement? Hasn't the Supreme Court already rejected attempts to lump apples together with oranges?

Symplex might retort that it is getting sick and tired of Theftech trying to exempt all of its East Carolina activity on the basis of technical distinctions. It would stress the overall picture of a company doing not only general East Carolina business, but directly involved with the other party to the lawsuit!

Now it's your turn. Which cases are relevant, and how? Are there flaws with either argument? Who is likely to prevail?

PART THREE

Life After Law School

Passing the Bar

Imagine yourself as a marathon runner. Having shaken off the fear and disorientation of the first leg, struggled through endless stretches of miles and braved Heartbreak Hill, at last you stumble across the finish line—exhilarated and victorious, collapsing into the embrace of family and friends. Then the judge taps you on the shoulder. You're expected for the 800 meters, see the hurdles going up around the track? Mustn't tarry.

That's sort of what it's like to graduate law school with the prospect of the bar exam looming two or three months ahead. What's it all mean? What's it like? Will you pass? What if you don't? How much preparation will you need? Do people really take more than one of these at a time?

Whoa! Catch your wind, marathon person! One question at a time.

* * *

From the outside looking in, the bar exam may resemble an archaic rite of passage, a cynical device to restrict the ranks of practicing professionals. Look at it this way. The courts are clogged, the people are confused, the government is busy looking busy. Lawyers are supposed to reduce the chaos, not add to it. They have to know their way around the institutions they serve. Sure, some states have tougher tests than others—just compare pass rates (or ask a New York entertainment lawyer whether he enjoyed wandering the maze of income and estate taxation). But bar exams across the country are more alike than different, and their purpose is the same. Think of it as a service to the malpractice insurers. Besides, what now seems exclusionary may one day come to seem professionally responsible, even downright public spirited—particularly in the face of all those hungry neophytes clamoring for the opportunity to steal your clients.

The bar exam is really two tests: the multistate multiple-choice part, which everyone takes, and an essay part that varies from state to state (and year to year). The multistate tests your knowledge of "majority" law and your eye-hand coordination as you decorate 200 little ovals with a No. 2 pencil. That's one full day (six hours of decorating). Another day, the "local" day, tests your knowledge of whatever the bar examiners consider important that year—state law, a local slant on multistate topics, "majority" law not on the multistate. The local day almost always has you writing; essays vary in number and size, and are combined with the multistate into a score that's usually graded on a curve. States may soon replace or supplement their essay questions with the "multistate performance test," or MPT. This format is supposed to simulate the actual practice of law. Examinees are furnished with a case file and a mini-library of legal source materials, and asked to have a crack at a memorandum to a senior lawyer, write a client letter, or create a negotiating proposal or discovery plan.

Many states also require the "multistate professional responsibility examination," which tests your ability to parse the subtleties of betrayal, deceit, and malpractice. If you can distinguish between representing clients and ripping them off, you won't have much trouble.

The bar exam is generally administered twice a year: in July, to prevent new law-school grads from becoming reacquainted with the concept of recreation; and in February, when tall snowbanks hide the desolate return of those who didn't pass in July. Either way, you won't hear a thing for three to four months after it's all over.

You might feel a twinge of apprehension at the prospect of studying for the most comprehensive, career-determining exam *after* law school—without the discipline of classes and syllabi, deprived of your study buddies. Well, don't worry. Bar preparation has become an industry. As graduation approaches, you'll find yourself rich with the entreaties of both local and national review courses. Then the bar reviewers become rich. These courses are expensive and time-consuming. Figure on several hours a day of lectures for two weeks or more, taking you through the "black-letter law" of the subjects you'll be tested on. Also figure on hundreds of pages of reading to round out the lectures. Then include some more weeks of sample questions, sample answers and more reviewing. The lucky graduates, the ones with jobs awaiting them at big firms, don't have to pay for any of this. Their future employers pay for the course, for the examination, and some even pay a living stipend.

The big players in the review biz include, most prominently, the West Bar Review and Bar/Bri. While national in scope, these courses also cover the specifics of the state (or *states,* if you are truly masochistic) where you plan to sit for the bar. Local courses vary from state to state and year to year. Like all standardized test-prep courses, bar reviews have attracted their share of controversy. Their boasts of stratospheric pass rates have caught the attention of the folks who design bar exams, and guess what? They've made the tests harder. Thanks at least partly to the bar reviewers, pass rates have climbed steadily upward, so the testmakers figure they've been getting soft. Of course, harder tests mean that the incentive to take one of these courses is greater than ever before. And naturally, that's easiest for the well-hired or well-heeled.

Must you feed this upward spiral? If you went to one of those "national" law schools, you probably don't have much of a choice. Your curriculum wasn't designed to teach you the law of a particular jurisdiction; you just spent three years learning to "think like a lawyer." Now you've got to learn what the law actually *is*. Pick the course with the best instructors and the fewest lectures delivered by videotape. Even the big bar reviews vary in quality from state to state. Ask around. Sterile classes make a difficult task excruciating.

If you went to a "regional" law school—no school will admit to being merely "local"— you really do have a choice. In a sense, you've already taken the mother of all bar-review courses, three years' worth. You've had classes in most, if not all, the subjects on the exam. Maybe you were heads-up enough to save the most difficult bar-exam subjects for your last semester. Think you can discipline yourself to pace your studies evenly and review diligently? Then save that final tuition payment and go it alone (although you still might consider a scaled-down review course just for the multistate).

Suicidal as the prospect may seem, some people take more than one bar exam at a time. The multistate is given on the same day nationwide. Some states administer the local portion of the exam the day before the multistate, some states the day after. That means you can hit the road before or after the multistate and take another local test somewhere else. A word to the wise: don't do it just because you have some vague career aspirations and the timing happens to be right. Studying for two exams lessens your chances of passing either. Besides, many states have "reciprocity" with one another, meaning that practice in one state for a certain number of years makes you automatically eligible for admission to the bar of another state. Check the relevant reciprocity provisions. Then ask yourself whether it's really likely you'll jump jurisdictions before you'd be able to do it without even taking another bar exam.

What if, after all the preparation and studying, you don't pass? It all depends. From a purely mechanical perspective, some states let you "bank" a passing score on the multistate, so next time around you need only sit for the local day. Other states require a complete encore. As far as stigma is concerned, it's naturally worse in states where the pass rate is high (93 percent in Wisconsin, February 1994, and 95 percent in Illinois, July 1994) than where it's low (53 percent in New York, before the great migration to Wisconsin and Illinois). But wherever you find yourself, in a law firm or clerkship or government post, someone somewhere has blown it before you. The trail to forgiveness has been blazed. People will understand.

Just don't do it again.

┌─────────┐
│   10   │
└─────────┘

The Traditional Options

NOT ALL NEWLY MINTED law-school graduates end up as lawyers. Attorneys Henri Matisse and Wassily Kandinsky became better known for color schemes than courtroom scenes.[1] And even those who at first actively pursue a career in the law sometimes stray from the beaten path, ending up as consultants, business managers, or investment bankers.

But everyone starts somewhere, and for those just out of law school that somewhere tends to be in a private law practice or in a corporation. Here we will discuss these two career paths, which involve more choices than you might at first think.

10.1 Life in a Large Firm

Here's what you've heard about large firms: the work hours are crushing, the money embarrassingly abundant, the partners rich[2] and unapproachable, and the chances of becoming one of them vanishingly small. As it actually turns out, all large law firms are different; while many resemble the stereotype to varying degrees, each has its own

---

1. Paul Cézanne never even got that far—he dropped out of law school.
2. How rich? The 1996 Am Law 100 survey, which attempts to canvass the financial health of the nation's one hundred highest-grossing law firms, reported New York's Wachtell, Lipton, Rosen & Katz as having the largest average per-partner profit at $1,595,000, as well as the highest overall revenue per lawyer at $1,005,000. Skadden, Arps, Slate, Meagher & Flom, although lower in the per-partner profit pecking order (at a paltry $885,000), nonetheless took in the most revenue overall: clients forked over $635 million to the 1001-lawyer firm.

147

personality. Complicating matters further for the initiate trying to make a career decision is the fact that even considered as a group, large firms have changed quite a bit in the last decade. Older assumptions are giving way to new realities.

To understand any particular law firm, recognize first that it is run as a business. If the men and women in charge of the enterprise make poor business decisions so that firm profits decline, the best and most productive lawyers will leave for (literally) greener pastures. Thus, it is usually a mistake to view harsh policies as a reflection of pure greed; often, it's a matter of survival. Bear in mind also that firms compete with each other in two distinct markets: the one for legal services (what the firm sells to clients) and the one for legal talent (you). These markets prevent a firm from pursuing policies that could damage its reputation either as top-notch counsel or a decent place to work.

How Large Firms Are Organized

Nearly every law firm is organized as a partnership, which has customarily meant that each partner (a) owns a piece of the firm, (b) accepts liability for the firm's debts, (c) bears legal responsibility for harm caused by the screw-ups of every other partner, (d) has a voice in how the firm is run, and (e) enjoys some sort of tenure. Some of that is changing. More and more states are recognizing the "limited liability partnership" (LLP) and "limited liability company" (LLC) alternatives to traditional partnership and corporate forms. The members of an LLP are liable for their partners' screw-ups only to the extent of their capital investments in the firm, so at least the house is safe if the founder's forgetful son lets another statute of limitations slip by. The notion of having a voice and job security as a partner is also changing, as we'll see.

But these developments haven't altered the fundamental facts of partnership life, chief among which is that partners' fortunes are tied to the firm they own and run. The more work that gets done, the greater will be the spoils. Because partners can't do all that work themselves (and for other reasons we'll get to soon), they hire a corps of attorneys, usually called associates, as employees. Associates do not share in the ownership of the firm until (and unless) they are promoted to partnership after a period as apprentices. Lacking tenure, they can be fired whenever it suits the partnership.

Most big firms practice several different kinds of law. Responsibility for each separate specialty belongs to a department or practice group. Such groups operate quite autonomously. Often they are (or seem) competitive—the corporate lawyers viewing litigators as histrionic egomaniacs, and the 'gators gritting their teeth as they spend long nights trying to bandage deals the corporate lawyers seem to have bungled. But interdepartmental rivalries and banter frequently mask the underlying reality. In the end, the position of any department is dictated by economics. The more productive ones receive a greater share of firm resources (including partner compensation), more seats on the executive committee, and see more of their associates promoted to partnership; this is not lost on the other departments, which can grow quite resentful if the disparity gets out of hand.

Large, diversified enterprises are rather complex organisms. Ambitions aside, not every partner in a big law firm can be CEO. Oversight must be delegated. Committees of partners, usually elected by the partnership as a whole, supervise different aspects of firm operation and periodically report back to the entire partnership. The subjects of committee oversight tend to involve matters of firm policy, strategy, or professionalism, such as financial practices and ethics. Day-to-day aspects of firm operation, on the other hand, are now frequently entrusted to nonlawyer management professionals, usually called executive directors. Not only are these individuals better at coordinating routine activities than lawyers (who tend to make lousy business decisions) used to be, but their involvement frees attorneys to pursue what they were trained for—the practice of law.

The idea of democratic participation in the decision-making process, one of the hallmarks of partnership, is also giving way to the need for decisive action in a changing economic climate. A firm with revenues in the tens of millions of dollars and capital assets in the hundreds of millions cannot risk paralysis by allowing the entire partnership to bicker over relatively minor business decisions. Many of the largest firms have appointed managing partners or small executive committees whose dominion extends from where to open branch offices to the color of the carpet in the main reception area. The nonlawyer executive director may also have more of a say in the running of the firm than most partners. And the power held in these few hands can be quite durable. At a recent seminar on the future of the legal profession, the managing partner of one of the nation's largest firms was unable to remember whether a mechanism even existed for his removal by the other partners.

Is this trend desirable? That depends on your perspective. In a very large firm, there may simply be no workable alternative. If you don't mind practicing law in an environment where even partners view themselves as corporate shareholders, and you have confidence that management of the firm is in capable hands, such delegation of responsibility may not seem so bad. But for those of you who see yourselves succeeding to an increasing share in the decision-making process as you progress,[3] look carefully at the size and structure of the firm before you sign on. How many committees does the firm have, and how have these changed over time? Are they all elected by the partners, or are some self-perpetuating? Is a partner's distribution fixed by the partnership as a whole, or by a small coterie that operates in secret? How committed are the partners to preserving the firm's democratic character? React (privately) with skepticism when you are told that a firm is run based on one partner/one vote. Which decisions are made by the firm as a whole, and which remain the sole preserve of the management committee, executive committee, or managing partner?

Finders, Minders, and Grinders

In successful firms, the way in which partners are compensated serves to promote the interests of the partnership as a whole. Ideally, the amount of a partner's distribution, or share of the pie, reflects that partner's contribution. This can be measured in a number of ways. Lawyering is an hours-crunching race to push out the product clients want and a never-ending

---

3. After the collapse of the mammoth New York firm of Finley, Kumble, Wagner, Heine, Underberg, Manley & Casey, erstwhile younger partners ruefully compared their experience with that of cultivated mushrooms: "Kept in the dark and fed bullshit."

chase after new clients who demand ever more product. That's the only way a large firm, with large overhead, can survive. Keeping clients plentiful and happy requires the sustained efforts of individuals having very different talents. What are these talents, and how are they rewarded?

The *finders* in a firm are the few, the proud, and the frequently lucky who have attracted some of the biggest clients, and who show every likelihood of attracting more. Without them the firm will shrivel and die, and the finders know it. They receive generous compensation because they can always take their business elsewhere, and the other partners know it. Cross them and they will squash you like a bug.

Finders are sometimes born, but more often made. Clearly, those whose family or previous business connections and natural charisma engender instant confidence have a leg up on everyone else. But the majority of these "rainmakers" are entirely self-created. Having established a personal reputation for excellence over a period of years or decades, they have managed to amplify their prominence over an entire region or beyond.

Of course, this widespread name recognition does not arise on its own. It takes years of sustained, relentless self-promotion—giving lectures, writing articles or books, actively participating in civic organizations, playing golf with the right people. So who's keeping the clients happy at tee-off time? Other partners—the *minders*—who send out the bills, supervise staffing of projects, and hold the client's hand when the going gets tough.

This is not an easy job. It takes tremendous organizational ability to keep track of all of the goings on affecting even a few large clients; when the vice president of any of them calls, the minder must be ready with the answer. "I'll get right back to you" is not an acceptable response. Since they are also likely to head the important negotiations and sign papers filed in court, minders must be top-notch attorneys who have, in addition, developed the considerable diplomatic skills needed to avoid alienating fussy corporate clients. If a big client decides to walk, the minder will be squashed like a bug.

Minders are also critical to the firm's success and often emerge as the next generation of finders. They are not as highly paid as the most successful finders but do quite well.

Responsibility for the actual work and close day-to-day supervision of associates lies with the *grinders*. These partners are the back-room lawyers with tremendous legal minds and little interpersonal skill. They will never bring in a significant amount of new business. Nonetheless, ultimate responsibility for client satisfaction rests on their shoulders. They train beginning associates and mold them into effective lawyers. They work hard and generate significant revenue for the firm, since most of their time is billable (which may not be the case for minders and is certainly not for finders). But unlike finders, the grinders can be replaced. There are many more of them out there (and also rising through the associate ranks) than there are rainmakers. Thus, their compensation reflects their personal effort levels. If the firm is successful and the grinders willing to work hard, their rewards will be significant; the absence of either of these conditions results in reduced draws and increasing disparities in partner-compensation levels.

All of this represents a substantial change from the way most law firms used to compensate partners. Back in the old days, the shares of partners in large firms were determined solely (or nearly so) by seniority; each partner's compensation increased lock-step, year after year. This seemed fair, since the business community viewed the firm as an institution, and the role of any partner in shaping the firm's reputation would naturally increase as the longer he (or she, but usually he) had been around. It also avoided unseemly competition and bitterness among the genteel partners.

Today, clients are more sophisticated and discriminating. They send business to a particular lawyer rather than to a firm. This personalization of legal services, and the economic power it provides to much-sought lawyers, accounts for the recent adoption in many, if not most, large firms of compensation schemes based at least somewhat on performance. Yet even the most hard-nosed and profit-oriented among them have some provision for recognizing value that goes beyond billings. A strict "eat what you kill" policy based solely on rainmaking may be fine for independent practitioners sharing office space, but can hardly suffice for a law firm where associates need to be recruited, trained, and provided with work; where the practice of the firm must be managed; and where clients need to be exposed to the capabilities of all the firm's departments.

The Ever-Changing Pyramid

Regardless of where they stand in the pecking order, partners in large firms tend to make large numbers of dollars. How do they accomplish this, if there are only so many available to bill hours in a given day? *Ah, tender initiate, that's where you come in!* Partners are profit-takers; associates in large firms are profit-makers. Typically, an associate generates revenues of at least three times his salary. What's left over after paying for his benefits, secretary, office space, and share of the library overhead is pure gravy. Consequently, if an associate is fully productive (a bigger and bigger "if" these days), he enlarges the pie that the partners carve up. But if the firm makes him a partner, he takes a slice of that pie instead of contributing to its bulk.

The number of associates employed by a firm relative to the number of partners who own it is often referred to as *leverage;* by dividing the total number of lawyers in a firm by the number of its partners, one produces the so-called *leverage ratio.* Highly profitable firms often have much higher leverage ratios than less-profitable ones. Their organization resembles a pyramid in its division between a few profit sharers on the top and many profit contributors on the bottom. But leverage is not without its risks. Associates get paid every week, whether the firm makes money or not. And while hiring associates expands the firm's *capacity* to undertake work, associates rarely bring that work with them—the firm must generate enough business to keep all of its associates busy. A highly leveraged firm, just like a company with a heavy debt/equity position, can suffer greatly if business begins to erode.

Helping to maintain healthy leverage ratios has been the traditional up-or-out career path. If, after a fixed number of years, an associate in a large firm failed to demonstrate the right stuff for partnership, he was fired. Gone. Despite its severity, this policy appeared justified on a number of grounds other than maximizing partner profits. First, experience tended to confirm the reliability of evaluations based on seven to ten years' exposure. Second, because younger lawyers generally have an easier time finding new jobs than older ones, early termination can—somewhat perversely—appear humane. Finally, why should a passed-over associate want to stay? Someone who has just seen his partnership chances evaporate can hardly be counted on to provide enthusiastic service for clients; why, he might even *work fewer hours* than associates still chasing after the grail. With only so much work to go around, it seemed like a better idea to fatten the lower associate ranks and simply lop off unwanted portions at the top.

But executive directors and management consultants, who run rings around lawyers when it comes to bean-counting and statistics, pointed out that associates become more profitable as they advance. A higher proportion of their billable hours are "good hours" that can actually be charged to clients. Moreover, each of these hours is charged at a comparatively high rate, since hourly prices tend to reflect seniority. Firms learned that by following an up-or-out policy, they were chasing some of their most productive assets right out the door.

And the business mavens offered further observations. The growth of the 1980s will not persist into the 1990s, they said. Sophisticated and cost-conscious clients, a general leveling-off of demand for legal services, and expansion of the number of practicing attorneys have placed limits on the extent to which billing rates can increase. Nor can the pyramids continue to grow endlessly. If the firm wants to preserve the size of each existing partner's slice of the pie, fewer associates can be promoted to partnership; the bottom of the pyramid won't grow quickly enough to finance new partners' distributions without impact on those of existing partners.

Law firms therefore began to adopt policies that further lengthened the road to partnership, but stopped short of encouraging competent—though not superstar—associates to leave. They have also started to take a hard look at existing partners, questioning the time-honored concept of tenure. The result has been a radical transformation of the traditional law-firm profile, and that profile continues to evolve. The most obvious change is the increasing difficulty of making partner.

Except at the toniest firms, young associates once began practice with the expectation that loyalty and selfless devotion to the partners would be repaid with their patience during the sometimes-painful learning process, and that eventually they would themselves become partners. If you did what you were told, kept your nose clean, and didn't screw up big-time, you could capture the brass ring. That isn't true any more. Law firms are taking a much closer look at the competence, dedication, leadership abilities, and client-getting skills of partnership candidates. Furthermore, the brass ring has grown a bit tarnished. Associates can no longer count on earning, as partners, the kinds of sums that partners have earned in the recent past.

Partnerships have also restructured. Many big firms now employ a multitiered scheme, in which the customary attributes of partnership have been unbundled. Associates are first promoted to a diminished form of partnership and receive a title such as nonequity, income, or limited partner. These bottom-tier partners have restricted rights of participation in firm governance and/or firm profits. Limited in their immediate upside potential, such partners are ordinarily exempted from liability on firm debts and leaseholds to limit the downside. In the most common arrangement, nonequity partners vote only on admission of new nonequity partners, and their level of compensation is set by the equity partners. Most multitiered firms attach some degree of tenure to the lower tier. This provides nonequity partners with significantly more job security than they enjoyed as associates.

Nonequity partners are usually considered for elevation into the equity ranks after a fixed period of time. If initially refused admission, they can generally request reconsideration after another fixed number of years. But to be promoted, nonequity partners must demonstrate significant leadership and business-generation ability—often well in excess of that exhibited by many existing equity partners who were "grandfathered" into the upper tier when the partnership was restructured.

Proponents of multitiered arrangements view them as a way for the firm to be more flexible in their criteria for admission to some form of partnership. Excellent lawyers who might not yet fulfill enough of the partnership criteria to deserve a full ownership stake can nonetheless acquire a variety of membership. These proponents also observe that in many firms, opportunities for genuine participation in partnership governance are already limited. Critics, on the other hand, see multitiered arrangements as needlessly subjecting associates to the punishment of Tantalus, hoisting the true fruits of partnership even further beyond their futile reach. They see the cost in morale damage as exceeding any financial benefits. Other opponents question whether flexibility is such a good idea at all. The availability of a lower tier may encourage admission of less-than-spectacular candidates, since they won't be "real partners" anyway. But to the outside world, partners are partners, and such admissions might dilute the firm's reputation for promoting only the best of the best.

Another innovation that many law firms have introduced is, simply, refraining from firing passed-over but productive associates. These individuals, who are respected (and fully chargeable to clients) for their technical proficiency but, in the firm's view, will never meet the criteria for partnership, receive the opportunity to stay on as permanent associates (or, more euphemistically, as senior attorneys). The characteristics of permanent associateship are set forth in a written agreement. Typically, these attorneys earn slightly more than they did as ordinary associates. Their salaries rise by the rate of inflation or thereabout and may be augmented by bonuses for significant efforts or sacrifice. Permanent associates can also receive a degree of job security. But their chances of becoming partners have been largely foreclosed.

The infinite possibilities of creative contracting are not reserved solely for associates. Many firm letterheads list a few names under the heading, "Of Counsel." This nebulous designation can signify any of a number of nonpartner relationships. For partners who have been hired laterally from other firms, it connotes a sort of purgatory. During a probationary period, the firm pays such individuals a flat salary or limited participation in the profits they generate; they are then considered for full partnership. Of-counsel status can also serve as a holding tank for unproductive senior partners, whose contribution to the firm has fallen below some objective or subjective minimum. No longer part-owners of the firm, such individuals receive a fixed compensation rather than a share of the profits.

Laterally-hired partners having more clout may be engaged as "contract partners" instead of on an of-counsel basis. Contract partners attend partnership meetings and may also be given a vote. The contract runs for an agreed-upon term, after which it can either be renewed or the contractee considered for full equity partnership.

Is a Big Firm for You?

In the face of tremendous time commitments, intense competition among associates, and diminishing partnership prospects, why would anyone want to join a large firm? There have always been a number of compelling reasons, and these remain valid today. The legal profession has consistently been a stratified one. By and large, big firms perform the most exciting cutting-edge work the profession has to offer. Lawyers in such firms find the deals and litigation they work on reported in the national press. The training they receive serves as a powerful hiring inducement to other prospective employers should they decide to leave. And starting salaries, while flattening, are still enormous.

If you decide to pursue opportunities with large firms, it is important to make educated assessments of these institutions even as they evaluate you. If you think you know which department within the firm you would want to join, determine whether that department expects to hire new associates. You don't want to sign up assuming you will be working on mergers and acquisitions, only to find yourself cast into trusts and estates the day you show up. Also, inquire about the composition of your chosen department. What is the partner-to-associate ratio? If it is more than the overall firm ratio, question department members about upward mobility. How do these people view the department's capacity to absorb future partners?

Talk to associates, both present and departed (your law-school placement office or alumni center can help you locate associates who have left a particular law firm). Ask about the department you're interested in, and find out how it is perceived by the other departments. Explore quality-of-life issues. For example, most firms require a minimum annual number of billable hours. Is this the amount needed to succeed, or merely to avoid getting fired? Does the firm listen to its associates? Is it responsive to the concerns of its work force? Inquire regarding issues of firm governance, and don't be too shy to ask about partnership-compensation arrangements. If the firm has a multitier structure, what are the stated (and the *real*) criteria for tier-jumping? You must doggedly examine everything about the firm that you feel important to your future professional development, happiness, and sanity.

10.2 Life in a Small Firm

To many law-school students approaching graduation the decision whether to practice in a large or a small firm looms like a brooding menace, stern and unforgiving, that will irreversibly fix an entire professional career. It is commonly assumed that while jumping from a large to a small law firm is typical, the opposite leap is flatly prohibited at the quantum mechanical level. Therefore, if you decide to join a small firm at the outset, the option of large-firm practice vanishes on your first day of work...forever.

Small firms are also assumed to possess certain immutable characteristics that distinguish them from their larger counterparts. In fact, you will often find the characteristics of small firms defined as points of distinction from large firms, rather than as attributes in their own right. Thus, it is said, small firms offer more challenging work earlier on, greater client contact and involvement, a more personal atmosphere, and broader opportunities for participation in governance than can be found in a large firm.

But the constellation of possible differences between given small and large firms is much larger than this and stems from sharp contrasts in economic realities and organizational philosophies. These contrasts allow small firms to differ *from one another* to a far greater degree than can large firms and, in the process, contribute to a widening trend toward smaller organizations generally. Not that large firms are disappearing—far from it; but as the ranks of the legal profession grow, the proliferation of small firms has begun to outpace the growth rate among large firms. In addition, economic pressures have forced many medium-sized firms to conclude that survival requires expansion into a large firm or downsizing into a smaller form.

What do small law firms offer, and how do you determine which of the congeries of possible characteristics applies to a particular firm? Read on.

How Big Is Small?

Whether a law firm can be considered small is less a quantitative issue than a state of mind. Small firms reflect particular styles of practice and a certain organizational feel. Nonetheless, numerical figures do provide some insight, if only to sketch the perimeters. And while it is misleading to try to define small firms solely in terms of their differences from their larger siblings, people do tend to categorize small and mid-size firms (in a given city) by reference to the size of the average large firm. This is not necessarily unreasonable. Business tends to sort itself out among firms on a relative basis, so a ten-lawyer firm in Baton Rouge may handle the same kinds of cases as a forty-lawyer firm in New York.

Generally, a law firm can be considered small if the city's average large firm is at least eight to ten times bigger. In this calculus, the size of the average large firm can be taken as the arithmetic mean of the five largest firms' legal staffs. There is also a numerical limit. When a firm grows above forty lawyers, it inevitably acquires a degree of overhead and bureaucracy that precludes practice as a true small firm. Again, these lifeless parameters reflect generalities; falling within them cannot guarantee "smallness" any more than their violation can preclude it.

The Personalities of a Small Firm

The two cornerstones of small-firm practice are specialization and low overhead. These factors combine to establish successful market niches. A potential client can be seduced from its large, general-practice firm by a highly focused group that offers special expertise in a particular area of law and/or favorable prices. In fact, some practice specialties can only sustain themselves in modest settings.

In this context, specialization can mean many things. Most obviously, it refers to acumen and experience in a narrow, perhaps exotic field. Traditional specialties of this type include intellectual property (a fancy term for patent, copyright, trademark, and trade-secret law), bankruptcy, admiralty, personal injury, and practice before specific governmental agencies (e.g., representing pharmaceutical companies before the Food and Drug Administration or power companies before the Federal Energy Regulatory Commission). But specialization can also mean political connectedness, unusual geographical location, or a truly exemplary reputation in a not-so-unusual area of law.

At first blush, it may seem odd that the costs, per lawyer, of running a small firm should differ significantly from those in large firms. The microeconomic fact, however, is that bigger organizations generate larger average costs of doing business. Like tall buildings, sizable firms require more elaborate scaffolding to support themselves than do smaller ones. The space needed to house one or two hundred lawyers and support staff may exist only in the most expensive office-buildings in town. A large firm must usually hire staff members such as messengers to facilitate interoffice communication as well as various coordinators to prioritize and service requests for photocopies, taxicabs, telecopier access, and meals. And frequently, the per-lawyer cost of technology—telecommunications, computers for word processing and accounting, and high-volume duplication equipment—actually increases as the firm grows larger.

So, in terms of fixed costs, small firms can have an advantage. For practices such as debt-collection or personal-injury law—where fees for a case typically depend on the size of a recovery rather than the number of hours worked—such savings can mean the difference between prosperity and disaster. But costs are only part of a profit-and-loss statement. Recall that time is a lawyer's inventory. Fewer lawyers means a smaller pyramid; by and large, small firms do not have high leverage ratios. Do lawyers in small firms simply make less money than those in large firms? Quite often they do, although expertise in an exotic specialty can justify premium (i.e., expensive) fees that offset the need for leverage.[4]

But that's relatively unusual. Survey after survey shows that, on average, lawyers in large firms earn more than their colleagues in small environments. In other words, while small law firms can have higher profit *margins* than large firms, their net per-partner profits tend to be lower. For associates, the effects of these economic discrepancies assert themselves in two ways. Given their lower profitability levels, it's not surprising that small firms typically pay their associates less than large firms. But with reduced overhead constraints, smaller firms can offer better training and broader work experience. Partners feel less pressure to make their associates profitable immediately upon arrival.

So, for example, a partner in a small firm may invite more than one associate to attend a deposition or motion hearing, even though he knows that only a small portion of the associates' time can be billed to his client. These associates learn as they watch the partner parry and thrust, attempting to smother the adversary with deft maneuvering. By contrast, a large-firm partner, mindful of high associate salaries, expensive rent, and an ever-diminishing tolerance on the part of clients for inflated bills, may hesitate; she knows that her client will likely offer less resistance to paying for an associate to proofread document than to serve as a spectator. So proofreading may be the order of the day, with the possibility of learning by observation yielding to the bottom line.

Associates may also get relatively early hands-on experience in a small firm. This is due to the kinds of cases often handled by such firms. Large outfits need substantial cases to generate big fees. Smaller firms can, and often must, make do with less. But for an associate, less can mean more. Because modest cases or transactions do not require as much strategizing, document management, behind-the-scenes maneuvering, or open-the-flood-gates paper-chasing as do the big ones, a young associate can be given greater responsibility. With adequate supervision, she may even be able to take charge completely.

The downside to all of this, of course, is the fact that while the actual day-to-day work may be interesting, the cases themselves might not be. Leading-edge cases that require adroit strategy and management are often fascinating to be involved with, even if that involvement is peripheral. Some small firms, particularly those serving unusual practice areas, get such cases; but then, the opportunities for participation may differ little from those in a large firm.

---

4. For example, in the 1996 Am Law 100 Survey, merger-and-acquisition specialists Wachtell, Lipton, Rosen & Katz ranked first in profitability despite a low leverage ratio of 2; Cravath, Swaine & Moore, a general-practice firm, ranked second with a leverage ratio double that of Wachtell, Lipton.

These are some of the ways in which small-firm and large-firm practice styles diverge. But remember that we said small firms have personality characteristics of their own, characteristics that go beyond mere differences from large firms. These stem from the individual personalities of an organization's leaders. In most small firms, the name partners are very much alive and strong—a notable contrast from established big firms, where all that remains of the original founders are legends and the names forever embalmed on the firm's letterhead. When the old order passes in a small firm, the new order wants the transition broadcast loudly. Small-firm leaders have greater power to articulate the culture, values, and hierarchies of their organizations.

Often, small firms were first created or rejuvenated by one or a small group of energetic, successful entrepreneurs. They belong to every imaginable civic organization, regularly appear in local newspapers, earn awards for community service, and consistently bring in the big business. In a large firm, these partners would be highly visible finders; but, surrounded by few (if any) rivals to share the spotlight, they tower over a small firm's landscape like skyscrapers. Their relationship with the firm determines its organizational temperament. If the firm leader views himself as manager of an institution—that is, an enterprise whose importance extends beyond the size of his distribution and which will outlive his tenure—he will recognize the need for group decision-making and participation in governance. His organization will reflect a healthy, noisy, democratic character. If, on the other hand, he sees himself as a burdened chieftain, grudgingly but with a sense of beneficent mission presiding over his otherwise helpless flock, the firm will build little in the way of loyalty and bonding.

And loyalty means a great deal in a small firm. The peaks and valleys of profitability tend to be sharper in small firms than in large ones, since individual clients can each account for a significant proportion of revenues. Without cohesiveness among partners, the firm's viability will depend mostly on its continued economic vitality; the leader's colleagues will see little incentive to make sacrifices in hard times.

Beyond issues of structure and governance, the dominant lawyers' personalities can pervade the firm's very soul. Leaders are viewed as role models. Regardless of practice setting, younger attorneys often emulate both the lawyering styles and life-styles of their superiors, out of admiration, envy, the desire for advancement, or a combination of these motives. But in a small professional environment, the leaders are more visible and their behavior patterns more prominent than they would be in a more crowded arena. If the top partners drive Ferraris and live flamboyantly, these values will enter the firm culture. Likewise, should you join a small firm where the leaders are dour geeks, don't expect much levity around the water cooler.

The entrepreneurial origins of most small firms also carry implications for partnership. Imagine approaching the guiding light of a successful small firm after years of loyal service and asking for a partnership position. What unstated thoughts might shoot through her mind at that instant? *Partnership, you say? Who is this young upstart, voicing such an impudent*

158

request? Does he think he is underpaid? Where was he when I built this enterprise? Did he sit nervously by the phone during the lean early days, waiting and hoping for clients to call? Besides, how many of my clients would follow him if he were to leave?

Obviously, this caricature represents a parochial and, in its undiluted form, relatively uncommon view. But you get the idea. Firm leaders with an institutional mindset take pleasure in the progress and promotion of associates, seeing advancement as the mechanism by which the firm renews itself and grows. Those who see their partners and associates as hired help obviously behave differently.

Regardless of the leaders' attitudes, the fact remains that the procedures for making new partners in small firms tend to be less formalized than those of large firms. If you distinguish yourself with early signs of success, the road to partnership may be relatively short. But small firms with loose review policies can just as easily delay advancement decisions. They may demand more in the way of current business (in contrast to large firms, where good prospects for attracting clients *in the future* often suffices), or insist on deferring consideration until the firm's fortunes improve.

Is it possible to make the lateral transition from small to large firm? Answering this question requires some knowledge of large-firm hiring criteria. Recall from chapter 8 that credentials reign uppermost in the minds of large-firm recruitment partners. If your law-school performance was superior, large firms will remain interested in you. But as you progress, the willingness of a potential new employer to invest in your training diminishes. They want someone who can be plugged into transactions or lawsuits immediately. Associates who work for another large firm have probably received good training and know the ropes of large-firm practice. Small-firm associates must make more of a case for themselves and for the training they have received from their present employers.

But the situation changes dramatically if your small firm practices a legal specialty of interest to the large firm. In that case, it can be assumed that you have received intensive, nonstop immersion in the fine points of this specialty. You may well be viewed as a more attractive candidate than your counterparts at large firms, who have probably gained only passing experience in your practice area.

Before you join a small firm, you should pose a number of questions both to yourself and to your prospective employer. Do you think that the firm's specialty will survive over the next ten to twenty years? Or does it exploit a regulatory or economic fluke that may soon wash away? During the mid-1980s, many firms viewed privatization—the transfer of traditional municipal functions to private hands—as a growth area for legal work. That all changed with a stroke of the legislator's pen, namely, the Tax Reform Act of 1986, which sharply reduced the tax incentives for such transactions. Leveraged buy-outs made many law firms rich during the 1980s, but won't during the 1990s.

During your interviews, ask partners how they share responsibility. In particular, ask the managing partner what powers he alone wields and which are shared with other members of the firm. Is there a limit to the degree that the highest-paid partner's distribution can exceed that of the lowest-paid partner? What period of time typically elapses before an associate is considered for partnership? Specifically, how long had the three most recently admitted partners toiled as associates before their elevation?

10.3 Life on Your Own

You may not realize this, but fully half of the lawyers in the United States practice on their own. These are people who eschew having decisions made for them, tireless mavericks who hate doing anything by committee. They tolerate risk easily, don't require very much sleep, and have a deep need to take full charge of their own destinies.

Many such individuals have been attracted to solo practice by the desire to be their own bosses. But that's a different story and in some ways the ultimate illusion. No lawyer is his or her own boss, least of all those who practice alone. Every client, judge, clerk, and agency chief directs the life of the solo practitioner. That European vacation you paid for? Can't go if the judge won't reschedule the hearing. Family emergency? The cash flow will suffer. Solo practitioners may not have to contend with other lawyers for decision-making authority, but their own bosses? Forget about it.

Clearly, solo practice is not for the financially faint of heart. Every iota of work results from personal marketing efforts, every dollar of revenue is self-generated. The lawyer practicing alone must contend with the crush of legal competition as well as skepticism among clients who are reluctant to entrust their work to a single individual. What can they offer to differentiate themselves from the infinite variety of law firms aggressively seeking the same business? Personal attention and low overhead. The successful solo practitioner is the supreme handholder. Clients know she will never delegate their work to unseasoned associates. She is also in a position to take risks with young, struggling companies. Without the need to support a large bureaucracy and high rent, the solo practitioner can be creative when it comes to fee arrangements. And as the consummate entrepreneur, she has steeled herself to the ebb and flow of fluctuating work demands, income, and future business prospects.

Yet even a sparkling personality and an entrepreneurial spirit cannot guarantee prosperity. Clients don't come pouring in the day a lawyer hangs a shingle, and that's why all solo lawyers start out with a preexisting book of business. Anyone considering solo practice needs a secure source of work that will survive the transition to independence. Such survival cannot be assumed. Present clients must be queried with frankness and candor: will they remain willing to do business with a single individual, and can their current level of business be expected to remain constant over the next twelve to eighteen months?

That source of work also needs to be augmented. Going solo means having enough rainmaking abilities to renew and replenish your client pool over time; existing clients become former clients as they move, go out of business, or attract investors who insist on big-firm representation. Only in rare circumstances can a law practice sustain itself over the long term with its initial stable of clients.

The sole practitioner must possess great and well-justified confidence in her managerial and organizational skills. She must be able to establish a realistic budget and stay within it, maintain various bank accounts, oversee support staff, prepare and collect all her own bills, negotiate with landlords and equipment suppliers—and, of course, provide legal services. The prospective solo lawyer should first prepare a pro forma twelve-month budget, including start-up costs, expenses of business operation, and expected personal (or family) expenses. This budget can itself provide some insight into whether solo practice is a realistic option.

Start-up costs include office equipment and furniture, an initial cache of office supplies, library materials, and security deposits. The office equipment must include a photocopy machine, a typewriter, telecopier and, unless you want to work in pre-information-age torpor, a computer system that includes word-processing and billing software. Sound substantial? Add to this the initial investment in what will become ongoing expenses, including malpractice insurance, your own health and life insurance, support-staff salaries, rent and related office expenses, telecommunications, and enough operating capital to cover client disbursements such as postage, messenger service, court costs, and administrative filing fees.

Then there's marketing. Many solo shops put out a newsletter to keep clients and (within ethical guidelines that govern lawyer advertising) potential clients informed of interesting legal developments, and which just may also have the salutary effect of motivating them to see their lawyer. Other marketing activities include your initial open house, networking in local organizations, giving seminars, running for part-time political office, and keeping the reception area rife with handouts. In addition to requiring the investment of time, all of these cost money. And money is what frequently motivates solo practitioners to share office space and resources with other like-situated professionals. Even four quarrelsome lawyers who could never work together as partners can easily stand the thought of sharing library space and books, a high-capacity photocopy machine, and two secretaries. They might even wind up consulting with one another on matters in which their respective areas of expertise complement one another.

In sum, solo practice means supervision and management of every aspect of legal practice. It means providing your own resources for every ounce of research, drafting, negotiating, and counseling, while leaving adequate time to keep up with legal developments and to market your practice. It requires you to squeeze your family or social life between professional and business demands. But it affords you complete control over the direction and character of your practice, if not its daily routine.

10.4 Life as an In-House Lawyer

Corporate Evolution

Not all that long ago, it was virtually unheard of for a corporation to hire lawyers as employees. Lawyers were seen as risk-averse *impedimenta* who utter cautions, restrain deals, and wag their index fingers a lot. When needed, such individuals could always be found at the company's law firm. And back in those halcyon days, lawyers didn't even charge all that much—young associates were billed out at, say, five bucks an hour. Although one need not go back more than a few decades to recall this state of affairs, things have changed so dramatically that it seems like ancient history. Think of that era, its corporate landscape barren of in-house lawyers, as the Ice Age.

The great thaw came as legal fees began to skyrocket just when corporations started to experience an ever-increasing need for legal services. Due to expanding governmental regulation and increased private litigation, larger American companies found themselves budgeting significant fiscal sums for recurring legal matters. Corporate executives, comparing the growing legal-services budget with the salaries of well-paid managers, realized that bringing a few lawyers under the corporate roof would save a lot of money.

The success of in-house lawyering programs often exceeded the expectations of executives and newly hired attorneys alike. The attorneys, freed from the hours-based economics of law-firm practice, found themselves working less while enjoying good salaries (particularly when benefits unavailable at law firms, such as stock options, were taken into account). And corporate executives discovered that not all lawyers are stuffy fussbudgets. Some, in fact, exhibited great business acumen, moving easily into traditional management and executive positions and leaving the world of law behind forever. This was the Neolithic Period of corporate counseling.

And like our forebears learning to work with new tools, company executives found more and more ways to make use of in-house lawyers. In addition to discharging the routine corporate housekeeping tasks for which they were originally hired, the lawyers began to participate in strategy sessions and board meetings. Satisfied executives responded by expanding the lawyers' ranks. Instead of maintaining a single group of attorneys to serve an entire company, corporations began to provide separate divisions and subsidiaries with their own counsel. Yet even as the number of in-house lawyers increased, the volume of legal work increased faster—particularly during the 1980s. Predictably, one response was to hire even more lawyers. That was often fine with the existing legal sachems, who thereby acquired more underlings and a bigger empire.

Another response to the increasing workload evolved from recognition that not all legal expenses recur. Particular kinds of lawsuits aren't started with sufficient regularity to justify hiring a retinue of specialist lawyers. Corporate managers resigned themselves to the fact that they could not efficiently reduce the need for outside legal help below a certain minimum; excessive hiring inevitably produces diminishing returns. So they began to assign in-house counsel the tasks of overseeing utilization of private lawyers, scrutinizing their bills, and devising ways of getting more service for less money. Many of the top company lawyers—the general counsels—were uniquely suited to the task, having been recruited as partners from the same law firms the company continued to use, and were therefore eminently familiar with sources of waste. With the size of in-house legal departments beginning to stabilize, the task of mananging relations with outside law firms gradually assumed a greater proportion of the general counsel's duties. Welcome to the Dawn of the Modern Era.

Today's corporate legal departments are, in many ways, similar to law firms. Lawyers account for their time by "billing" hours to fictitious accounts, enabling managers to assess utilization and efficiency. They have secretaries, word processors, file clerks, and wear suits to work.

Corporate salaries no longer trail far behind those offered by private law firms, as was the case in Neolithic days. Not surprisingly, lawyers' time commitments have increased. The growth of in-house legal departments has also reduced the amount and diversity of interaction among lawyers and nonlawyer managers. Corporate executives now pretty much understand how best to utilize lawyers and where they can provide maximum value to the company. This maturation in the relationship between lawyers and other personnel seems to have lessened opportunities for lawyers to move laterally into management positions. Lawyers are now hired to provide specific types of service and satisfy particular corporate needs; there are plenty of people with MBAs to fill executive slots.

As mentioned above, the Modern Era has also brought with it a leveling off in the sizes of in-house legal departments. This reflects increasing management sophistication. In happier Neolithic times, general counsels could successfully argue for expansion of the legal ranks by multiplying each lawyer's fictitiously billed hours by a representative billing rate and then subtracting the lawyer's actual salary. The difference was portrayed as dollar-for-dollar "savings" and seemed to justify increased hiring. Eventually, executives realized that their companies were going broke saving so many dollars, and they began to look more closely at what the in-house lawyers were actually *doing* rather than how many hours they worked. Hence the leveling off.

It is this same sophistication in lawyer utilization that appears to have narrowed possible career paths for in-house lawyers. Such narrowing is particularly apparent in very large companies or for lawyers with specialities. Company lawyers can't strive for the brass ring of partnership, and only one attorney can be *the* general counsel. But jobs without advancement paths tend to achieve little popularity—particularly among those who have spent a great deal of time and money pursuing professional training. So companies have reorganized to expand opportunities. Many supervisory legal positions are now considered management spots, making those who fill them eligible for special bonuses and other compensation incentives; for example, the head of legal services for a corporate division might be considered "general counsel" to that division. Corporations also attract legal personnel by offering nontraditional work arrangements. Many have embraced part-time and flex-time employment to a far greater degree than have private law firms. Some companies provide child-care benefits, either in cash or through on-premises daycare centers. Others permit job sharing or working at home.

Serving Two Masters

Any company large enough to sport a legal department will employ a large and diverse work force. Unlike a law firm, the company sells a product having nothing whatsoever to do with legal services. Organizational charts and military metaphors replace the language of law firms. Each corporate division has a "mission," not a specialty, and managers try to sell their pet projects to superiors as "mission-critical." Customers are provided with "solutions," not legal representation. Procedures are paramount. And hierarchical relationships can be much more complicated than a bifurcated world of associates and partners. While every individual in the company has a "direct-line," or immediate, responsibility to a superior, they may also have "dotted-line" indirect relationships to other company personnel.

These features of company organization have special relevance to in-house lawyers. Whether she practices in a corporation or in a private law firm, an attorney serves a client. Precepts of professional responsibility require attorneys to exercise care and loyalty toward their clients. An outside attorney representing a corporation, for example, must tend to corporate interests and not those of a particular officer or director; if these interests clash, the attorney cannot let personal feelings toward individuals overcome the duty of loyalty owed to the client entity. Rules of professional responsibility preserve the attorney's independence, enabling her to dispense objective, unbiased advice. That's why people pay lawyers, after all.

Imagine how much more immediate and pervasive these conflicts can become in a corporate environment. Frequently, in-house general counsels refer to different company divisions as individual "clients." A division's top attorney, as "general counsel" to that segment of the business, probably reports directly to the division chief; he may have a no more than a dotted-line responsibility to the company's overall general counsel. So what happens when the interests of the division diverge with those of the company at large (or with those of other divisions)?

From the perspective of a junior attorney, the pressures can be severe. A junior attorney's salary level may be set largely or even entirely by the division head—his immediate "client." And that client wants to get things done. She may grow impatient with lawyers who tell her what she can and can't do. The junior attorney may perceive—rightly or wrongly—that the division chief wants a rubber stamp more than detached advice. The chief's patience may grow even shorter when the source of the attorney's hesitation lies in his perception of the larger corporate interest. It is one thing for the attorney to point at a statute and explain,

"Look, it says right here that you can't do that." It is quite another for him to say, in effect, that the division chief can't put herself ahead of the company's shareholders.

Yet that's precisely what professional responsibility requires. To whom does the attorney turn? To his supervisor, the division general counsel, of course. But the division general counsel also reports directly to the division chief. The dotted line that connects him to the general counsel must be sturdy indeed to withstand the frustration of his immediate supervisor. If it's not, then the corporation isn't getting what it pays for—effective, independent professional counsel. For this reason, lawyers in well-run legal departments are periodically reviewed both by their business *and* legal supervisors. But oversight mechanisms and day-to-day service are different animals. In-house attorneys must constantly balance and reconcile competing demands for their loyalties.

More on Career Paths

As we said before, the partition between the legal department and the executive suite has probably grown less porous during the Modern Age. But that's only a general observation. Some situations offer greater potential for intracompany mobility than others. It all depends on the degree of similarity between legal work and the product sold by the company. Take financial institutions, for example. In-house lawyers who review loan documents, prepare term sheets, and negotiate closing papers operate close to the heart of the company's business. Their work substantially overlaps that of executive dealmakers, enabling the lawyers both to develop relationships with those individuals and also to learn how the business runs. The dividing line between doing business and providing legal services is indistinct in such a setting, and so lateral movement remains a clear possibility.

Contrast this situation with that of a patent attorney hired by a technology company. Sure, the attorney will grow familiar with every nook and cranny of the company's products. She will know all of the engineers and help negotiate key license agreements. But all of this has relatively little immediate relationship to selling products, which is what drives company profits. Besides, the attorney was hired to fill a very specific employment niche—if she doesn't produce a certain number of patent applications annually, company executives may wonder why they put her on the payroll. The incentive to maximize utilization of a specialty employee only widens the gulf between her and company executives.

On the other hand, the specialty lawyers have the best chances of entering (or reentering) private practice. For generalists, this can be a difficult transition to make. The primary reason is suspicion on the part of law-firm hiring partners. Some will always think of corporate practice as a soft cradle that envelops and gradually drains the ambition from even the most energetic initiates. While this may remain true in a dwindling few corners, the stereotype is largely anachronistic; the Modern Age has imposed significant limitations on corporate fat. Nonetheless, the perception remains.

A more reasonable source of hesitation on the part of private law firms stems from differing skill sets acquired by in-house and private attorneys. Basically, in-house lawyers deal with a single client. Associates in private law firms learn to juggle the interests of many clients and develop the interpersonal skills necessary to attract more clients. These faculties are necessary for long-term success. They tend not to be part of the training provided in company legal departments, however.

Such negative factors recede in importance if the in-house attorney possesses much-sought expertise in a legal specialty. In that case, the mere dearth of comparable candidates from private practice may persuade a hiring partner to take a chance on an in-house lawyer. That inclination will be further strengthened if the candidate has established a network of contacts in the industry—contacts that may translate into future business. In this sense, freedom to jump from corporate to private practice resembles the ability to leap from a small to a large law firm; in both cases, the burden rests with the candidate to motivate a prospective employer.

11

Getting Your Foot in the Door

11.1 Interviewing

Law students usually begin interviewing for summer positions in the fall of their second years, and for permanent placement the year after. The process of obtaining and scheduling interviews varies from school to school. Most allow employers to review students' résumés and select only those applicants they wish to see. Other schools take the position that all of their students are well-qualified candidates, so employers shouldn't get to make a first cut prior to the interview. These schools employ a lottery system in which students compete for interview slots awarded by chance.

Baring your soul to an employer's law-school emissary is never easy. Neither of you really wants to be in that interview room. For you, the process mercifully ends in twenty to thirty minutes; for your interviewer, who may speak with up to twenty candidates in a single day, the process never seems to end. Interviewers come in all shapes and sizes. Some are plastic, some kind, some mean, and some start off kind and become mean as the day wears on. Your interviewer's personality says a lot about the firm he represents. His partners have dispatched him to campus because they think he'll make a great impression. They consider him a real people person, a charmer. If he snarls and spits, and he's the best they've got, well, that says something, right?

The atmosphere of an interview is necessarily artificial. It's not a social situation, although you must appear to treat it as one. In a few short minutes, you want to give the interviewer enough confidence in your poise, demeanor, and bearing to earn an invitation to the firm for a more formal set of interviews. You must distinguish yourself from all the other applicants he will see that day.

It's not as hard as it may seem. Because the interview routine is so contrived, most candidates ask the same questions, give the same responses, and get lost in the noise level of the interviewer's memory. There are ways to avoid this. Research the firm well in advance of the interview. Start with the firm's résumé and NALP questionnaire, both of which are on file at your school's placement office. Then go to the library and haul out one of the huge *Martindale-Hubbell* volumes, which provides specific biographical information on each lawyer in the firm. If you can learn the interviewer's identity before you meet him, study his biography with particular care. Ask third-year law students who worked at the firm as summer associates about their impressions—what's the firm's specialty, what clients does it represent, what big cases has it won recently?

Now that you've got some raw data, prepare some questions you just know the interviewer will want to answer. The on-campus interview is not the place to gather information to help *you* make *your* decision. Your sole objective, from the time you walk into the room until you leave, is to make a good impression. Nothing else. So ask the interviewer about his recent testimony before the House Ways and Means Committee, about his firm's decision to open an office in Berlin, and what impact he thinks that recent Delaware case will have on premerger disclosures. Have some opinions of your own ready in case he turns the tables on you and asks, "What do *you* think?"

Interviewers sometimes ask questions that seem combative, vague, or just plain stupid. But that doesn't make the attorney across the table any of the foregoing. Your interviewer is merely trying to throw you off poise, to see if you know how to play the game. Don't disappoint. Avoid arguing the premise of a combative question. If the interviewer observes that he has yet to meet a physics major who can write a quality brief, tell him you're the exception that proves the rule, and you'd like an opportunity to prove yourself. If the question is vague, choose a reasonable interpretation and answer specifically. And do your best to make stupid questions seem intelligent. Give the answer that puts you in the best possible light. For example, the classic "What do you see as your most negative characteristic?" captains the all-star team of dumb questions. What are you supposed to do, announce your attraction to monster-truck matches and the mosh pit? Of course not. When you're asked about negative characteristics, make them sound positive to the workaholic you're talking to: "Oh, sometimes I get overeager and take on so much work that I forget to eat or even complain."

Never appear obsequious. Don't bring the interviewer a brownie, don't express concern at the mound of cigarette butts accumulating in the ashtray. Lawyers instinctively know when you're trying to cultivate them. It doesn't work.

Follow the interview with a short, personalized thank-you letter. Tell the interviewer *why* you enjoyed meeting him, what interests you about the firm, and why that should interest the firm in you. Remind him of something specific in the interview. Close by expressing gratitude and stating that you look forward to hearing from the interviewer.

Up to this point, you've only sold yourself. When do you obtain information about a firm that's important *to you?* From your preinterview research and during the call-back interviews. Receiving an invitation to visit the firm is cause for optimism, since your chances of receiving an offer have increased substantially. You'll probably speak with five or six lawyers at varying levels of seniority; each such chat lasts about half an hour. Ask questions to establish rapport, just as you did during the on-campus interview, but feel free to probe more deeply into the firm's philosophy (along the lines set out in the last chapter, for example). Firms will often send you to lunch with a couple of junior associates before or after the office interviews. Sure, they'll be evaluating you, but interview lunches offer a relatively relaxed atmosphere—the closest thing in the recruitment world to true social interaction. You won't pry loose any firm secrets but, if you ask some honest questions, you might be able to get a sense of how associates are treated.

11.2 Preparing and Broadcasting Your Résumé

Résumés deliver your credentials to prospective employers. They are the currency of your self-marketing efforts. Those in the business world devote great thought and care to their résumés, describing career goals and offering glowing accounts of their accomplishments. Candidates for business positions fret over choice of paper and typeface.

You're not part of that world, even if your goal is an in-house corporate position. Lawyers will evaluate your résumé, and lawyers could care less about packaging. They want to know why they should hire you. Give them the facts. Tell them about your education, confess your GPA, describe the experience you've had *that relates to a legal career.* Don't bother including your age, marital status, religion, political affiliation, or whether you have children.

A legal résumé has three to five elements.

1. *Your name, address and telephone number.* If your law-school address differs from your permanent address, put the former on the left, the latter on the right side of your résumé.
2. *Education.* List your law school first, followed by any graduate education (the most recent degree first), and then college. Under each heading, include separate "bullet" paragraphs for the date you received the degree, your GPA, honors and activities. If you participated in a slew of societies and organizations, select the ones that might make an impression on a cynical partner (debating society, yes; nude decathalon, no).

3. *Experience*. This section is more than an employment history. It should tell a story whose most natural ending is legal employment. So be selective about entries. You may have had unpaid experience (a legislative internship, volunteer counseling) that will count for more than the two summers you spent painting houses.

Under each item describe, preferably in just a couple of energetic one-line sentences, what the job required and what you achieved. Start each sentence with a past-tense verb, and give some careful thought to those verbs. They must portray you as a future junior attorney, signal your readiness to assume legal responsibilities. What do lawyers like their underlings to do? "Research," "organize," "lead," "resolve," "analyze," "draft," "represent," "manage," and "supervise." "Assisting" and "preparing" are all right, too. Concepts like "coordinating," "effecting," "launching," and "strengthening" come across as vague. But above all, be truthful and accurate. Résumés are sales documents second, biographical statements first.

4. *Publications*. If you've got 'em, list 'em. Lawyers are the ultimate word processors. Any recognition that you've attained for your written expression lifts you above the ruck in a key area.

5. *Interests*. Most résumés list a few hobbies. They give you a personality. And who knows, there may be a hiring partner out there who also enjoys solo Himalayan spelunking.

The proper résumé format is not all that different if you graduated from law school a while ago and now look to escape from your current legal position. Just confine the "Experience" section to legal employment, and add sections for bar and bar association memberships.

Here's a sample law student résumé:

GILBERT N. SULLIVAN

5004 Governor's Square
Williamsburg, VA 23188
(804) 123-4567

109 Medway Street
Providence, RI 02906
(401) 123-4567

EDUCATION

College of William and Mary Law School
J.D. Expected May 1999
GPA: 3.5
Activities: Mediation Project

Brown University
A.B. Political Science, *magna cum laude,* May 1996
Honors: Phi Beta Kappa Society
Activities: Editor, *Brown Daily Herald*
              Program Director, *WBRU* radio station

EXPERIENCE

Senator Edward L. Burke, Boston, MA
Legislative Intern, Summer 1995
  Researched proposed legislation
  Drafted position papers, press statements
  Managed constituent correspondence

Brown University Art Department
Assistant Slide Curator, Fall 1994–Spring 1996
  Organized and managed collection of 200,000 slides
  Monitored circulation of 34,000 slides per year
  Assisted users of the collection

Freelance Photographer since 1991
Work published in *The Providence Journal, The New Paper*

INTERESTS: Camping, Racquetball, Tennis

Most résumés are one page in length. The eyes of résumé readers tend to glaze over if they must flip a page, particularly if your entry is at the bottom of a three-inch stack. If you feel compelled to exceed a single page, make sure it's for a good reason—namely, to present qualifications that directly advance your cause. As for paper, no need to get fancy; white or ivory is fine. Times Roman or Helvetica typefaces look neat and appropriately bland.

Before on-campus interviews, résumés automatically reach the hands of prospective employers through the efforts of the placement office. But not all firms will visit your campus. If you're going to school in California but want to work in Cleveland, you might have to do a bit of hunting. Start at the placement office. They may have résumés and/or NALP questionnaires from Cleveland law firms who have interest in the school but lack the resources to send someone out. Obtain copies of weekly periodicals directed toward the Cleveland legal community; these frequently contain help-wanted ads with specific positions, as well as articles about law firms you might not otherwise have heard of.

You may also fail to qualify for an on-campus interview. Most law firms don't interview first-year students at school for summer positions, even though many accept a small number. And a lottery system virtually guarantees that you won't get interviews with firms that might otherwise have been receptive. In these situations, you have no choice but to take matters into your own hands. Follow the same preinterview research strategies outlined above, but put the results into a cover letter. Call the firm to learn the name (and position) of the individual who reads résumés. Make a case for yourself in the letter. Tell the reader why they want you.

Follow up in a week or two with a phone call. Would the firm like additional information to help them with their decision? Are there any questions you can answer? This is obviously a more difficult route to employment than the on-campus interview. You may find yourself sending out quite a few résumés before you get a bite.

The search for employment can be an ego-deflating experience. Yours is never the only résumé in the pile. Try to be realistic about your expectations, give each opportunity your best shot, and be persistent. All you need is one offer—the right one—to start your career on track.

11.3 Summer Positions and Judicial Clerkships

Summertime Dreams

Picture it: an enormous salary, glamorous lunches, "dream evenings" where your every gustatory and entertainment fancy is yours for the asking, and precious little responsibility for turning out quantity or quality work. Such are the myths, anyway, of law-firm summer programs. A relatively recent innovation, such programs have been adopted as a recruitment device by law firms, large and small, looking to lure commitments from the best students well in advance of their graduations. Summer associates receive the same salaries as beginning lawyers, as well as the opportunity to sample the firm's atmosphere and personality. The firm, on the other hand, hemorrhages money. Time is too short and summer associates too green to accomplish much that the firm can bill to clients, so those fat salaries can't be recouped. The firm also sacrifices otherwise productive time to the care and feeding of restless rookies.

But no matter, these firms figure. If they come to love us now, these currently useless nudniks will be back when they graduate, eager and billable, and then...well, you know the rest. Although populated mostly by law students with two years behind them, summer programs occasionally host a few first-year finishers with impeccable credentials. Big firms have the biggest and most lavish programs. They're also the most competitive. Smaller firms have smaller hiring needs but tend to be more flexible when it comes to academic records. What all summer programs have in common is the least anxiety-ridden atmosphere in the business. The purpose, after all, is mutual evaluation. In addition, they all offer a certain degree of extravagance (at least when compared with the fare of actual practice).

Should future cultural anthropologists suspect the veracity of legends surrounding various summer programs, they need look no further than the supplement to each October issue of the *American Lawyer*. That publication distributes questionnaires to summer associates in the largest firms nationwide, asking them to rate their firms both numerically and verbally in such categories as importance of work, length of an average work week, amount of client contact, and quality of feedback. The October supplement contains the statistical and anecdotal results.

Although all quarters tend to view the *American Lawyer* ratings with suspicion—firms seem to bounce from last place to first with little rhyme or reason—two messages are clear. First, the firms that enjoy consistently high ratings are not the ones that throw the wildest parties, but the ones that give their summer charges a realistic glimpse of life as it's actually lived there. Second, the burden of fear has shifted. Several years ago firms would automatically bestow an offer of permanent employment on every summer associate, regardless of performance, both because the bodies were needed and also to avoid scaring off future participants. Once you were in, you had it made.

All that has changed. Today law firms can offer fewer permanent slots and feel less inhibited about using the summer program as a genuine opportunity for appraisal. Not everyone will wind up with an offer. That may sound terrible, but it's actually all to the good. Life as a lawyer ain't a party. Summer associates who smugly ignored deadlines or turned in sloppy work may in the past have received offers, but they also earned the thinly veiled contempt of their future superiors. And while the pursuit of an offer does engender a certain degree of hyperactivity, the spirit of camaraderie usually prevails over competitiveness. There's just too little authentic work to support real competition.

During your interviews for summer positions, you will invariably talk with relatively junior associates. Don't shrink from asking candid questions about the summer program. What kinds of experiences did your interviewer have when *she* was a summer clerk? What percentage of last year's summer group received offers? As you pursue your summer tenure, use the suggestions outlined in the next chapter to guide your work habits; get to know your employers and treat them with respect—the right approach and spirit will reinforce your chances of getting an offer. At the same time, recognize that you've been awarded a valuable fact-finding opportunity. You must judge even as you're being judged. Try to cut through the forced smiles to see what life at the firm is really like. And finally, enjoy yourself. Trimmed-down summer programs are still unrealistically fun, and much later, as competitive pressures mount and tolerance for mistakes dwindles, alumni of these programs will continue to pine for those splendidly contrived days and wonder what the hell they were thinking when they signed up as real associates.

Playing Judge

Top law students with an interest in litigation frequently spend a year or two after graduation working as assistants for judges. Such clerkship positions always look good on résumés—just how good depends on the prestige of the court—and private firms usually give partnership-track credit for time spent at the judge's side. All clerks review briefs and other papers, research the law they present, and help judges write their opinions. But that's where the similarities end. Different judges and different courts make for a large variety of possible experiences.

Prestige tends to follow judicial hierarchy. Also, a federal clerkship is likely to impress to a greater degree than one in a state court. Those are the dry facts. But the court's prominence should not be the only factor you consider. Clerks for lower-court judges observe the juicy trials, see witnesses break down on the stand, watch the convicted felon cry in anguish as the judge hands down sentence. Sound like fun? Lower-court clerkships also tend to involve the greatest management role. These clerks act as go-betweens for the judge and litigants' attorneys, setting schedules and keeping cases on track. Appellate and high-court clerks lead much more academic lives. Their management roles are minimal, but they see the opinions they help write published more often than their lower-court counterparts, and appellate opinions tend to garner a lot more public attention. Whole academic careers have reputedly been built on authorship of a footnote. Or so they say.

Of course, it is the personality of the judge that has the greatest effect on a clerk's day-to-day life. Some judges work harder than others, and so do their clerks. Some let their clerks do all the opinion writing, others just want citations checked. You'll love some, feel different about others. The only way to obtain insight on any particular judge is to call former clerks—one of your professors, perhaps?—to get the real story.

And if you're unsuccessful in your attempts to gain access to a summer program or judicial clerkship spot, remember those volunteer programs. Though they won't line your wallet, they'll provide you with worthwhile experience. Even students on tight budgets often find ways to combine volunteer efforts with paying jobs.

$$\boxed{12}$$

Starting Out As a Lawyer

12.1 Positioning Yourself for Success

The transition from law student to legal practitioner is not easy. Anyone who doesn't feel anxiety and disorientation upon first beginning life as a lawyer should consider finding a new profession. As a new entrant, you cannot possibly deliver the kinds of advice and services that clients pay for—at least not at first, and not without help. Yet inevitably, the most important component of your performance (and the one upon which you will be judged most severely) is the degree to which clients value your efforts. A law firm survives on the satisfaction of its clients. And that's why your overriding goal as a new lawyer is to develop your skills.

This, you can be sure, is easier said than done.

Your short-term goal is to deliver quality work that's polished and free of embarrassing mistakes. How? Step one is to follow the research and writing guidelines outlined below; this will help you produce the well-reasoned, fully researched analyses that warm partners' hearts.

But watch how fast those hearts turn to ice if your writing contains typos or missing verbiage—especially if a client will see it. So step two is to review everything one last time before you submit it. Don't assume that your secretary or the word-processing center made all those corrections you requested. Your final review should include one proofreading and a subsequent, additional reading for overall sense and meaning. Sound excessively fastidious? It really doesn't take long, and may even give you some additional ideas or expose a reasoning flaw you hadn't noticed. And unfair though it seems, partners (or higher-ups in the general counsel's office hierarchy, if you're working in a corporation) are more likely to criticize your trivial errors than praise your brilliance—they already expect the latter in exchange for your salary.

Step three applies to documents destined for a client's eyes. Supervise and be supervised. Pass anything but the most routine correspondence before the eyes of a superior prior to sending it out. That superior need not be a partner; senior associates know their way around the office, and they don't bite. Obvious errors spotted by a senior associate generate far less anxiety than those spotted by partners, who fill out the performance evaluations. Make sure you copy the partner in charge on all client correspondence, and explicitly list his or her name as a "cc"; that way, the client will see that you're getting proper supervision, and the partner won't think you're getting uppity.

Now to your own supervisory responsibilities. Scrutinize that letter or memorandum. Is the client's name spelled correctly, and is her title accurate? Is the transaction you're working on sensitive enough to warrant completely secret correspondence? And if so, has your secretary marked the envelope "Personal and Confidential" or verified that the client's fax machine is secure? Check the contents of the package: Are all the enclosures there? Have all the copies been made? Is the "Saturday Delivery" box properly checked on the Federal Express label? Call the client to follow up. Did she receive everything? Does she have any questions?

So much for short-term goals. Your first long-term goal is to produce those terrific pieces of work efficiently, with minimal waste of time. It is here that the interests of clients and associates converge—you want to spend a sane amount of time in the office, and the client wants to avoid large bills. Efficiency is partly a function of experience; the longer you're at it, the quicker you'll do it. But good work habits also promote efficiency. The day you first report for work, you should carve out a roomy place in your file drawers for a precious set of folders or hanging pockets. Into these folders you deposit examples of contracts, memoranda, motions, briefs—whatever it is you deal with day-to-day—as examples for future reference. Label the folders and you've got what's known in the trade as a precedent file. Compulsive though it may sound, maintaining a well-stocked precedent file can save you enormous headaches and hours of searching later on, when you just know you've worked on a debenture indenture but can't remember the name of the file...

Use senior associates as resources. They can help you in myriad ways besides sight-checking your work. Ask them for advice when you feel stuck or confused. The fact that they're still around means they did the same when they were new and tender, so they won't mind giving you a hand. And their advice can save you more than just time. Because they've worked with the partners so much already, they know what's expected and can prevent you from turning in exactly what your supervising partner doesn't want. Of course, it goes without saying that you should be considerate and exercise discretion when bugging a senior associate; gather all your questions together before you knock on his door, and try to wait until he looks reasonably unharried.

All of which brings us to the subject of billable hours. Yes, they're important. And every firm has different expectations when it comes to the amount of "product"—i.e., chargeable time—their associates produce. You'll quickly learn the size of those expectations through the grapevine. If your firm is too small to have a reliable grapevine, ask a partner, but demand an honest answer; as noted in chapter 9, the firm may have absolute minimum and another minimum for those on partnership track. Don't shoot at an uncertain target.

And don't get carried away, either. Significant as billable hours are, you shouldn't build your career around them. Respect your firm's requirements, but strive for excellence and efficiency. While your firm as a whole may love lots of billables, individual partners evaluate only your performance on their projects. Don't juggle more assignments than you can handle well—high hours and low marks do not success make. Don't be afraid to turn down projects you can't realistically handle.

One way *not* to keep your hours high is to spend more time on projects than your supervisors expect. Clients won't accept inflated bills that reflect associate training costs. That means your performance will be evaluated based not on billable time (i.e., the time you record), but the amount of time partners actually charge out. And they *really, really* hate to write your time off when preparing their bills. It reminds them of how much you're being paid, which evokes wistful memories of that ski timeshare they passed up because quarterly profits were down. Make sure you know how much effort you should devote to an undertaking before you start—ask if you're not told. Then stay within this guideline. If you can't, request additional latitude *before* you charge expensively ahead, and be prepared to explain why that initial time parcel was insufficient.

Your second long-term goal is to demonstrate versatility and intellectual adroitness. As the legal industry retrenches from busier times, previously reliable practice areas may not continue in high gear. Managing partners speak discreetly about the need for lawyers to retool. At one time, it may have seemed advisable for an associate to specialize early on. She could become an expert, garner partner loyalty and respect, and allow the firm to provide efficient service in an important field. But more and more such fields are drying up these days. Don't get caught in a narrow specialty unless you feel confident in its longevity. And take some initiative of your own. If you can identify a new practice area of interest to the firm, educate yourself. You may not pull the clients in right away, but partners may know of some doors to knock on; they will certainly appreciate your efforts, and you will have a unique (and therefore valuable) proficiency.

The third long-term goal is development of communication skills. In addition to obtaining supervision, and beyond asking questions, learn to communicate with partners and clients. This is an acquired skill, harder to attain than you may first think. It's all too easy to retreat from the world when the going gets tough, and to sit back and relax once you've accomplished your mission. Keep your supervisor and client informed! Write them, fax them, e-mail them of your progress. Law is a service business, and that means understanding your customer's goals. Woe unto the lawyer who lets his own judgment overtake his client's interest; and double woe unto those who do so innocently, out of inadvertence, because they failed to communicate.

12.2 Resources

By now you've gotten the point that efficiency is key to success in law. Working productively and managing assignments with facility earns you glowing reviews and gets you out the door in time for a social life. You build that facility by mastering resources—the tools at your disposal to find answers and deliver the product.

And how those tools have multiplied! All law schools provide a course titled Legal Methods (or something equally imaginative) that teaches you the basic mechanics of conducting legal research, preparing legal documents, and delivering oral arguments. But those courses probably *don't* show you everything that's available, and they certainly can't show you what it's like to be a lawyer. After all, your professors and instructors have their hands full just giving you a guided tour of the law's terrain; they can't be expected to teach you what it's like to live and breathe in those precincts also. In actual practice, contracts must be negotiated (not merely drafted), research assignments fully grasped and pursued capably, and the extent of your efforts tailored to the importance of a project (as well as the ability— or willingness—of your client to pay). This section and the ones that follow highlight some of the most important resources available, and give you a sense of how to translate the skills you learn in law school into practice *as a lawyer*.

The newest resources come packaged in bits and bytes. Not that computers are a recent arrival; they overran legal practices some time ago. Pity those older partners who still marvel at the information revolution as if it's just begun. And seize the opportunity to impress them. Today you can discover, with a few clever keystrokes, answers that just a few years ago would have required limitless time and a journalism degree. Where yesterday's young associates once trudged and unshelved, today's savvy info-surfers can prospect from their desks. Learn how to make the most of your resources; they're what set you apart from the trudgers.

The Basic Toolkit

In most firms, especially those involved primarily in litigation, young associates spend much of their time doing legal research. That means getting an assignment and jumping headfirst into the ocean of case reporters, annotated statute books, and assorted research materials that fill your firm's library. In chapter 3 we discussed ways of making sense out of a set of related cases. But how do you get your hands on those cases in the first place? How can you be sure you've covered all the bases?

When venturing into a research project, the most important step is the one you take before ever cracking a book: understand your assignment! Legal research tasks can originate in one of two ways. Either a partner or a senior associate has no idea what the law says about a particular topic, or she already knows what she wants to argue and asks you to find authority to support her position. Regardless of how the assignment is presented to you, your approach is the same. *Get all the facts!* Ask questions. Take notes. Do not relent until you feel that you know just what you're looking for. Beware the lawyer who tells you, "I just know there's a case out there that says..." There probably isn't. Pin her down. Identify what she's really after.

Then ask specific questions about what's expected. Research projects typically require two to ten hours (and sometimes more) per issue. Can you comfortably devote that much time? Inquire about the form of the final product. Does your superior want a survey of the law? Or just an answer to a specific legal question? Should you prepare a memorandum or just copy cases and share your thoughts orally?

Once you really know your assignment, the key to successful research is to understand the tools you have available, what each can do for you, and the order in which to employ them. What follows is a survey of the basic research sources, their advantages, and drawbacks. Later we'll explore strategies for using them.

Legal Encyclopedias These are the most general and easily accessible sources you can find. You simply look up the topic you're interested in, and there you'll find an explanation along with oodles of footnote citations to relevant authority. Encyclopedias can be completely general[1] or focused on a specific area of law.[2] But their breadth is also their drawback; only rarely can they provide answers to specific questions, and those copious citations frequently do not include the best or most recent decisions.

One rather odd duck in the encyclopedia world is something called *American Law Reports, Annotated* (A.L.R.). This massive series contains summaries of decisions in a huge variety of areas. In contrast to other encyclopedias, A.L.R. treats specific legal questions and contains exhaustive citation lists. Unfortunately, the entries are not organized at all, and the so-called "Quick Index" is anything but. While an A.L.R. headnote directly on point can abruptly end your toils, the seemingly random universe of A.L.R. topics reflects the inclinations of its editors; your issue may never have been considered.

---

[1]The most common general encylcopedias are *American Jurisprudence 2d* (AmJur) and *Corpus Juris Secundum* (C.J.S.). AmJur entries tend to be better-organized and better-written than those in C.J.S.

[2]A widely used example is *Fletcher's Cyclopedia of Corporations*. Restatements, mentioned in chapter 2, can also be thought of as focused encyclopedias.

Treatises A treatise is a scholarly analysis of a specific area of law. Frequently recognized by their authors' names (e.g., *Nimmer on Copyright* or *Wright and Miller's Federal Practice and Procedure*), treatises vary in scope, detail, and readability. They may occupy one or many volumes. Some are highly readable, others (especially the older ones) painfully dense. Although treatises contain far more information than general encyclopedias, an author may be more interested in scholarly aspects or the law's historical development than its practical operation; obviously, this limits the usefulness of such treatises as research tools. The publisher's willingness to furnish updates also bears heavily on a treatise's value. Infrequently updated treatises must be used with great care, while entirely outdated volumes are best left to rot on the shelf.

Law Reviews Law-review articles, notes, and comments are mini treatises. Their authors intensively analyze specific legal issues or even particular cases, and it's usually easy to tell from the outset whether an article offers the kind of practical analysis you're looking for. The problem is that it can be difficult to get a sense of the author's focus from the article's title, and there tend to be a lot of titles out there.

The West Keynumber System The ubiquitous West Publishing Company reports most (though certainly not all) of the significant decisions handed down by judges all over the country. Using West's materials provides access to their keynumber classification system, which indexes entire fields of law according to numbered topics and subtopics. Each reported case contains a series of headnotes that describe the legal issues and provide the relevant keynumbers. By referring to West's case digests, in which the headnotes of all reported cases are gathered and classified under their respective keynumbers, you can locate other cases that discuss similar legal issues.

The keynumber system is invaluable for accessing a body of related cases, but is best used *after* you've found a few relevant cases using other tools. That's because the topics frequently overlap or contain general categories whose contents can be unpredictable. West digests can be cumbersome tools for uncovering those first, crucial cases.

Commercial Databases Legal materials—cases, statutes, law-review articles, you name it—can now be found on commercial electronic databases.[3] Using a computer to access this material, you can rapidly sort through entire bodies of law according to a search command of your own devising. Such commands may contain a key word or phrase, designate cases written by a particular judge within a specified period of time, or limit the search to specific types of decisions. The chief drawback of commercial computer-aided

---

[3]The two most important databases for ordinary legal research are LEXIS and WESTLAW, the latter maintained by—you guessed it—West Publishing Company. Although WESTLAW is the trickier of the two to use, it offers electronic access to the West keynumber system. You will learn the details of using databases in law school or on the job.

research is its cost. Database access is not cheap, and if your search retrieves a high proportion of irrelevant garbage, you'll spend a lot of expensive time gleaning through the pile. The Internet, discussed below, can provide a worthwhile and cost-effective supplement (or preliminary) to high-priced legal databases.

Shepard's Citations   These materials follow the fates of all reported American cases after they are first decided, telling you which courts subsequently cited a decision and in what context. "Shepardizing" a case you've found tells you whether it is still "good law," and also points you to more recent authority as well as A.L.R. annotations and law-review articles. You can also find Shepard's Citations for statutes, patents, trademarks, and law-review articles.

The Internet

Chances are, a few years ago you'd never heard of the Internet. And chances are that today, even if you're an unwired computer agnostic, you know about Web sites, browsers, and those funny monikers that say things like *http://www.something.or.other*. In those few years the Internet has become a treasure trove for law student and lawyer alike. Unlike commercial databases, which are maintained for profit, most information on the Internet is free for the taking (at least for now). And it's worldwide; you can as easily access the archives of a New Zealand research library as send electronic mail (e-mail) to your next-door neighbor.

Just what is the Internet? Think of it as a constantly growing, global system of computers that talk to each other over telecommunication links that don't affect users' phone bills. The larger computers—the "servers"—store huge hoards of information that can be accessed at any time by anyone else on the system. Every Internet computer knows what its name is, and the servers know not only their own names but the names of their stored files. Call out a name from your dinky little PC and the memories of the world's mightiest computers are yours in an instant. E-mail a message or a document file and it's zapped immediately to its destination. You can even talk over the Internet, although that's still a cumbersome and crude proposition.

As a law student or lawyer, you'll want to surf the Net, as they say, for several basic reasons: to look for answers, to communicate, to get help, and to find opportunities. And to these ends, you'll want to focus on just a few basic Internet resources: newsgroups, listservs, and Web sites. A *newsgroup* is an electronic discussion forum devoted to a particular topic. Participants ask each other questions and debate the answers; "lurkers" too shy or casually interested to post can read through the threads of typed conversation. Easy shopping and low commitment are the hallmarks of newsgroups. Using an Internet browser, which we'll get to below, you can search the ever-expanding population of newsgroups to find a thread relevant to your topic; then you can lurk or post to your heart's content.

A *listserv* also facilitates electronic discussion, but in a more private, less topic-specific fashion. Listservs are essentially group-specific mailing lists. Post a message to a listserv to which you belong and it's broadcast to everyone else on the list. In other words, everyone reads everyone else's mail. People can converse on a particular issue, but their exchanges are punctuated by the thoughts and exchanges of others. Listservs are also closed groups; you can't just browse your way into them. Sometimes admission to the listserv requires only a request, while other groups have restricted memberships. Listservs may also be moderated, meaning that messages are not automatically broadcast to the group; a moderator screens them first to ensure appropriateness. Like so much on the Internet, listservs come and go as membership waxes and wanes. Mostly you hear about them by word of mouth (or e-mail); there may be one local to your school, or to your practice specialty in the city where you work. Some popular listservs include the Law School Discussion List (*LAWSCH-L@american.edu*)[4], the self-explanatory *PRELAW-STUDENTS@lawlib.wuacc.edu*,[5] a list for law review staffs (*LAWJOURNAL-L@lawlib.wuacc.edu*),[6] and the Student Judicial Affairs Discussion List (*JUDAFF-L@bingvmb.cc.binghamtom.edu*).[7]

With newsgroups and listservs you can share thoughts, advice and pre-exam panic with like-situated sufferers far and wide. These facilities streamline communication and forge connections that would be impossible any other way. But they're not really resources; they're people gateways. When looking for raw information—court decisions, statutory text, company profiles—the best place to start is the World Wide Web. There's nothing exotic or mysterious about the Web. It's just one of many Internet communication protocols. But its recent exponential surge in popularity has propelled the Web to the forefront of the Internet; indeed, to many, the Internet is synonymous with the Web. On the Web you will find tremendous information repositories. Much of what you can find on commercial electronic databases is also there. So, too, are library catalogs, the contents of popular and scientific journals, newspapers—the list of resources is endless and growing. But the Web is also a vast landfill of unedited verbiage, only some of which is useful. The trick is finding the good stuff and ignoring the garbage.

Web-accessible information is usually found through a Web "page." This is a screen (or series of screens, the first of which is the "home page"), frequently rendered with slick artistry, from which you can call up documents or jump to other pages. That's one of the beauties of the Web—the ability to slither from page to page and back again using "hypertext" links. A link appears unobtrusively as an underlined portion of text in a page or a document; move your cursor over the underlined text and click, and *presto!* The link

---

[4]Subscribe by sending the following message to *listserv@american.edu:* subscribe lawsch-L *your name*.

[5]To subscribe send, to *listserv@lawlib.wuacc.edu*, the message: subscribe prelaw-students *your name*.

[6]To subscribe send the following to *listserv@lawlib.wuacc.edu:* subscribe lawjournal-L *your name*.

[7]Subscribe by sending the following message to *listserv@bingvmb.cc.binghamton.edu:* subscribe judaff-L *your name*.

executes and the linked document or page jumps onto your screen, doubtless with several links of its own.

To get on the Internet, you sign up with an Internet service provider, such as AT&T Worldnet, or an online service, such as America Online, that offers Internet access. Law students can usually plug in through their schools. Once on the Internet, you use a "web browser," such as Netscape Navigator, to access Web pages, documents and hyperlinks. You feed the browser the URL—that is, the "uniform resource locator," one of those gibberishy *http://* character strings—of the resource you're after, and the browser finds it for you, wherever it is. Then you're off and clicking.

What follows are lists of Web sites useful to anyone doing legal research, to law students specifically, and to recent law-school grads. These aren't exhaustive lists, nor could they be; so many Web pages are added every day, and plenty bite the dust, too. We'll stress it again, and we'll stress it now: you just can't count on the accuracy, completeness, or continued availability of materials you locate on the Internet. Commercial databases are bastions of spell-checked order and cite-checked comprehensiveness; perform a keyword search and you can be nearly certain you'll retrieve every case matching your search. That's why they can charge the big bucks. The Internet, by contrast, is still the anarchic, unruly frontier. There are no rules and no guarantees, but (usually) no charge, either.

So keeping that in mind, get hold of your mouse and surf.

Legal Research   The pioneer Web site for matters legal is maintained by Cornell Law School. Established way back in the early mists of time—1992—the Legal Information Institute is devoted to delivering free legal information over the Internet. The collection includes full-text versions of recent Supreme Court decisions, the complete United States Code, various other federal and state materials, analysis of some court decisions, law review articles, and a smattering of international material. The offerings are varied and expanding. Find them at *http://www.law.cornell.edu*.

Also check out the LawLinks site (*http://www.lawlinks.com:80/lawlinks.html*), which provides not only its own collection of legal materials, but hyperlinks to other sources (such as Cornell). The result is a very broad array of subject matter organized by category. The index reads like a well-stocked catalog of law-school study aids, from administrative law to workers' compensation. You'll find entries for various foreign countries, an international spin to topics such as criminal law, and unusual topics such as substance abuse, militias, and cults. The retrievable materials themselves are a polyglot of cases, commentaries, statutes, news reports and pointers to other Internet resources. This is an excellent place to start.

If your research project involves a specific governmental entity, such as an administrative agency, maybe they have a Web site. More and more do. The Patent Office is at *http://uspto.gov*. You can find the Copyright Office at *http://lcweb.loc.gov/copyright/*, where you can download information and registration forms. The U.S. Congress has a site (*http://thomas.loc.gov*), as do the White House (*http://www.whitehouse.gov*) and the Department of Justice (*http://www.usdoj.gov/*).

And if it's a state-law question your pondering, maybe one of that jurisdiction's law schools maintains a site. These tend to be rich in state-oriented materials. The Indiana University School of Law, for example, makes available the Indiana Code and constitution, legislative news, and some case law. They're at *http://www.law.indiana.edu*. More generally, you can also scour the holdings of numerous public libraries at *http://library.usask.ca/hytelnet/sites1a.html*.

Support for Law Students   Although your best sources for answers in law school are your professors and fellow students, there are a few Web sites out there that can provide some information and point you to worthwhile organizations and opportunities. Chief among these is Hieros Gamos (*http://www.hg.org/*), which maintains a chunky page devoted entirely to law students. Some of the entries are just links to sellers of commercial study aids, but you'll also find guides to law-school listservs, law-student organizations, admissions information, and a few legal periodicals of interest to students. You might also have a look at the Princeton Review's home page (*http://www.review.com*), and in particular their directory of pointers to student-oriented Web sites.

Employment Opportunities   Legal recruiters—the "headhunters"—amass fortunes taking the awkwardness out of the post-graduation employment routine. Like a shy adolescent at a mixer, the average associate unhappy with his present position is reluctant to take the initiative; contacting another law firm to see what opportunities prevail risks rejection and smacks of desperation (or so it seems). The law firm, chary of being accused of raiding, won't take the initiative either. So those headhunters with their hearty voices and opportunities that are always perfect play matchmaker, placing endless calls, nudging prospects along, discreetly cajoling and wheedling.

What if the awkwardness were to disappear? Suppose job postings were instantly accessible and clearly explained, and lawyers in search of lateral opportunity could post inquiries conveniently, privately, without stigma or chance of detection by their current employers?[8] The marketplace for legal talent would open, expensive recruiters would find jobs telemarketing credit cards, and everyone else would be happier. That, anyway, is the vision behind an expanding number of employment-related Web sites. Thus far, these pages are little more than online classified ads; but even still, the idea of centralized, global want ads sure beats shopping through innumerable national, state, and local law journals. And one day, you can bet, the process will be completely automated; you'll just click on an entry, jot a cover memo and zap your résumé off. For now, check out the job listings at Hieros Gamos

---

[8]*Don't assume that e-mail sent from your office is beyond the reach of your employer!* It's usually archived and readily (and legally) accessible to systems administrators. Although Big Brother probably isn't monitoring your every transmission, your e-mailed thoughts aren't yours alone. If privacy is a concern, use your own Internet provider.

(*http://www.hg.org/employment.html*), which includes subdivisions dedicated to particular law schools as well as pointers to other online classifieds. The LJX Law Employment Center (*http://www.lawjobs.com/*) also offers numerous job listings, and the LawLinks site (*www.lawlinks.com:80/lawlinks.html*, click on Attorney Center, then click on Employment) has pointers to various job resources. You might also check the home pages of law firms in which you have an interest; more and more are setting up Web sites, and they frequently post openings.

There you have it, a snapshot of just a few of the Internet resources available at this moment in time. Problem is, there are so many more, and who knows how long any of the above sites will be around? Clearly, there has to be a better way to find things on the Net. And there is. It's called a search engine. You visit one of these just like any other Web site, and you're invited to post a keyword search. Submit the search, and in a flash, dozens, hundreds, or thousands of Web pages matching your search appear listed on your screen. You skim through them, clicking to visit the ones that seem relevant, ignoring the others. All free of charge. The search engine is constantly adding new listings to its repertoire.

The biggest and fastest search engine is Alta Vista, brought to you by Digital Equipment Corporation (find it at *http://altavista.digital.com*). Its listings cover tens of millions of Web pages, and it works at mind-boggling speed; you post your search and a moment later your screen is filled with the first ten of 200,000 candidate Web sites (which means it's time to refine your search). Alta Vista is ideal for brute-force searching. Say a merger deal has just come your way from on high. Perform an Alta Vista search to find out more about your client and the other company. Check their Web sites. Scan the newsgroups—maybe the investment jocks have already picked up the scent! If you're a litigator, see what you can find out about the opposition. Or their lawyers. Or the judge. You may find hits, for example, in online newspaper or periodical archives: nonlegal sources that traditional research methods would overlook, but which can add quite a bit of valuable context (and perhaps strategic advantage) to your efforts.

The other two major search engines are Yahoo! (*http://www.yahoo.com*) and Lycos (*http://www.lycos.com*). These engines let you search by category. If it's a particular site you're after, one you know is out there somewhere, use one of these. To find the Copyright Office Web site, for example, is a breeze using Yahoo! or Lycos; you just search the Government category, and you're there in a jiffy. Try that on Alta Vista and you'll surf the listings for weeks.

*   *   *

So, with all of those computational and paper resources under your belt, how do you deploy them reliably and efficiently when an assignment lands on your desk? Everyone develops his or her own style, but you might try beginning along these lines:

1. Consider starting with an Internet search. It's cheap and easy, and you never know what you'll find. Unless the assignment involves detached analysis of a specific point

185

of law, unexpected background information from sources far and wide can provide a worthwhile nonlegal supplement to your research. Begin at a search engine, then go to some of the law-related sites. These are a great place to try out your more exotic hunches and instincts, since you're not paying for each retrieval. Keyword-searchable sites yield their greatest rewards when the issue involves an uncommon or highly specific term of art. But remember the absence of guarantees on the Internet, and the consequent need to verify what you find.

2. Now return to the world of paper. Begin with the general: try a treatise first. If none is available or helpful, grab the *Index to Legal Periodicals* and look for law review articles. Although it's hard to tell how useful an entry will prove merely from its title, confining yourself to the most recent articles will help thin out the field. If the issue is simple or very basic, consult a legal encyclopedia. These sources should provide you with your initial harvest of relevant cases.

3. But maybe not. If, after all that, you've hit nothing but a series of dead ends, try a commercial database.

4. When you've obtained a smattering of cases directly on point or at least fairly close, examine their headnotes and write down the keynumbers. Look up these keynumbers in West's state and federal digests to find additional relevant cases.

5. Shepardize the most relevant cases to find even newer cases and, just as important, A.L.R. citations.

If it's a statute you're researching, it's likely to be on a Web page somewhere, possibly with annotations. Even commercial database searches of statutory law tend to be quite efficient, since you can home in on cases that interpret the specific provision without also dragging out too much junk. You might consult an annotated version of the statute that contains case citations; these are rarely comprehensive, but will at least get you started. In either case follow through with a keynumber search, and then Shepardize the important cases.

12.3 Writing Like a Lawyer

Legal writing rarely makes for popular reading. Ask anyone to characterize lawyers' prose and the response will probably include such adjectives as "turgid," "rambling," and "incomprehensible." In part, this can be explained by the need for precision and caution. But only in part. Sure, there may be times where the difference between *considerable* and *not inconsiderable* is important. Operative documents like contracts generally require highly refined terms and definitions, in contrast to advocacy documents like briefs, where presentation is key. But plain English should be your goal in anything you write. Avoid unnecessary verbosity, eliminate lawyerisms, and eradicate redundancy. Shun pretentious-ness. Critics of the legal profession already think we write unintelligibly just to cloak ourselves in mystery and justify high fees. You will find, as you progress, that no one appreciates pompous twaddle—not your superiors, not judges, and especially not clients.

Everything you write as a lawyer serves a purpose: to convey information, to argue a position, to memorialize a transaction. The writing style must reflect your commitment to that purpose. In the remainder of this section we'll explore the most common kinds of documents that lawyers write, and the right way to go about writing them. You'll also encounter a couple of examples.

Research Memoranda

After you complete the library phase of a research project, it's time to put pen (or dictaphone or word processor) to paper in the form of a memorandum. But before we discuss research memos, a preliminary warning. Stoutly resist the temptation to provide your supervisor with an unsolicited glimpse at your progress before you've completed the research. Sometimes you don't find the most important case until you're almost done; you probably don't Shepardize the ones you have found until then, either. A new, important decision or the unexpected demise of a leading case can invert your conclusion completely. Why risk humiliation or, worse, the possibility that your supervisor will recklessly pass your tentative thoughts onto the client as gospel? *Keep your mouth shut until the research is done!*

Before you begin to write, decide how you will organize the memo. Most are built around four topic headings: Facts, Issues, Conclusions, and Discussion. This presentation enables the reader to get the information she needs, fast, and to verify that you've addressed the right topics.

The Facts section should not be too long. Its only purpose is to give context to your analysis by concisely summarizing the legally important factual information. The process you use to distill the facts into a few terse sentences closely parallels the way you've digested cases into briefs. Keep only what's necessary. Try to use the active voice (a topic to which we'll return). If the facts aren't right, it means you didn't do a good job asking questions at the outset...and the reader will not be pleased.

Boil the legal questions down to succinct, one-sentence questions, and list them under the Issues heading. Once again, if you asked all the right questions when you first received the assignment, you should have walked out of the assignor's office with the issues already sketched out into your mind.

Set out the results of your research, issue by issue, in the Conclusions section. Ideally, each one-sentence issue question receives an equally succinct conclusory answer. You may need to add some qualifiers or alternatives, but try to give the reader what she's looking for— simple answers to direct questions.

In the Discussion section, you provide the rationale by which you arrived at your conclusions and cite the authorities that support your analysis. If the memo addresses more than one issue, break this section up into separately titled subsections.

Your goal in presenting each analysis is impartiality. Give the pros and cons. Even if your superior has asked you to produce an argumentative piece that supports a specific position, make sure any contrary authority nonetheless comes to his attention—somehow. Anything less is malpractice. Of course, even an impartial lawyer wants to win his case, so try to maintain a positive attitude (if that's possible) in your analysis. You could say, "Three factors limit the availability of relief in this case," but you'll earn greater appreciation by saying, "We can demonstrate liability by overcoming the following three factors." Get the idea?

Attention to a few stylistic points will further enhance your presentation.

- *Watch those citations.* You can cite cases or statutes in text or in footnotes. Although convention frequently motivates the authors of briefs and judicial opinions to pack their authorities right in there along with the text, too many of them can turn an otherwise neat presentation into Oscar Madison's bedroom. Important points get lost in a welter of citations. But the most crucial consideration regarding citations is accuracy. Whether you include them in text or banish them to footnotes as recommended here, make sure the citations are Blue Book perfect.
- *Stick to the facts.* In contrast to the abstract philosophy of many law-review articles, research memos are rigorously practical documents. Your writing will help the memo's reader assess position and plot strategy. Keep that in mind as you draft. Maybe you can move beyond detached analysis and make practical suggestions. Whose deposition would help resolve a factual issue? What information appears to be missing from the client's story?
- *Keep your sentences uncluttered.* This goes back to avoiding pretentiousness. Minimize word clusters ("the fact that," "notwithstanding the foregoing") and compound prepositions ("in the event that"). Make your sentences efficient and to the point.

Let's suppose you've been hauled into the office of a senior partner with a hot assignment. Although he's demanding, he relieves his associates from the need to ask questions by providing them with all the information they need (remember, this is pure fantasy). He tells you:

"Our client is a professional photographer, Xavier Stieglitz Kitsch. He takes pictures of cute, folksy scenes and sells them to greeting-card companies who produce cute, somewhat tacky reproductions. Two years ago our client photographed a farmer, his wife, and their prize pig Arnold just after Arnold won the blue ribbon at the county fair. He sold the photo to the Acme Greeting Card Company and earned a decent profit on sales.

"About three months ago our client was shocked to find his photograph on the cover of the calendar section of the Sunday *Times*. At least he thought it was his photograph. As he read the cover story, he learned that the artist Gottfried Ulrich Snöwd had created a sculptural version of Arnold and his proud owners—a three-dimensional reproduction of our client's picture. What appeared in the newspaper was a photograph of that sculpture.

"Snöwd is a 'conceptual artist,' meaning that he cares less about his subject or the art object than the idea behind it. In fact, he never even gets his hands dirty—he pays high-priced craftworkers to make reality of his ideas. But the art world considers him a genius and collectors pay big bucks for his creations. In this case the sculpture appeared in a show that satirized contemporary values and life-styles. Snöwd sold an edition of three of the sculptures for over $350,000—many times what our client has earned from his photograph. We've learned that Snöwd had the sculptures produced in Italy. He provided his craftworkers with a note card bearing our client's photograph and instructed them to make a sculptural duplicate.

"Snöwd's response to my outraged letters was that his recent artwork depends on appropriation to convey its message, that appropriation is a recognized artistic genre, and that if he has to step over a few bodies to make his point, so be it.

"Assuming our client has complied with all the necessary copyright formalities, what are his rights? Take all the time you need for this assignment. Give me a balanced memo that analyzes both sides of the issue."

After diligently cracking the books, you might produce a memo like the one beginning on the next page.

Briefs

At least where writing is concerned, briefs are a litigator's finest hour. It is here that the arguments are delivered, the judge convinced, the case won. Because a brief is an advocacy piece, a document whose purpose is to persuade, it should contain a minimum of legalese and be practically twaddle-free. Good brief-writing skills can only be learned over a lifetime of practice, so we won't dwell on the fine points. What follows is a short sketch of the way you should approach the drafting of briefs. We conclude with an example that shows one way to turn the objective memorandum presented above into a weapon for your client.

Presenting an argument in a brief isn't all that different from writing a good exam answer. You begin by telling the court what you want it to do. Then you move to the applicable legal standards—the major premises of your argument. Since major premises get lonely without the minor premises that give them life, you explain why the facts of the case obviously fit (or cannot possibly fit) the rules you've laid out. Now anticipate your opponent's response. Preempt her arguments and put the best spin on unfavorable facts. Then move on to policy. Tell the court why failing to do what you've asked will not only be contrary to law, but unwise public policy as well. Finish with a short conclusion that essentially restates your request.

MEMORANDUM

To: L. Excelente
From: J. Valdez
Re: X.S. Kitsch v. Gott U. Snöwd

FACTS

Our client, X. S. Kitsch, photographed a bucolic scene and earned a modest return from sale of the photograph. He properly complied with all copyright formalities. Gott U. Snöwd, a financially successful entertainer, commissioned sculptural versions of the Kitsch photograph. He sold the sculptures without Kitsch's permission and for many times the return Kitsch could ever hope to derive from the photograph.

ISSUE

Did Snöwd's conduct violate copyright law?

CONCLUSION

Kitsch should succeed in an action for copyright infringement because the Snöwd sculptures represent derivative works, and it is unlikely that Snöwd will persuade a court to excuse his conduct.

DISCUSSION

Kitsch's ability to recover damages from Snöwd for copyright infringement will turn on three issues: (1) whether Kitsch's photograph is protectable under copyright; (2) if so, whether Snöwd's sculptures constitute unauthorized copies of Kitsch's photograph; and (3) if so, whether the nature of Snöwd's work nonetheless qualifies it as a noninfringing "fair use."

Protectability of the Kitsch Photograph

Copyright protection extends only to original expressions, not to underlying ideas[1] or unadorned facts.[2] However, the standard of originality is easy to meet,[3] and it is well-settled that copyright law protects a photographer's originality in executing

---

[1] *See, e.g.,* Baker v. Selden, 101 U.S. 99 (1879).
[2] *See, e.g.,* Hoeling v. Universal City Studios, Inc., 618 F.2d 972, 979 (2d Cir. 1980).
[3] *See, e.g.,* M. Kramer Mfg. Co. v. Andrews, 783 F.2d 421, 438 (4th Cir. 1986) (characterizing required level of originality as "minimal" and of "a low threshold").

photographic expression.[4] While it may be a fact that Arnold is a cute pig and that he won a blue ribbon, the manner in which Kitsch arranged his subjects, lit them and carried out the photographer's art should easily qualify for copyright protection. A photograph need not be fanciful or abstract to be original and the Kitsch photograph is no more "idea-laden" or "fact-laden" than many other photographs that courts have protected under copyright.

Do the Sculptures Represent Copies?

Only the copyright owner may prepare or authorize preparation of "derivative works," which are defined in the Copyright Act as works "based upon one or more preexisting works, such as [an]…art reproduction,…or any other form in which a work may be recast, transformed or adapted."[5] Clearly, this language covers a sculptural rendition of a photograph.

Snöwd may argue against a literal reading of the statute, reasoning that copyright protection should be limited to the medium in which a work is originally produced; in other words, that photographs should be protected "as photographs" and no more. But courts have uniformly held that transforming a work from one medium to another (e.g., from two dimensions into three dimensions) will not avoid copyright infringement.[6] Although the cases are not terribly recent, it is difficult to conceive of any worthwhile policy a contrary result would advance.

Snöwd may also try to find minor discrepancies between his sculpture and the Kitsch photograph and use these to argue that he did not "copy" the photograph. But the test under copyright law requires only "substantial similarity," not slavish equivalence. The obvious correspondence between the two works, coupled with Snöwd's explicit instructions to his craftworkers, should defeat this argument.

The Fair Use Exception

Even if the Kitsch photograph qualifies for copyright protection and the Snöwd sculptures represent copies, Snöwd cannot be held liable for infringement if his appropriation constitutes "fair use." This concept is defined in 17 U.S.C. §107, which lists four non-exclusive factors that courts must consider in determining whether the "fair use" exception applies:

(1) the purpose and character of the use, including whether such use is of a commercial nature or is for nonprofit educational purposes;
(2) the nature of the copyrighted work;

---

[4]*See, e.g.,* Burrow-Giles Lithographic Co. v. Sarony, 111 U.S. 53, 55 (1884).
[5] 17 U.S.C. §101.
[6]*See, e.g.,* King Features Syndicate v. Fleischer, 299 Fed. 533 (2d Cir. 1924) (toys based on cartoon characters); Fleischer Studios, Inc. v. Ralph A. Freundlich, Inc., 73 F.2d 723 (2d Cir. 1934).

(3) the amount and substantiality of the portion used in relation to the copyrighted work as a whole; and

(4) the effect of the use upon the potential market for or value of the copyrighted work.

Courts have also been willing to find fair use in cases involving parody or satire.

In this case, Snöwd's goals are obviously commercial; Kitsch's work is creative rather than factual; Snöwd has appropriated the entirety of the Kitsch photograph; and sale of his sculptures interferes with Kitsch's ability to market similar adaptations of his photograph. Therefore, it will be difficult for Snöwd to show fair use according to the terms of §107.

With respect to satire, Snöwd's desire to parody contemporary values cannot justify appropriation of the entire Kitsch photograph. Although the cases are not uniform, courts tend to hold uses that do much more than "conjure up" or recall the original to fall outside the scope of fair use.[7] Even the more generous decisions draw the line at wholesale copying.[8]

Another line of satire cases also applies to Snöwd's appropriation. These cases hold that fair use applies only where the work copied is itself the subject of satire.[9] Snöwd aims to satirize contemporary culture, not Kitsch's photograph. Snöwd's argument that appropriation, as a popular artistic genre, merits exemption from copyright law obviously proves too much. Courts have consistently held that merely because something is art does not necessarily make it right.

---

[7]Berlin v. E.C. Publications, Inc., 329 F.2d 541 (2d Cir. 1964); MCA, Inc. v. Wilson, 677 F.2d 180 (2d Cir. 1981).

[8]*See, e.g.,* Warner Bros., Inc. v. American Broadcasting Cos., 654 F.2d 204 (2d Cir. 1981).

[9]*See, e.g.,* Metro-Goldwyn-Mayer, Inc. v. Showcase Atlanta Coop. Prods., Inc., 479 F.Supp. 351 (N.D. Ga. 1979).

The stylistic suggestions set out above for memos also apply to briefs. Here are some additional pointers:

- *Use the active voice.* Someone once said that a brief should march and sing, leading the reader with strength and conviction, inspiring rather than lecturing. The passive voice ("summary judgment *was* requested *by* the plaintiff") is flabby and inspires only yawns. It can also produce skepticism if it looks like you're trying to avoid saying who did what to whom. The active voice ("the plaintiff requested summary judgment") stirs your reader's heart and tells him you're not pulling any punches.
- *Learn to adore verbs.* Avoiding the passive voice requires that you replace those "to be" conjugates with other verbs. But keep them punchy. Weak verbs, supported by adjectives and adverbs, do little to free your ideas from the prison of excess verbiage. Use concrete verbs to keep your brief singing. In fact, take a lesson from singers. Rock-and-roll dancers *twist and shout,* they don't move in a rotating fashion and utter loudly; rock singers break on through, slip out the back, hop on the bus, get themselves free of boring verbs.
- *Limit prepositions.* This goes back to the idea of keeping sentences uncluttered. Prepositions add weight to sentences. Saying "jury trial" instead of "trial by jury" eliminates a preposition; so does saying "the court's ruling" instead of "the ruling of the court." And when you need to use a modifier, make sure it's placed correctly— usually right next to what you want to modify. In the sentence, "The judge ordered the witness to leave the courtroom cursing and spitting," we're unsure who's misbehaving and we don't know whether the judge has ordered or responded to the indiscretion.

The organization of a brief can vary considerably, depending on the status of the case and the rules and customs of the tribunal. Let's assume that the recipient of your research memorandum has decided to move for *summary judgment.* This is a way of sidestepping the usual long and winding road to trial by convincing the court that a trial isn't even necessary, given the vigor of your case. In the example on the next page, we've spared you from slogging through the text of the motion itself, as well as the statement of facts and procedural context that usually precedes the argument.[9] We've also omitted the fair-use analysis, since it involves some rather involved evidence issues. In accord with the usual custom, case and statutory citations appear within the text.

Contracts

The way lawyers draft contracts bears almost no resemblance to the way they write briefs. Contracts are built up in layers. The first layer is a general approach to the problem at hand, a set of basic clauses that capture the essence of the deal the parties have struck. The additional layers arise from more detailed thought about the transaction, negotiation among

---

[9]In fact, we've left out even more by limiting the argument to the substantive issues of copyright law explored in the research memorandum. In a real brief, you would also need to address the appropriateness of the summary-judgment remedy itself, and make frequent reference to affidavits or other evidence. Real briefs also tend to contain many more citations.

IN THE UNITED STATES DISTRICT COURT
FOR THE SOUTHERN DISTRICT OF NEW YORK

)	
XAVIER S. KITSCH,)	
Plaintiff)	
v.)	Civ. Act. No. 92-1
GOTTFRIED U. SNÖWD,)	
Defendant.)	
)	

MOTION FOR SUMMARY JUDGMENT

Introduction

[Statement of facts and applicable law, description of parties, discussion of court's jurisdiction]

Argument

I. COPYRIGHT LAW FULLY PROTECTS THE KITSCH PHOTOGRAPH

Copyright law encourages the production and distribution of creative works by protecting their makers against unauthorized duplication. Specifically, 17 U.S.C. §§501-509 impose strong criminal and civil penalties on those who misappropriate original expressions. Photographs unquestionably qualify for this protection. For over a century courts have unanimously treated photographic expression like that of any other artistic medium, applying the full measure of copyright authority to original photographic works. See, e.g., Burrow-Giles Lithographic Co. v. Sarony, 111 U.S. 53, 55 (1884).

Courts have characterized the level of originality required for copyright protection as "minimal" and of "a low threshold." See, e.g., M. Kramer Mfg. Co. v. Andrews, 783 F.2d 421, 438 (4th Cir. 1986). The Kitsch photograph reflects considerable originality both in terms of its artistic organization and its technical execution. All three of the subjects were arranged for precise compositional harmony. The poses and facial expressions convey a unified sense of bucolic pride. Indeed, the lighting on Arnold's pink snout reflects particularly careful attention to color balance and shadow management. As a result of Kitsch's lighting efforts, Arnold appears to be smiling, the proud winner of a high honor. The farmer's bald pate rendered this effect especially difficult to obtain, given the tendency of a shiny surface to reflect excessive amounts of light. Clearly, the artistic and technical skills evident in the Kitsch photograph more than satisfy the originality requirements of the Copyright Act.

II. THE SNÖWD SCULPTURES REPRESENT UNAUTHORIZED, INFRINGING COPIES OF THE KITSCH PHOTOGRAPH

A. The Snöwd Sculptures Are Derivative Works

Under the terms of the Copyright Act, only the copyright owner may prepare or authorize the preparation of derivative works. The Act defines a "derivative work" as one that is "based upon one or more preexisting works, such as [an]…art reproduction,…or any other form in which a work may be recast, transformed or adapted." 17 U.S.C. §101.

That the Snöwd sculptures represent three-dimensional duplications of the Kitsch photograph is beyond question. The appearances of the subjects are identical, down to the afterbirth stains on the farmer's sleeves and the details of his wife's considerable girth. To say that the sculptures are "based upon" the photographs is an understatement; they are alike in every sense except medium.

But the medium is not the message in copyright law. An infringer does not elude liability merely by copying into a different material. The plain language of the statute, as well as an unbroken line of cases extending over a century, hold a change in medium to be irrelevant. See, e.g., King Features Syndicate v. Fleischer, 299 Fed. 533 (2d Cir. 1924) (toys based on cartoon characters); Fleischer Studios, Inc. v. Ralph A. Freundlich, Inc., 73 F.2d 723 (2d Cir. 1934). This reflects not only settled law, but sound policy as well. The fruits of Mr. Kitsch's creative labors appear no less in sculptural form than in pictorial form. If the creator of a work does not possess an inherent right to exploit that work in all media, the possibility of alternative-media competition will dramatically reduce its value without any corresponding public benefit. Moreover, were this Court to confine copyright protection to a single medium, how could such a medium be defined? Artists consider lithography and photography to represent different media, yet virtually all copyright infringements of photographs utilize some form of mass-duplication lithography. Perhaps photocopying an entire book would also be allowable, since xerography and press printing utilize different media. Copyright protection becomes a cruel hoax if infringers can escape liability by choosing the reproduction technique most convenient to their infringements.

These considerations strongly compel a finding that the Snöwd sculptures are derivative works based on the Kitsch photograph.

B. The Defense of Fair Use Does Not Apply in This Case

The Copyright Act permits certain limited uses of copyrighted works under the rubric of "fair use."

*   *   *

Conclusion

In light of the foregoing, we ask this Court to grant the Plaintiff's Motion for Summary Judgment, as well as such other and further relief as the Court considers just.

Respectfully submitted,

_____

L. Excelente, Esq.
J. Valdez, Esq.

the parties and, more often than not, the insights of older and wiser lawyers who review your initial efforts.

First and foremost, the layers must be well-crafted. Think of contracts as clothing. Shoddy clauses tossed together look about as good on paper as a suit of rags would look on you. But good drafting is readily learned. The most difficult part of writing contracts is getting the layers to work together. If they relate to one another only obscurely or not at all, once again you have not produced a contract; what you have is an expensive Halloween costume. It may be an impressive costume, if the layers are nicely written, but it's not what your client pays you for.

Your task, therefore, in drafting contracts is to produce neither rags nor costumes, but merely to wrap your client in layers of protective language to secure him against the cold, cruel business world. The layers need not have designer labels—there is no need to deploy gratuitous legalisms—and they can't be so thick as to stifle your client. The idea is to dress him neatly and thoroughly, but not to overdo it.

When the bargaining starts, you must either find a way to accommodate the concerns of the other side while protecting your client's interests, or be able to stand firm. Of course, it's easiest to stand firm when your client has the economic upper hand. Negotiation can sometimes turn into a patterned dance, as you helplessly follow the choreography toward an outcome preordained by the parties' relative bargaining strengths. But the key is *sometimes*. More often than not, even a strongly positioned adversary will listen to your point of view, and weaklings can unexpectedly walk away from a deal if they feel stepped on. Standing firm always means being able to offer persuasive arguments for your adamance.

To see how contracts are assembled, let's suppose, once again, that you're a junior-level associate who has this time been asked to draft a contract clause. "Don't worry about the rest of the contract; that's already been negotiated," the partner in charge assures you. "The basic concept is this. Our client, Swelled Head Institute of Technology, has developed—or rather, one of their professors has developed—a therapeutic agent that clears clogged arteries by breaking up atherosclerotic plaque. They're tying to hook up with a pharmaceutical company, Drugs Drugs Drugs Inc., to test and commercialize the material. Problem is, the Institute is afraid of liability. Suppose someone dies from this stuff? So DDDI has agreed to insure itself and the Institute, beginning at the start of clinical trials. Your assignment is to draft a clause that keeps everyone happy. Should be a snap. Show me a draft before you send it off to DDDI's lawyer." And with that, she tosses the contract on your desk.

The first thing you do, once again, is to define the scope of your efforts, learning how much time you can realistically spend on the project. Then you read through the definitions section, which comes at the beginning of the contract. Those definitions include:

The "Institute" shall mean Swelled Head Institute of Technology, the licensor hereunder.

"DDDI" shall mean Drugs Drugs Drugs Inc., the licensee hereunder.

The "Agent" shall mean the biologically active form of the pharmaceutical developed by the Institute for treatment of atherosclerosis.

And so you begin by drafting a concise statement of what it is you think the parties have agreed to:

Not later than the time of initiating clinical trials of the Agent, DDDI shall procure adequate liability insurance naming the Institute as additional insured.

"You didn't ask me enough questions when we last spoke," says the partner as she reviews your work. "Liability insurance against what? What does 'adequate' mean? Would your clause prevent DDDI from canceling the insurance the day after clinical trials begin? And how do we even know whether they've gotten the insurance at all? Let me give you a few pointers..."

You listen, and then you try again:

Not later than the time of initiating clinical trials of the Agent, DDDI shall procure *and at all times thereafter maintain* liability insurance, *in an amount not less than $10,000,000, and which* names the Institute as additional insured *against all claims, suits, obligations, liabilities and damages, based upon or arising out of actual or alleged bodily injuries, death, or other damage to person or property caused by the Agent. As often as requested by the Institute, DDDI will furnish to the Institute a certificate from its insurance company or companies establishing that the insurance is in full force and effect.*

"Are you nuts?" steams the lawyer for DDDI when he receives your proposed clause. "We will never agree to this provision. DDDI is just as afraid of liability as the Institute, but we won't bankrupt ourselves to buy insurance. You're just going to have to trust our business judgment as far as amount goes. And what do you mean, 'at all times thereafter'? Do you mean forever? Statutes of limitation do run out at some point, you know. My client also won't accept the language about certificates of insurance. They've got more important things to do than chase documents for the Institute."

"Hey, pipe down," you reply. "Your point about statutes of limitation is reasonable. I'll draft some new language. But you're dead wrong about certificates of insurance. The Institute has every right to assurances that DDDI is maintaining its insurance, and only DDDI is in a position to get that information from its insurance companies. But, if it will make you more comfortable, we can limit DDDI's obligations to 'reasonable' requests by the Institute. As far as not naming a specific amount goes, I'll just have to check with my own client first."

"Fine," the other side grudgingly responds, "but DDDI won't provide certificates more than four times a year."

When you report back to the partner in charge, she decides it's time to call the Institute. "Yeah, we can live with all of that," says the director of the technology licensing office. "But they'd better use *prudent* business judgment about the amount of insurance."

And so your final handiwork looks something like this:

> Not later than the time of initiating clinical trials of the Agent, DDDI shall procure and maintain, *at all times until the expiration of all applicable statutes of limitation,* liability insurance in an amount *dictated by prudent business judgment* and which names the Institute as additional insured against all claims, suits, obligations, liabilities and damages, based upon or arising out of actual or alleged bodily injuries, death, or other damage to person or property caused by the Agent. As often as *reasonably* requested by the Institute, DDDI will furnish to the Institute a certificate from its insurance company or companies establishing that the insurance is in full force and effect*; provided, however, that in no event shall DDDI be required to provide such certificate more than four times in a single year.*

Were this the real world, your next step would be to integrate the final clause within the rest of the contract, placing it in a logical location and making sure that its terms remain consistent with the overall framework.

But rarely will you be asked to write a single clause in isolation. Typically, assignments involving contracts require formulation of an entire draft agreement, with varying degrees of responsibility for negotiation thereafter. How on earth can a novice hope to produce a serviceable document out of thin air? By locating the right resources and going back to basic principles.

Books on contract drafting and negotiation have been written for virtually every field you can think of, from computer-related transactions to mergers and acquisitions to commercial leases. Your law firm's library, or a public law library, will have them. When an assignment takes you into strange territory, these books will help you chart the terrain. They tell you what clauses are important and provide simple forms.

Another source of wisdom, once again, is your firm's crew of senior associates. Seek one or two of them out and tell them what your assignment involves. They may be able to provide you with contracts from neighboring fields that can be turned into the agreement you need, or at least provide language for key clauses.

By and large, law schools don't do a very good job preparing you to draft contracts. Law professors teach you how to analyze, not how to write. But don't think you've wasted the three or four years of legal education. Contract assignments are the ultimate issue spotters. They're tougher than the ones you encountered on law-school exams, however, because the facts have not been contrived in advance or presented to you neatly. Instead, *you* must get the facts by asking the right questions. The idea of an insurance requirement seems simple enough; but as we've just seen, it encloses a number of different topics that you must first unpack and identify before you can address them.

12.4 Effective Oral Expression

As a lawyer, the need to express yourself verbally arises constantly—in court, in negotiations, and in your everyday dealings with clients and partners. Polished and persuasive speaking is the successful lawyer's hallmark. It elicits confidence in those on your side, reins in the adversary, and persuades neutral arbiters.

Most of us have what it takes to deliver competent oral presentations and engage in spoken argument, but few have taken the time to develop these skills by the time we get to law school. The key is organization. If you've got time to prepare a presentation, use that time wisely. Draft an outline. Rehearse before a colleague. Will questions be asked at the end? Anticipate them and prepare answers. But avoid reading directly from an outline or prepared notes. Talk to your audience, watch their responses.

When pursuing an exchange with an adversary or skeptical partner, *s l o w d o w n!* Once again, organization is critical. Think through your response before you say anything. Don't let your thoughts overtake your ability to express them. Remind yourself of your next point as you begin to speak.

Watch an experienced litigator make an objection. Chances are he'll rise slowly, affording himself a brief moment of organizational thought before straightening up and facing the judge. Even the highly charged and fast-paced atmosphere of trial offers opportunities for quick mental preparation.

Then there are some pitfalls to avoid. Do you tend to speak in a monotone? Be honest, now. If you do, find some patient soul who loves you, strap him to a chair, and make him listen to you deliver a speech. As you speak, think punctuation. Pause for the commas, pause for the periods, and pause when your audience begins to doze off. Force yourself to emphasize the important points. Let your voice rise and fall. Then wake your audience up and ask how you did. Keep at it until he doesn't snooze anymore or leaves you for good.

A related pitfall is the monotonic cadence, where a speaker's voice rises and falls rhythmically in singsong fashion without regard to what's being said. Train yourself to emphasize the important points. Exaggerate the emphasis as you rehearse and, once again, find a willing spectator who will help you gauge your improvement.

Finally, don't be so hard on yourself that you become nervous or develop an implacable hatred of public speaking. Relax, try to improve, and you'll do fine.

Index

Index

General statement vs. universal statement, 75–76
Gilbert outlines, 119
Government. *See* Federal government
Government agencies, 127, 183. *See also* Administrative agencies
Grades, law school, 123–24
Grinders, 150
Guilford v. Yale University, 24–26, 32
 brief of, 107–8

Hanson v. Dencla, 132
Harris v. McRae, 46–47
Hawaii Housing Authority v. Midkiff, 54–55
Hieros Gamos, 184, 185
Holding, 32
Home pages, 182
Hornbooks, 115–17
Hyde Amendment, 46–47
Hypertext links, 182–83

Inductive reasoning, 82–83. *See also* Deductive reasoning; Legal thinking; Logic; Reasoning
In-house lawyers, 162–66
Insider trading, 37
Internal Revenue Code, 44–45
International News Service v. Associated Press, 88
International Shoe Co. v. Washington, 92, 130–31, 136–37
Internet, 127, 181–86
 browsers, 181, 183
 commercial databases, 180–83
 job listings, 127
 for legal research, 183–184
 service providers, 183.
 See also Computers; World Wide Web
Internships, 127
Interviews with employers, 167–69
Issue, 31–32

Jobs. *See* Employment
Journals, 182
 legal, 125
Judges, 84–85
 federal, 14
 state, 16
Judicial clerkships, 172–74
Judicial review of administrative agencies, 20–21
Judiciary branch, 11–18. *See also* Federal courts; State courts

Jurisdiction of federal courts, 13
Jurisprudence, 85
Justice Department, U.S., 8–10
 Web site, 183

Langdell, Christopher Columbus, 85
Law firms, 147–65
 interviews at, 167–69
 large, 147–55
 associates, 151–53
 compensation, 147n, 148–51
 leverage ratios, 151–52
 organization of, 148–49
 partnerships, 148–54
 small, 155–64.
 See also Employment
LAWJOURNAL, 182
LawLinks, 183, 185
Lawmaking process, 5–7
Law professors, 105–6
Law reviews, 125, 180
Law school, 105–6
 prestige associated with, 123
Law School Discussion List, 182
Law students
 outlines and, 110–14
 study groups and, 109–10.
 See also Internet; Study aids
Lawyers, in-house, 162–66
Legal-aid, 127
Legal encyclopedias, 179
Legalines outlines, 119–20
Legal Information Institute, 183
Legal issue, 31–32
Legal realism, 91–95
Legal recruiters, 184
Legal research. *See* Research
Legal themes, 33–39
 normative empirical distinction, 35–37
 objective vs. subjective approach, 37–39
 slippery slope, 33–35
Legal thinking, 84–101
 conceptualism and, 86–90
 economics and, 95–97
 feminism and, 98–99
 formalism and, 85–86
 natural law and, 97–98
 realism and, 91–95
 retrospectivity and, 99–100.
 See also Deductive reasoning; Inductive reasoning; Logic; Reasoning
Legislature, 4–7

Index

State constitutions, 11–12
State courts, 14, 16. *See also* Courts; Federal courts
State judges, 16
State laws, 11–12, 184
State v. Boon, 44–45
Statutes, 39–47
  intent of drafters of, 39, 44–45
  resolving ambiguities in, 43–47
    conflicts among statutes, 46–47
    techniques of judicial construction, 45–46
    unclear provisions, 43–45
  wording of, 40–42
Statutory construction, 39–40, 45–49. *See also* Strict construction
Statutory law, 11
Strict construction, 45
Student Judicial Affairs Discussion List, 182
Student Lawyer magazine, 126
Study aids, 115–22
  cassette tapes, 122
  flash cards, 121
  hornbooks, 115–17
  on Internet, 183, 184
  Nutshell series, 117–18
  prepared briefs, 121–22
  substantive outlines, 118–21
  topical outlines, 121
Study groups, 109–10
Substantive facts, 25–31
Substantive outlines, 118–21
Summer positions, 172–74
Sum & Substance outlines, 119
Supremacy Clause of the U.S. Constitution, 12
Supreme Court. *See* U.S. Supreme Court
Syllogism, 69–71
  categorical, 79–80
  conditional, 80
  disjunctive, 80

Tautology, 76
Tax Court, 14

Tax law, 44–45
Topical outlines, 121
Treatises, 180

Uniform Commercial Code, 41–42
Uniform Resource Locator (URL), 183
U.S. Congress, 4–7
  administrative agencies and, 18–19
  Web site, 183
U.S. Constitution, 12. *See also specific clauses and amendments*
U.S. Supreme Court, 9, 14, 17–18. *See also specific courts*
Universal statement vs. general statement, 75–76
Unjustified conclusions, 75–76
URL (uniform resource locator), 183

Veto power, 7
Volunteer programs, 127

Want ads, 184
Web sites, 181
West Bar Review, 144
West keynumber system, 180
White House Web site, 183
Willow River case, 77, 88
World-Wide Volkswagen Corp. v. Woodson, 132–34, 136–37
  brief of, 108
World Wide Web, 182. *See also* Computers; Internet
Writing, 175, 186–99
  briefs, 189–93
  contracts, 193–99
  research memoranda, 187–89
Writing contests, 126
Writ of certiorari, 14

Yahoo!, 185

Steven J. Frank, Esq., is an honors graduate of Harvard Law School who has practiced in both large and small firms. A partner in the Boston law firm Cesari and McKenna, Frank has written articles on law and technology for major magazines and frequently lectures on the subject